# Contents

# Preface

The educational situation of migrant workers' children is a source of wide concern for a variety of reasons. There are at present no agreed educational policies for solving the many problems it raises. However, it seems to us that to reach an agreement on concepts of educational policy at the European level is a matter of less urgency than to develop a number of different national schemes, carefully and flexibly linked, that could be brought into operation in specific problem situations in response to specific demands. This need not mean, however, that such developments should take place independently of one another and without cross-fertilization.

Yet even within the individual countries, where there are unified political institutions and no language barriers, exchanges of information prove problematic and laborious. Differing political and educational outlooks, professional rivalries, the emergence of conflicting schools of thought on the education of ethnic minority children, and not least the plethora of communication, constantly impede the flow of information. And it would be naïve to suppose that the rapid development of global communication systems was anywhere near to putting an end to pedagogical parochialism: if anything they tend to make it more difficult for us to look across the borders of our own education system. For harmonized information, reduced to the lowest common denominator of formal definitions, is more likely to get blocked than to flow freely along these international channels, and as a result it is usually deprived of that element of singularity to which successful educational innovation owes its force. The view across the border must not, of course, be impeded by defensive mechanisms, whether of our own or others' devising: it is easy to perceive what is all too familiar and never changes, and, conversely, it appears that we find it hard to endure the critical scrutiny of those who look across the border in our direction and see things in unfamiliar ways, having been reared on different experiences.

These remarks should not be misconstrued: what we are insisting on here is the uniqueness of educational innovation, while at the same time noting the customary stubborn adherence to traditional thinking and practice; we are not, however, preaching a kind of pedagogical parochialism which digs itself in behind time-honoured custom. Enlightened pedagogical tradition is alive and productive when it is working away at the boundaries which it will have to cross if it is to realize its full potential. In this context a contribution may be made by comparative educational study, but in order to do so it has to refrain from drawing hasty conclusions.

* * * * *

We do not see the Directive issued by the Council of the European Communities on 25 July 1977 as an instrument for the imposition of educational norms, but as an attempt to define minimal standards – which were long overdue – for the education of migrant workers' children. Were it up to us, we would gladly pitch these minimal standards higher than they appear in the wording agreed by the Communities, which was necessarily somewhat bland in order to secure unanimity, but such is our commitment to plural development that we would be equally glad to leave it to those immediately concerned to decide on how such standards should be achieved.

Our study has to be seen in the context of the resolution of the Council and the education ministers present on 9 September 1976 in favour of a programme of action in the sphere of education. In this resolution the ministers mention, among other things, an exchange of information and experience on the designing of suitable forms of teaching to be carried out in a limited number of pilot projects, making possible the assessment and comparison of these forms of teaching (*Official Journal of the European Communities*, No. C38, 19 February 1976). Since then, pilot projects have been set up in all the member states to try to find solutions for fairly precisely defined aspects of the schooling of migrant children.

The first pilot projects in this programme were mounted in Genk (Belgium), Bedford (England), Paris and Leiden (The Netherlands). We should perhaps give a preliminary account of what these projects involved. Those in Genk and Leiden were concerned with trying out forms of reception teaching for migrant children, while in Bedford and Paris experiments were carried out in mother tongue teaching. Three of the projects began in the academic year 1976/77, one in 1977/78. Three ran for three years, but the Bedford project was extended for a fourth year. Early in 1978 the ALFA Research Group was charged by the Commission of the European Communities with carrying out a comparative evaluation of these pilot projects. The evaluation exercise began in April 1978 and ended in June 1980, when we submitted our final report.

Our terms of reference were as follows:

-   to provide a critical assessment of the pilot projects within the framework of the education systems of the countries concerned, paying attention to the different social conditions prevailing in them;

-   to compare the pilot projects with one another and with the experiences of other member states of the EC and in non-member states;

-   to draw up recommendations for the further development of reception teaching and mother tongue teaching for the children of migrant workers in the countries involved;

- to assess the applicability of the findings of the pilot projects to the education systems of other countries, paying attention to their varying social conditions.

This is what we have tried to do.

* * * * *

In order to clarify the circumstances in which the study was carried out, we first outline the basic features of the proposals and guidelines for the improvement of the schooling of migrant children emanating from various supranational European bodies. We begin by describing the minimal European consensus as to what is considered desirable, without any attempt to describe the reality. In the next chapter we present our reflections on the methodological problems of comparative evaluation. These are intended to establish our attitudes to the pilot projects, to summarize the experiences we gained during our work and, not least, to make it possible for the reader to follow the stages by which we proceeded.

There follow detailed accounts of the individual pilot projects, each preceded by a brief survey of the education system of the country in question as it was at the time of the pilot project. Attention is focussed especially on the pilot projects, since we hope, by describing the success or failure of pedagogical innovations, to go beyond a mere summary of information and illustrate concrete possibilities for future developments.

We next try, in a moderately abstract discussion of selected problem areas, to compare the pilot projects and identify "growth points"; we also examine various proposed innovatory strategies in order to determine the extent to which they might contribute to the realization of equality of opportunity. Our definition of "equality of opportunity" here is purposely kept sufficiently abstract for it to be understood within the various frames of reference of the national education systems. In the final chapter we summarize our basic critique of the merely administrative measures so far pursued in "migrant education policy" and try to set against what was conceived and achieved by this approach various concepts and realizations that go beyond it; these take the form of proposals for intercultural education, which in our opinion is bound to be involved in any future educational reform.

## Acknowledgments

The education of migrant children is a controversial field in which there are continual clashes between differing interests and opinions. We are therefore grateful to the Commission of the European Communities, and especially to the General Directorate XII, which not only generously financed more than two years of research, but respected our independence and enabled our work to go ahead without any outside pressure. In our collaboration with the Commission we greatly appreciated and benefited from the openness and spirit of partnership we met with at all times.

We are grateful also to the many parents, teachers, scholars and officials in Belgium, England, France and the Netherlands who found the time and the patience to answer our sometimes naïve, sometimes insistent and sometimes irritating, but always inquisitive questions. We are especially indebted to our colleagues in Genk, Bedford, Paris and Leiden, who had enough good humour to put up with our visits, even when they were overburdened with pressing problems connected with their own work. We would mention in particular Serge Boulot, Gordon Burrows, Jean Clévy, Henk Everts and Marie-Claire Rosiers-Leonard, who gave us much invaluable support in our work.

Hardly a page of this book was written by less than two authors; usually there were more. It would be hopeless to try to identify the originators of particular ideas or formulations in almost five years of discussions. Some of the credit goes to Peter Groenewold, Louise Jansen and Katharina Kuhs, who collaborated in our project for different time spans and whose contribution to the present study is still discernible.

Annette Chmielorz, Stephanie von Frankenberg, Ingrid Gogolin and Renate Henscheid made valuable comments on the content and formulation of the present text, compiled the bibliography **and** read the proofs. Without their help the appearance of the book **would** have been delayed even longer.


Essen and Landau, January 1983                    Ursula Boos-Nünning
                                                     Manfred Hohmann
                                                      Hans H. Reich
                                                      Fritz Wittek

# Preface to the English edition

When this book first appeared in German in 1983, we were aware that some of the information contained in some chapters had already been rendered out of date by developments that had taken place since the end of our research in 1980. This applied mainly to the chapters outlining the educational position of ethnic minority and migrant children in Belgium, France, the Netherlands and the United Kingdom. Readers should therefore exercise caution when reviewing the information. To update our findings, however, would have required new research for which we lacked both the time and the resources. In any case, these chapters are intended mainly to provide the backcloth against which the individual projects are to be seen, and thus to help the reader to come to a fuller understanding of these innovations within their specific context. Requirements of both methodology and fairness to the original projects made it necessary for us to present them within the context from which they had in the first place emerged, and within which they were trying to make their specific contribution to educational change. Nevertheless, the mention of some major events may help the reader to form a rough picture of the kind of changes that have occurred in the four countries concerned.

In Belgium an integrated structure of secondary education has been gradually introduced which might in some ways be likened to what one is accustomed to calling comprehensive education. Although the Catholic, provincial and communal sectors have not yet started to implement this reform, it seems likely that they too will ultimately be obliged to do so.

France has seen a substantial investment by the Socialist government in the *Zones d'éducation prioritaire (ZEP)*, an institutional approach which was largely - indeed directly - inspired by the philosophy that has underpinned the Educational Priority Areas approach, which was developed in Great Britain in the wake of the Plowden Report as a strategy to combat inequality of opportunity in education. However, judging by what has happened to some other reforms introduced by the Socialist government, and in the absence of any indication that equality of educational opportunity is a top priority of France's present government, we are inclined to think that the *ZEP* will soon have to be seen as no more than an episode in the history of French education. The few modest reforms which the Socialist government introduced with regard to the legal status of migrant workers and their families are currently being scrapped and replaced by a new policy framework of unprecedented rigour, which will undermine whatever legal security the minority communities achieved in the early eighties.

More lasting changes seem to have been introduced in the Netherlands, where the right to vote (and to stand as a candidate) in local elections was granted to the ethnic minorities by a constitutional reform of 1984. Clearly this is no more than a first step, but one that is unlikely to be undone, as it had the support of all the major parliamentary parties. We should also mention the introduction, by law, of the intercultural approach as a universal principle of primary education; this is a further recognition of the fact that the Netherlands have irrevocably become a multicultural society. Readers in the United Kingdom may judge what this means in terms of the transformation of actual educational practice in schools.

As it appears to us, the British education system cannot now be described in quite the same terms as in 1983. Central influence seems to have increased substantially since 1980. The Schools Council has been dismantled, and the position of the teaching profession appears to have been weakened. The Rampton and Swann Reports, for all their sometimes contradictory conclusions, have certainly helped to unify official thinking on education for the multicultural Britain of today, and some recognizable progress has been made since they were published. At the same time, the fact that several LEAs have gone well beyond the recommendations of the Swann Committee in their policy-making demonstrates that centralization in the British education system has still some way to go. What seems most notable to us, however, is the development of an increasingly articulate movement for anti-racist education. In our analysis, this is not due so much to the fact that "race" as an issue in politics is more "visible" in the United Kingdom, as to the relative security which most ethnic minorities there enjoy, at least in legal terms. This may help ethnic minorities to develop into articulate and cohesive communities with an impact of their own in the political balance.

Not a single continental country is anywhere near such a situation, and significant educational change is therefore likely to be delayed on the continent even longer than in the United Kingdom. For surely, while educational thinking and experimentation in schools, as we have attempted to analyse it, may serve to enhance the credibility of the demand for educational equality, the struggle over the content and direction of educational change is decided by the general balance in society as a whole. Where we are heading in intercultural education will largely depend on the position which ethnic minorities manage to win for themselves in the political game, and what allies they find.

This brings us to another issue which we feel should be raised here - that of terminology. There has been, and still is, considerable debate among sociologists and educationalists about the 'correctness' of the terms used to designate those groups of workers who have moved from developing areas of the world to the highly industrialized countries of Central and Northwestern Europe during the last thirty years or so. Terms like "aliens", "foreign workers", "guest workers", "migrant workers", 'immigrants", "immigrant workers", "ethnic minorities" and - in the case of the United Kingdom - "Black British" have all been proposed, used and rejected on various grounds. A good deal of this debate would seem to be due to the sheer range of diversity in the legal, socio-economic and overall political situations prevailing in different countries. Another aspect of the controversy is related to the fact that, even in one country, none of these terms will cover all dimensions of the complex social reality. Hence, the decision as to which term to use will depend on the specific angle - legal, sociological, educational, etc - from which the issue is viewed.

Yet the final and most important dimension of the debate resides in the ideological and political connotations of any given terminology. Inasmuch as language reflects and shapes the way in which we perceive and classify social reality and members of society, many sociologists and educationalists feel concern over the potential reinforcement of existing social power-relations through the use of terminology which reflects them too directly and too uncritically. Efforts are therefore being made to develop terminologies which will rather emphasize the potential for change which is also inherent in all social relations. Yet the side-effects of this can be unexpected. As different and often conflicting schools of thought on the education of ethnic minority children (or, as Swann puts it, "Education for All") emerge, terminology tends to degenerate into a set of shibboleths which are used more and more to identify an individual writer as a subscriber to this or that school of thought, as an adherent of this or that ideology, or - in the worst case - as a member of this or that academic or political clique. The dividing line between the descriptive and the prescriptive element in such terminology is becoming increasingly blurred, and thus the proper use of terminology seems to be not so much an instrument of analysis and communication as a weapon in internecine academic warfare. This is not our concern.

Moreover, such terminological over-sensitivity is particularly obnoxious in cross-cultural sociological and educational analysis, where the use of any "correct" (and therefore necessarily uniform) terminology may in the end serve to obfuscate the complexity of issues that appear in the very diversity of situations. Thus, to use the term "ethnic minority" indiscriminately throughout our study would have been tempting, as it seems to be widely accepted in present English usage and would hence have passed virtually unnoticed. Yet to do this might also have masked a disturbing reality, namely that on the continent "ethnic minorities" are being ascribed the status of migrant workers, not just by some vague and uninformed "public opinion", but by law. Also, a term like this, in comparative analysis, is not without its own ambiguities. To cite just one example: it would be difficult to find an Algerian worker in France who would wish to be described as belonging to a *minorité ethnique*. In French this term is so redolent of colonial paternalism - indeed of outright racism - that it has become entirely unacceptable. We cannot analyse or even describe the reasons for this situation, but we cannot ignore it either. This diversity of situations (and hence the social meaning of the "terminology") was something we did not wish our English readers to lose sight of, and so we have been at some pains, with the help of June Geach and David McLintock, to ensure that the use of a diverse terminology should remind them of the diversity of the situations we describe.

The debate is ultimately about hoped-for social outcomes of the use of a "correct" terminology in terms of the options for different and often conflicting patterns of identity which are available to the people concerned. It seems to us that such decisions should be left to those who are directly affected by them, and that we might therefore spend less energy on evolving a legitimate language and more on supporting those who are still struggling for the recognition of their elementary human rights. We must not allow ourselves to forget that the social destiny of "ethnic minorities" is shaped by factors other than the use of "correct" language.

* * * * *

Finally, we should like to express our thanks to CILT: to John Trim, the Director, for undertaking the publication of this edition, to June Geach, the Linguistic Minorities Information Officer, for much valuable professional advice, to Ute Hitchin, the Publications Officer, for steering the work through its various stages with tact and firmness, and to David McLintock, who translated the book into English.

Essen and Landau, August 1986                    U. B.-N.
                                                 M. H.
                                                 H. H. R.
                                                 F. W.

# The EC Directive on the teaching of migrant workers' children

## Migrant workers' children as an issue in European education policy

The increasing mobility of labour between the European countries, due not only to the freedom of movement enjoyed by workers in the member states of the EEC, has given rise to problems of educational policy, affecting principally those children who join their families abroad, but also those born in the host countries. This was taken up as a political issue by the international organizations in the sixties and seventies and soon assumed central importance in the supranational debate on educational policy.

At an early stage, the **Council of Europe** began to be intensely concerned about the education of migrant children and passed resolutions dealing primarily with the situation of the workers themselves. Since 1953 it has demanded that they should enjoy the same social and financial conditions as indigenous workers. In 1966 it decided to appoint a subcommittee on the education of migrant workers' children and instituted a survey of their schooling and vocational training.

Resolution (68)18 demands that migrant workers and their families should be taught the language of the host country, and recommends the development and provision of methods and media appropriate to the learning situation of the migrants; Resolution (69)7 demands provision should be made for their possible return to their countries of origin through the creation of jobs in these countries, but also through bilaterally approved vocational training courses and mother tongue teaching in line with the curricular requirements of the countries of origin.

Resolution (70)35 on the education of the children of migrant workers, which was adopted by the Council of Europe on 27 November 1970, sets out the following basic objectives:

- support for migrant children within the national school systems;

- provision for the maintenance of the migrant children's linguistic and cultural links with their countries of origin;

- provision for the smooth reintegration of such migrant children as may return to their countries of origin.

Resolution (70)35 gave rise to the following projects:

- the development of a standardized international school and health certificate;

- the setting up of special reception classes (experimental classes) by the Council of Europe; such classes were set up in most of the host countries; attendance at these classes should not exceed one year, and at the end of each school year a report should be drawn up on objectives, on the recruitment of pupils and teachers, on methods of home-school liaison and on the diagnostic instruments used;

- the preparation of expert recommendations to be used as a basis for information pamphlets on the training and further training of teachers.

The **Standing Conference of European Ministers of Education**, to which the education ministers of all member states of the EEC and Portugal belong, also took up a position on the education of migrant workers' children. At its seventh meeting, held in Brussels in June 1971, it was agreed to devote increased attention to the problem. The results of the *ad hoc* conference on the "education and training of migrant workers", held in Strasbourg on 5 to 8 November 1974, influenced the content of the draft directive of the EC Commission. The essential demands of this conference were:

- to prevent the segregation of migrant pupils, except in the case of special preparatory classes and for the purpose of mother tongue and culture teaching;

- to make use of the presence of migrant children to promote international understanding and to provide live information about their countries of origin - an idea which hardly emerges at all in this form in other political statements.

In its recommendations, the conference drew up a more extensive list of concrete demands for the education of migrant children. The Ministers of Education were urged to request the member states

- to ensure that all pre-school facilities were available to migrant children, that pre-school facilities were provided to cater specifically for their needs, and that the migrants should be informed about such facilities in their own languages;

- to ensure that all migrant children were subject to the compulsory schooling required in the host country and attended school regularly; in preparation for the transition to mainstream education in the host countries they should be taught together in short-term reception classes; they should also receive teaching in their mother tongues, though this should not delay the transition to mainstream classes;

- to provide the children, free of charge, with the schoolbooks of their home countries (supplied by these countries) and with the schoolbooks and other materials used in the host countries (supplied by the host countries);

- to accept the Council of Europe's draft of the standardized school and health certificates and, for an interim period, to allow migrant pupils to move up into higher classes, irrespective of their degree of competence in the language of the host country;

- to ensure that the language of the host country was taught by methods which take account of the mental and psychic make-up of the children; in countries which had more than one official language migrant pupils in primary schools should be exempt from having to learn the second (third) language;

- to ensure that migrant children could learn their mother tongue or improve their knowledge of it and to provide the necessary materials, teachers and lesson time; the content of the education available in schools, especially as regards mother tongue teaching, should be of the same standard in both the host country and the country of origin, and each country should recognize the other's certificates and leaving qualifications.

There are also demands for the setting up of national documentation and information centres, schemes for the in-service training of bilingual teachers in both the host countries and the countries of origin, and special training schemes for teachers from the host country wishing to specialize in the teaching of migrant children.

At the 9th conference, held in Stockholm in June 1975, the governments of the member states were advised to initiate bilateral moves in pursuit of the following objectives:

- to guarantee and/or promote equality of opportunity and access to educational facilities;

- to give the migrants and their children opportunities to acquire a knowledge of the language and culture of their countries of origin and of the host countries, and to extend this knowledge;

- to take measures which would enable migrant children of all age-groups to receive general and vocational education; for this purpose it was recommended that preparatory classes or other schemes preparatory to mainstream education should be set up, that school-books should be provided free, scholarships awarded, standardized school reports introduced, leaving qualifications reciprocally recognized, teachers trained to deal with the problems of migrant children, and migrant parents encouraged to collaborate with the schools;

- to set up co-ordinating committees;

3

- to provide adequate funding for research into the problem areas of language teaching for migrant workers and their families; to initiate and fund measures which would help them in adapting themselves to the new social environment and to improve the supply of information available to them. (Council of Europe 1979, 86)

At a convention held in 1960 **UNESCO** came out against discrimination in education and in favour of the right of ethnic minorities to preserve their culture of origin through measures provided in the schools. In the resolution of the General Conference of UNESCO in 1972, all member states were called upon to take concrete measures to ensure that migrant workers' children had the same access to educational facilities as indigenous children and that the quality of their education was improved. In October 1973 the first conference of experts took place in Paris. UNESCO subsequently mounted further conferences and initiated research projects and recommendations, especially on the social problems of migrant workers and their families, on the preparation of statistical material, on the teaching of the language of the host country, and on mother tongue teaching and the promotion of the migrants' culture of origin.

The **OECD** sent observers to the conferences of other international organizations when the teaching of migrant children was being discussed, but until 1977 it confined its activities to general migration and employment policy, the problems of re-emigration and the preparation of statistical material. Only in 1978 did it address itself to educational questions and promote national studies on the teaching of cultural and linguistic minorities in the countries of the OECD.

The **International Labour Office** put forward agreements and recommendations on the access of the children to the educational facilities of the host countries, on school counselling, and on guidance in vocational training.

The international debate led to a basic consensus on general aims: opportunities should be opened up to migrant children in the school systems of the host countries – the same opportunities as were available to indigenous children. At the same time they should be enabled to maintain contact with the culture and language of their countries of origin. This last objective was at first linked largely with the need for the children to retain the possibility of reintegration (a matter which was stressed above all by the Council of Europe). A further aim, supported especially by the Standing Conference of Ministers of Education, was to stimulate and influence indigenous children.

Whereas originally the statements and recommendations emanating from these bodies were concerned chiefly with young immigrants who had only recently arrived in the host countries, later documents tend to address themselves increasingly to the task of providing suitable education for second- and third-generation immigrants. It must be stressed that there was an early awareness of the risk of segregation connected with the setting up of special preparatory classes, and that such segregation was declared to be undesirable and even dangerous. Until about 1972 official statements tended to lay more stress on the fear that the migrants might forfeit their own culture, but subsequently the demand for their integration into the education systems of the host countries was brought more into the foreground.


**The history of the Directive**

The treaties which laid the foundation of the European Economic Community in 1958 were concerned primarily with economic development. They contain no specific statements on education and provide for no regulations on educational issues. Schemes or recommendations in the sphere of education policy thus have to relate to or be derived from those areas covered by the treaties, for instance from Article 49 of the EEC Treaty, which relates to freedom of movement for workers.

In Regulation 1612/28 (L 257/2 of 19 October 1968), the demand for special training for the children of migrant workers who are nationals of member states is derived from their basic right to freedom of movement for themselves and their families. Article 12 states:

> "The children of a national of a Member State who is or has been employed in the territory of another Member State shall be admitted to that State's general educational, apprenticeship and vocational training courses under the same conditions as the nationals of that State, if such children are residing in its territory.

> "Member States shall encourage all efforts to enable such children to attend these courses under the best possible conditions."

This article contains two requirements: children from EEC countries must enjoy equality in these countries with the indigenous children, and special measures must be taken to achieve "the best possible conditions". From this the authorities of the Community derived the right to initiate innovations in the sphere of the education of migrant workers' children and to make these binding upon the member states. It was at first disputed whether it was permissible to derive recommendations on education policy from economic and social considerations, but this question was settled in the Council's socio-political action programme of 21 January 1974. The action programme went substantially farther than Regulation 1612/68: its measures are extended to include all migrant workers, including those of non-member states, and are directed towards creating a school education with fair opportunities for the children of migrant workers both from member states and from third countries. Commitment to education was reinforced by a judgment of the European Court which made it clear that the

5

education policies of member states could not restrict the effects of Community measures: Community measures lay down the conditions under which the individual states shape their policies, including education policy (judgment of 3.7.1974, cause 9/74).

On 6 June 1974 the education ministers described the creation of better opportunities for the general and vocational education of nationals of the member states and non-member states as one of the most important collaborative undertakings in the field of education. The central demand was for an active bilingual command of the mother tongue and the language of the host country. In order to realize the aims of the action programme the Commission laid down certain principles to which it sought the assent of the member states:

- Children of migrant workers have a right to an education suited to their situation;

- they should be helped by special pedagogical measures during their integration into the educational and social system of their host country;

- the mother tongue and culture must be represented in the timetable;

- reintegration into the school system of their countries of origin must be possible;

- no distinction must be made between nationals of member states and nationals of third countries with regard to their admission to schools and their school attendance.

From these principles the Commission derived a series of further concrete demands, above all the creation of a sufficient number of preparatory and remedial classes, the improvement of teaching methods and materials, the introduction of schemes which would as far as possible enable the mother tongue and culture teaching to be given during normal school hours, the introduction of measures which would allow of the children's reintegration into the school systems of their countries of origin, the training of specialist teachers to work with migrant workers' children, the appointment of bilingual teachers capable of giving tuition in the mother tongue and culture of their countries of origin, the guaranteed inclusion of the children in national training schemes, intensified social work designed to ensure regular school attendance; in addition there were demands for the encouragement of bilateral and multilateral agreements between the host countries and the countries of origin to facilitate co-operation in educational affairs, with special regard to the appointment and training of specialist staff.

From 1974 onwards, draft directives were submitted and fully discussed at various levels. On 28 July 1975 a final draft was laid before the

Council, and on 24 September 1975 an opinion was expressed by the European Parliament. On 29 January 1976 the Economic and Social Committee made its views known, including in particular the demand for measures to be taken which would remove any discrimination against migrant workers, guarantee their children access to all forms of education and prevent the emergence of ghetto-like conditions. It was stressed that the setting up of schools intended mainly or exclusively for the education of ethnic minority children was rejected as undesirable because it would make their integration into the community of the host country more difficult. The Committee agreed to the setting up of reception and remedial classes.

Political discussion about the Directive took place principally in the Committee of Permanent Representatives of the Member States. This has the task of doing the preliminary work for negotiations in the Council and thus supports the work of the Council, whose decisions can be signed only by the ministers themselves. The group specializing in social questions, which had to do the crucial work on the proposed Directive, subjected the Commission's proposal to thorough scrutiny at thirteen meetings held between 24 September 1975 and 18 May 1977, working through it repeatedly article by article, introducing modifications, and submitting detailed reports on the results of its work to the Committee of Permanent Representatives. The Committee then reported to the Council; the most important reports are dated 28 June 1976, 30 November 1976 and 14 August 1977.

It is significant that, from 11 February 1976, the German delegation to the groups dealing with social questions included not only members of the Permanent Representation of the Federal Republic of Germany at the EC and the Federal Minister for Education and Science, but also representatives of the Conference of Ministers of Education.

**The debate on the Directive**

There was a number of controversial points on which a compromise had to be found. Most of these problems were discussed at the meeting of the Council on 24 September 1976 and impeded the passage of the Directive.

The Commission's proposal and the Directive are set out here side by side:

| COMMISSION | COUNCIL |
|---|---|
| Proposal for a Council Directive on the education of the children of migrant workers | Council Directive of 25 July 1977 on the education of the children of migrant workers |
| *(Submitted to the Council by the Commission on 28 July 1975)* | (77/486/EEC) |

7

THE COUNCIL OF THE EUROPEAN
COMMUNITIES,

Having regard to the Treaty
establishing the European
Economic Community, and in
particular Articles 49 and
235 thereof;

Having regard to the proposal
from the Commission;

Having regard to the Opinion
of the European Parliament;

Having regard to the Opinion
of the Economic and Social
Committee;

Whereas in its resolution of
21 January 1974 concerning a
social action programme, the
Council included in its
priority actions those designed
to improve the conditions of
freedom of movement for
workers, particularly with
regard to the problem of the
reception and education of
children;

Whereas, moreover, the same
resolution fixed as an
objective the achievement of
equality of treatment for
Community and non-Community
workers and members of their
families in respect of living
conditions;

Whereas in their resolution
of 6 June 1974 the Ministers
of Education, meeting within
the Council, also achnowledged
as a priority matter the
development of better
opportunities for cultural
and vocational training for
nationals of other Member
States and of non-member

THE COUNCIL OF THE EUROPEAN
COMMUNITIES,

Having regard to the Treaty
establishing the European
Economic Community, and in
particular Article 49 thereof,

Having regard to the proposal
from the Commission,

Having regard to the opinion
of the European Parliament,

Having regard to the opinion
of the Economic and Social
Committee,

Whereas in its resolution of
21 January 1974 concerning a
social action programme, the
Council included in its
priority actions those designed
to improve the conditions of
freedom of movements for
workers, particularly with
regard to the problem of the
reception and education of
their children;

countries and their children;

Whereas it is necessary for the children of migrant workers to receive an education suited to their particular situation and to be guaranteed access to all forms of education and vocational training;

Whereas it is necessary to provide the children of migrant workers with a crash course in the language of the host country so that they can be integrated as quickly as possible into the the educational environment or the vocational training system of the host country;

Whereas it is advisable that the children of migrant workers receive tuition in their mother tongue and their culture of origin, in order to ensure the full development of the personality of children situated between two cultures and to maintain the possibility of reintegrating them into the educational system and the social and economic life of their country of origin;

Whereas application of the system of education thus envisaged should be extended to all children of migrant workers residing in the Community, irrespective of their country of origin and the nature of the occupations of the persons responsible for them; whereas the system thus conceived is such as to contribute towards improving living and working conditions in the Community; whereas the Treaty has not provided all the powers of specific action

Whereas in order to permit the integration of such children into the educational environ- and the school system of the host State, they should be able to receive suitable tuition including teaching of the language of the host State;

Whereas host Member States should also take, in con- junction with the Member States of origin, appropriate measures to promote the teaching of the mother tongue and of the culture of the country of origin of the abovementioned children, with a view princi- pally of facilitating their possible reintegration into the Member State of origin,

9

necessary to bring about this
objective; whereas recourse
should therefore be made for
this purpose to the
provisions of Article 235,

HAS ADOPTED THIS DIRECTIVE:

HAS ADOPTED THIS DIRECTIVE:

### *Article 1*

The Member States shall facilitate within their territory
the gradual adaptation of the
children of migrant workers to
the educational system and
social life of the host
country whilst ensuring that
the cultural and linguistic
links are maintained between
the children and their country
of origin.

For the purposes of this
Directive, children of migrant
workers are children who are
the responsibility of any
national of another Member
State or non-member state
residing on the territory
of the Member State where the
said national is employed or
pursues a professional or
trade activity.

### *Article 1*

This Directive shall apply to
children for whom school attendance is compulsory under the
laws of the host State, who are
dependants of any worker who is
a national of another Member
State, where such children are
resident in the territory of
the Member State in which that
national carries on or has
carried on an activity as an
employed person.

### *Article 2*

For this purpose the Member
States shall make all the
arrangements necessary in
order to organize on their
territory appropriate gratis
initial education in
reception classes for the
children of migrant workers,
including, in particular, a
crash course in the language
or in one of the official
languages of the host country.

### *Article 2*

Member States shall, in
accordance with their national
circumstances and legal
systems, take appropriate
measures to ensure that free
tuition to facilitate initial
reception is offered in their
territory to the children
referred to in Article 1,
including, in particular, the
teaching – adapted to the
specific needs of such chil-

This education shall be
provided for such children
following compulsory
education on a full or part-
time basis as defined by the
laws of the host country.

dren - of the official language
or one of the official
languages of the host State.

Member States shall take the
measures necessary for the
training and further training
of the teachers who are to
provide this tuition.

### Article 3

The Member States shall also
make all the necessary arrangements to include in the school
curriculum gratis tuition in
the mother tongue and culture
of the country of origin of
children of migrant workers
suitable for achieving the
aims laid down in Article 1.
While the Member States
should make use of those
methods and techniques which
are best suited to the needs
of migrant workers' children,
such tuition must be given in
in accordance with the
education standards normally
applicable in the host
country, particularly as
regards the minimum or
maximum number of pupils per
class. This tuition shall
cover the entire period of
full-time compulsory
education as defined by the
laws of the host country.

### Article 3

Member States shall, in
accordance with their national
circumstances and legal
systems, and in cooperation
with States of origin, take appropriate measures to promote,
in coordination with normal
education, teaching of the
mother tongue and culture of
the country of origin for the
children referred to in
Article 1.

### Article 4

The Member States shall make
all the necessary arrangements to ensure the training
of teachers who are to
provide the crash course
in the language of the host
country and the tuition in
the mother tongue and culture

11

of the country of origin of
the children of migrant workers.
For the tuition in the
tongue and culture of the
country of origin, the
Member States shall, where
necessary, make use of
foreign teachers.

### Article 5

The Member States shall bring
into force within three years
following notification of this
Directive the laws,
regulations and administrative
provisions necessary to comply
with the Directive, and shall
forthwith inform the Commission thereof.

The Member States shall also
inform the Commission of all
laws, regulations and
administrative or other
provisions which they bring
into force in the sphere
governed by this Directive.

### Article 6

The Member States shall submit
to the Commission within four
years following notification
of this Directive all useful
data to enable the Commission
to report to the Council on
the application of the
Directive.

### Article 7

This Directive is addressed
to the Member States.

### Article 4

The Member States shall take
the necessary measures to
comply with this Directive
within four years of its notification and shall forthwith
inform the Commission thereof.

The Members States shall also
inform the Commission of all
laws, regulations and
administrative or other
provisions which they adopt
in the field governed by this
Directive.

### Article 5

The Member States shall forward
to the Commission within five
years of the notification of
this Directive, and subsequently at regular intervals at the
request of the Commission, all
relevant information to enable
the Commission to report to the
Council on the application of
this Directive.

### Article 6

This Directive is addressed
to the Member States

## The legal form of the Directive

A great deal of time was taken up by discussion of the legal form in which the Commission's proposals should be presented to the member states. The question was whether the text should be a directive or a recommendation. It must be borne in mind that the directive is one of the Community's instruments which have binding legal force.

Up to the last moment the British and German delegations had objected to a directive on the ground that a division of powers existed in the education systems of their own countries, so that on principle they could not agree to the introduction of binding regulations at Community level. The Irish delegation likewise preferred a non-binding instrument, though it gave no particular reasons. The Commission and the Italian delegation were in favour of a directive on the ground that a non-binding instrument would not create a new situation which went beyond earlier resolutions.

However, the question of the legal form of the text cannot be seen simply in relation to the non-centralized structure of the British and German education systems. In Articles 2 and 3 of the Commission's draft, special measures are required for migrant workers' children preparatory to their admission to the national system, and for tuition in the mother tongue. A directive would have been acceptable to Ireland, the Netherlands and Great Britain, however, only if its terms were relaxed on a number of points and member states were given greater freedom to plan their own measures. Agreement became possible only when the requirements contained in these articles were watered down and made relative to national conditions and national legal systems. These modifications having been introduced, even the British government withdrew its constitutional objections. The Federal Republic, which, as already mentioned, was represented in these discussions by members of the Conference of Ministers of Education, also gave its assent.

The adoption of this legally binding Directive was thus bought at the price of a whittling down of its terms on certain essential points which will be discussed below.


## The position of children of migrant workers from non-member states

The important question was whether the Directive should apply solely to the children of nationals of EEC states or include the children of nationals of other countries too, and whether it should apply only to children whose parents were actually employed in the country or also to the children of foreign residents with independent means and no gainful employment. In both cases the Commission had decided in favour of the more liberal interpretation.

The Italian delegation in particular was in favour of distinguishing between member states and other countries. Here it should be remembered that the applicability of the Directive to workers from member states can be justified by reference Article 49 of the Treaty, whereas Article 235 has to be invoked in the case of persons of independent means and nationals of third countries. The two countries most strongly opposed to a differential treatment of nationals from member states and third countries were Great Britain and Ireland. There was some discussion as to whether a directive should be adopted for migrant workers' children from EEC countries and a recommendation added regarding children from other countries, or alternatively whether an extension of the provisions to children from third countries could be achieved by a joint declaration.

In the final version the Italian view that nationals of member states should be differentiated from others carrried the day. In its preamble the Directive, unlike the draft, does not invoke Article 235, and the reference to equal treatment for workers from the Community and those from other countries is omitted. Also deleted is the express requirement that compulsory education must be extended to all children of migrant workers, irrespective of their country of origin and the type of occupation they follow. In Article 1 it is expressly stated that the Directive applies to those children who are liable to compulsory education according to the law of the host country, who are entitled to support, and who live on the territory of the member state in which the national in question earns or has earned a wage or salary. It follows that the Directive applies only to children of workers from EEC countries.

After the promulgation of the Directive an attempt was made to counter its potentially discriminatory effect. The Council took steps to ensure that its action programme in support of migrant workers and their families, envisaged in the resolution of 9 February 1976, also led to better educational and training opportunities for nationals of non-member states and their children, at the same time recalling the measures set out in the Directive. Also, in the report of 28 June 1976, it is stated that those delegations who were pressing for the wider application of the proposed measures should make declarations that when the Directive was implemented at national level all groups of migrant children would be included.

## Mother tongue teaching

Article 3 proved especially contentious. The main problem here was the division of responsibility between the host counties and the countries of origin in matters of educational policy and finance. The Federal Republic of Germany stressed the high cost that it would have to bear; Great Britain declared that the cost of measures which the host countries did not regard as priority matters, such as mother tongue and culture teaching, should be borne by the countries of origin. Some of the delegations took the view that the cost of such teaching should be shared.

It was maintained, however, that joint responsibility must not mean that co-operation with the countries of origin would infringe the competence of the authorities of the host countries. Apart from the German delegation, those of Luxemburg and the Netherlands, while not opposed in principle to the terms of Article 3, pointed out difficulties in the way of its implementation. The British delegation in particular attached great weight to the words "in accordance with their national circumstances and legal systems".

The effect of the statement that tuition in the mother tongue and culture of the country of origin should be shared between the latter and the host country may be that, if no collaboration takes place, there is no obligation on the host country to provide such tuition. The wording in the draft was clearly different on this point: there it was stated that the member states should take all measures necessary to ensure that such teaching was incorporated into the curriculum and that teaching methods should be developed which were suited to the particular situation of the children. It was further stated that this teaching should continue throughout the period of compulsory schooling, as defined by the laws of the host country. Article 3 is watered down even further in the protocol declarations which are part of the Directive. According to these, the children in the host country have no individual legal right to mother tongue and culture teaching. On the positive side, however, one should note that the Directive itself calls for the co-ordination of mother tongue tuition and mainstream teaching.

### Reception teaching

The Commission's proposal that appropriate reception teaching should be provided gratis for the children of migrant workers also did not pass without discussion and was not adopted without modification. The British delegation pointed out that for constitutional reasons the government at Westminster was not in a position to dictate to schools what their curricula should contain. Accordingly, this article too was made relative to national conditions: whereas it is stated in the draft that member states "shall make *all* the necessary arrangements", the Directive states that they "shall, in accordance with their national circumstances and legal systems, take appropriate measures".

### Appointment and training of foreign teachers

Article 4 of the draft was intended to regulate the whole complex question of teacher training and the appointment of foreign teachers. The Directive, however, speaks only of the obligation to provide for the training and further training of the teachers involved in reception teaching (this now comes under Article 2), and there is no mention of the obligation to train those who are to give mother tongue tuition. On this and on the question of the use of foreign teachers one must refer to the minute of 14 June 1977 on Article 3 of the Directive, which states that questions relating to the use of teachers from the countries of origin and the necessary in-service training of the teachers for this kind of teaching will be examined "in this framework". The phrase "in this framework" refers to the framework of the limitations set out under point 3.

Thus, as a result of the committee's deliberations, the binding nature of the Directive was restricted, especially by making it relative to national circumstances. A representative of the French delegation, which had shown the least resistance to the original version of the Directive after the impression aroused by the protocols, voiced the following criticism in the Social Committee: "The content of the Directive has been so attenuated that there is almost no Directive left, thanks to all the flexibility." This criticism is correct to the extent that the adoption of compromise formulas opened the way to the possible circumvention of the terms of the Directive when concrete measures were introduced and brought into force. On the other hand, it can be countered by the observation that the legal form of the Directive, which was bought at the price of various compromises, provides the Commission with the political means to pursue its original intentions within this more open framework. The member states will not find it easy to evade the demands in the field of educational policy that are set out here, even though they have left themselves considerable room for manoeuvre in the matter of their realization. The significance of the Directive in terms of educational policy will thus depend on the consistency of the policies pursued by the Council and the Commission, on the capacity and willingness of at least some of the member states to introduce innovations on their territory in the spirit of the Directive, and on the maintenance of a basic consensus among all member states regarding the general objectives outlined in the Directive.


## The initiation of pilot projects during the debate on the Directive

In the resolution passed by the Council and the Ministers of Education in February 1976, the Commission was given a mandate to carry out pilot projects in the member states in order to try out and evaluate certain aspects of the implementation of reception teaching, mother tongue teaching and forms of in-service training for indigenous and foreign teachers working with ethnic minority children. The setting up of pilot projects shortly before the adoption of the Directive naturally resulted in a link between the two from the point of view of content.

In a number of respects these pilot projects were experimental in character: they were the first attempts made by the Council and the Commission to initiate innovations in the member states by means of selective support and to examine the possibility of generalizing whatever solutions were found. This is linked to the notion that in this way it will be possible to encourage more countries to adopt these objectives in the sphere of educational policy. The following analysis of four pilot projects will attempt to show what progress was made towards these objectives.

# Reflections on methods

A comparative evaluation of innovatory schemes introduced in various countries can be of little interest to those concerned with educational science and educational policy unless it proceeds beyond mere analysis and juxtaposition. On the one hand, the specific character of the individual pilot projects can be understood only from within the educational traditions of the countries in which they were conducted; this context must therefore be understood and described. On the other hand, it is quite plausible, to say the least, to assume that certain problems which have so far proved intractable in these national contexts derive from comparable educational structures and are hence common to more than one system. Moreover, it is reasonable to presume that these problems, at least in the area of educational provision for migrant children, are generally recognized as not having been successfully solved. This is confirmed not only by the activities of supranational institutions, especially the Council of Europe and the European Communities, but also by the fact that a European debate, admittedly encouraged by these bodies, has begun among educationists, teachers and administrators – and even, at times, politicians – which has by now reached such an advanced stage that theoretical "recidivism" is no longer tolerated. In the context of this debate, the idea of "intercultural teaching" has prompted a truly impressive response throughout Europe, thus demonstrating – if demonstration were needed – that efforts to identify common structural shortcomings need not ignore the realities of the problems at national level.

Our present reflections, which perforce amount to no more than a brief synopsis, relate to three dimensions of analysis, which had to be kept separate during the planning of our research, in order to create a theoretical framework within which they could be related to each other in a consistent manner at a later stage. To use the language of sociological methodology, we were concerned, first, with microanalysis, i.e. with the study of individual pilot projects, and, secondly, with macroanalysis, i.e. the study of the political, legal, economic and social conditions of migrant workers in the host countries and of the situation of their children in the individual education systems; this is a subject which occupied far more of our attention than is suggested by the few pages that we are able to devote to it in the present book. Thirdly, our study had a comparative component, operating at a level between and above the dichotomy of microanalysis and macroanalysis. This means that, insofar as the problems derive from similar structures, the activities of the pilot projects – while always viewed with reference to their individual structure and their national context – are set side by side and compared with one another, in order to ascertain whether they can contribute to the solution of more widespread problems. Any assessments we make in this regard are related to our own stance, which we are at pains to make clear. Such assessments and comparisons are intended to suggest a new orientation and thereby stimulate further development: they make no predictions, however, about what is likely to happen if our suggestions are adopted and pursued under conditions other than those which gave rise to them. Thinking such processes through is a quite separate task, which we embarked upon when it became necessary to go beyond comparison and assessment and come up with recommendations. We are aware that our recommendations can be only tentative; but we thought it worth while to pursue these ideas a few stages further

There is something artificial about reconstructing the methodology of our research retrospectively, as though it had been evolved during a clear-cut phase of our work, and as though by the end of this phase we had to hand a set of accurate instruments ready for use in further investigations. The methodological reflections summarized here are at one and the same time pre-conditions and results of the procedure we adopted, in the course of which we repeatedly reconsidered problems of method, treating them not so much as questions of pure methodology, but as open questions to be subjected to research: what we sought to do was to pose questions of content as questions of method and, conversely, to examine questions of method in order to reveal their implications in terms of content. In settling for open procedures, we were also obliged to decide on a flexible application of the instruments of qualitative sociological and educational analysis. We were not involved in evolving the concepts behind the individual pilot projects, nor did we have any say in the modifications that were subsequently in'roduced. This meant that we first had to "get to know" the projects and be constantly prepared for modifications in their educational orientation. Hence, new questions arose whenever we learned something new about the projects, and in each case these had to be pursued by specific means. What is more, we finally found ourselves in methodologically uncharted territory: to our knowledge there have been no comparable scientific projects - and certainly not in the field of migrant education. We could not take it upon ourselves to evolve methodological standards for comparative evaluation research. It is true that our reading of existing theoretical studies in the field of comparative education, evaluation research and the methodology of comparative sociology provided us with valuable insights into individual problems connected with our work, but they also demonstrated to us that we had nothing like a solid body of methodological knowledge at our disposal. A few pointers in this direction were put forward by Wolfgang Nieke in the wake of the international colloquium at which we presented the report on our research in November 1980 (Nieke 1981, pp 96-128). In this chapter we will largely refrain from this kind of normative discussion of possibilities for future research, confining ourselves rather to straightforward reflections on method, so readers will be able to follow the results that are presented here. If from time to time suggestions are made which are of interest outside the immediate context, this need disturb them unduly.

## Description and analysis of the pilot projects

At first we had to take into account a few external difficulties which arose from the circumstances under which the comparative evaluation of the pilot projects was carried out Although in principle they all started at the same time, viz. at the beginning of the academic year 1976/77, mutual agreement as to their objectives was arrived at only in an extremely roundabout way, insofar as the various resolutions of the Council and the manner in which the Directive took shape could be interpreted – and were meant to be interpreted – as general indications of intent. However, one could no more speak of a uniform experimental programme, which might have made it possible to compare the projects according to strict empirical and analytical criteria, than one could speak of their having been co-ordinated. In fact, it was the Commission's intention to leave the national and local authorities all the scope they needed in order to adapt the projects to their own requirements. Moreover the projects were intended to explore different problem areas of migrant education, in order to allow a fairly wide spectrum of possible solutions to be evolved and tested. Also, we were in no position to influence the concepts behind the pilot projects in the direction of uniformity, since we did not begin our work until April 1978, when they had been running for almost two years. We were therefore not concerned with the question of whether such uniformity was desirable.

Under these given conditions it was clear that any evaluation of the projects was possible only "from the outside": the separation of our research team from those who were actively involved in the projects also precluded certain rudimentary kinds of field research. The time factor too relegated us to the position of "neutral" observers, able to analyse the development of the projects, but unable to intervene in their development.

We had countless informal discussions with those who took part or were more or less directly involved in the pilot projects – teachers, school heads, inspectors, consular representatives, indigenous and migrant parents, and also, where the language situation allowed, with the pupils themselves. In this way we informed ourselves about the educational concepts behind the projects, their internal structures, and the political, institutional and material conditions under which they were conducted. In addition, we made use of all the documentary material available to us: proposals for class projects, working papers of project groups, minutes of their meetings, personal files kept by the participants, school records, teaching plans, teaching and learning materials developed during the pilot projects, textbooks used in lessons, pupils' written work, etc. In some cases we had to insist gently on being given certain materials; in other cases we were shown documents that we did not know existed. Whenever we were asked to do so we treated the information we were given as confidential. (Our bibliographical references include only material that was publicly available at the time and still is.) At an early stage we agreed in general to use factual information only if it was confirmed by at least one other source. Where we have cited our informants' interpretations, this is is always indicated; the sole criterion for using such interpretations was their factual relevance to our own analysis.

From these conversations there emerged a great variety of partly overlapping and partly contradictory views of the pilot projects. We made it our task to analyse them and then reassemble them in order to arrive at our own assessment.

The contact our informants had with us, however, gave them a chance not only to give their own account of a particular pilot project, but also to reflect (in some cases not without embarrassment) on the part they played within their particular team. For us this meant above all trying to understand the information we gathered from these conversations as interpretations of the realities of the projects by particular people occupying particular positions - in other words, interpretations which we ourselves then had to interpret in order to differentiate between the facts themselves and the participants' perceptions of the facts. This must not be taken to mean that we treated their perceptions merely as raw material to be worked on by our own interpretative skills: on the contrary, we considered it essential to follow their interpretations as far as possible, lest the 'external evaluation" became restricted to viewing the pilot projects solely from outside. And our readiness to adopt our informants' perspective to a large extent was a prerequisite for our attempt to correct any ingrained ethnocentricity in our own patterns of interpretation.

In order to create a solid basis for such interpretative procedures, we decided, in the second phase of our investigation (after we had gained a detailed knowledge of the pilot projects), to carry out a series of extensive qualitative interviews; these were recorded on tape, and full transcriptions are available. We had previously discussed the idea of an agreed format for these interviews with the leaders of the pilot projects and the local evaluators and sent them a draft for their comments and further suggestions; suggestions for revisions were then incorporated into the version that was eventually used.

We sat in on lessons conducted by teachers belonging to the project teams in order to be able to compare their didactic concepts with the way in which they realized them; whenever possible we discussed our observations with the teachers immediately after the lessons. Having taken notes during the lessons and the subsequent conversations with the teachers, we had further discussions with other members of our team in order to decide what further observations needed to be made in subsequent lessons and what further questions should be put to the teachers.

The reports of the local evaluators constituted a special source of information. At the express wish of the EC Commission, the programmes of all the pilot projects included evaluation procedures which were entirely independent of our own. These became the object of a special part of our comparative evaluation; at the same time, the evaluators' reports on the individual projects furnished information which we could make use of in our own analyses.

What is true of the pilot projects as a whole is true to an even greater extent of the evaluations: tney were independently planned and lacked any uniformity of conception. Whereas the projects themselves were all influenced, at least to a small extent, by the educational policy underlying the Council's action programme and the Directive, there was not the least trace of agreed methods or objectives in the evaluations This demonstrated to us, on the one hand, the very limited degree to which professional standards have taken hold and, on the other, the advances that have been made in the establishment of "schools" of evaluation with relatively distinct methodological and pedagogical profiles. In the controversies between these schools it is often hardly possible any longer to discern a universally accepted frame of reference. It is probably to this curious situation, in which a diffusion of standards is combined with a basic rigidity of approach to questions of educational theory, that we should attribute the "lack or good and easily accessible evaluation studies" which was noted by Wulf as early as 1972 (Wulf 1972, p 264) and has still not been remedied even today Under these conditions every study that is published is subject to the most varied and scarcely predictable criticism and has little chance of commanding assent. Hence, the upshot of these abstract academic discussions remains intangible to practical teachers and school authorities. There is consequently a growing conviction that evaluation can generally be dismissed as a kind of arbitrary game; in favourable cases on the other hand, it is perceived as a means to be employed to secure legitimation for certain measures, while in unfavourable cases it is seen as a pseudo-scientific monitoring device employed by the bureaucrats, which should therefore be fended off. This mixture of incomprehension, distrust and indifference towards evaluation could be sensed in some of the pilot projects; it found expression not least in the fact that the local evaluation, relating only to the one project, was not planned until the "project itself" had been finalized. It was clearly not appreciated that evaluation might be a vital factor in educational innovation – indeed in educational activity as a whole Presumably one of the reasons for this is the intangibility of "evaluation". The remedy for this state of affairs is to spend less time lamenting the lack of published evaluation studies – and to publish more of them.

This minor reflection may serve as an example of how we attempted – at a comparative level – to make use of the advantages we enjoyed as outsiders. Other examples find concrete illustration in the case studies themselves, especially where the internal structures of the pilot

22

projects are involved. Here we must add a few further observations The
more opportunities we had to appreciate how those taking part in the
projects perceived their own roles and the problems facing them, the
more sensitive we became to the interactive dynamism which - often
behind their backs - created definitions of problems which they could
no longer evade. *What* had to be dealt with as a problem or task was
determined by consensus - though this consensus was sometimes fraught
with conflict: *how* these problems and tasks were to be understood
however, was not infrequently a matter of dispute among those involved.
By the time we made our first contacts with the pilot projects they had
already developed their own political and pedagogical identity; our late
arrival on the scene, our relative aloofness from the projects, and the
obligation we were under to make a comparative study served to make us
aware of this state of affairs and forced us to recognize it as an
issue in itself. The relation between the innovations that were
developed and tried out in the pilot projects and the ideas and
practices that were accepted in the school systems of the different
countries was generally characterized by a good deal of tension. This
was particularly obvious, for instance, where the position of the
bilingual teachers was concerned, especially in those cases where they
did not use the language of the country of origin as a medium for
subject teaching, but taught it as a subject on the curriculum: those
indigenous teachers who daily had to contend with the language
problems of the migrant children tended to consider every minute that
was not spent during subject lessons - at least indirectly - on the
acquisition of the language of the host country (in other words the
language of the school!) as a waste of time, and consequently found it
hard to see any educational sense in having mother tongue teaching as
a subject on the curriculum. The marginal position which the mother
tongue teachers occupied in the staff was a clear indicator of this. To
find a way out of this difficult situation, the pilot projects resorted
to the most varied strategies; these included withdrawing pupils from
mainstream classes, adapting the aims and content of mother tongue
tuition to the expectations of the indigenous teachers, and increasing
the amount of advice and back-up given to bilingual and indigenous
teachers alike. It was quite obvious that in all this the cohesion of
the project teams - both as regards the convictions they shared and
friendly personal relations they maintained - was a vital factor in
making it possible to plan and execute (or justify) offensive
strategies. On the other had, the cohesion of the project team was
really put to the test when schools reacted in an unenthusiastic or
even hostile manner to a proposed innovation, failing to see the sense
of it or finding it highly inconvenient.

Schools are conservative institutions which can seldom be induced to
adopt a proposed new measure solely by virtue of its inherent
plausibility and logicality. Consequently we had to regard these
conflicts as unavoidable and try to analyse them as "miniature test
cases" if we wished to arrive at a judgment about whether certain

measures could be introduced generally and what resistance might be expected if this were to be done.

This is an example of how an analysis can typically succeed only if there is a certain distance from the day-to-day action; it also exemplifies the fact, however, that precisely our distance from the pilot projects enabled us to understand that we had to get close to them if we wished to do them justice, that we could not circumvent the analysis of patterns of personal interaction which had developed and went on developing in the projects.

The analysis at this level brought us face to face with problems whose methodological and ethical dimensions could not be clearly delimited in the process of our investigation. It is true that at an early stage, in view of the material and practical conditions under which we were working, we had turned away from the idea of action research, and that we never intended to intervene in the pilot projects with active advice or criticism, let alone guidance, but we did arouse expectations in this direction among some of those taking part in them - expectations which expressed themselves all the more insistently, the closer we drew our network of information and interpretations around the projects. Such expectations came, for example, from teachers who had risked coming into conflict with their superiors and now hoped that we would throw our authority as evaluators (as they saw it) into the scale in their favour.

Wherever such wishes were expressed, we interpreted them as the reverse side of a phenomenon with which evaluators are not unfamiliar. It is true that there are considerable variations from country to country in the extent to which teachers are subject to bureaucratic monitoring structures, but such monitoring is never entirely absent, and its inhibiting effect is often palpable: teachers are not geared to evaluation, but to inspection, in other words to asymmetrical communication and power relationships. This encourages playing along dutifully and patiently with the exercise known as evaluation, even when the point of it is misunderstood; this weakens the desire to ask questions and makes it difficult to conduct a factual dialogue, even if it is controversial. We tried to explain our position and made a point of deferring, in one way or another, to those participating in the projects. Of course we could not always avoid being irritated, especially when we had to decide to disappoint their expectations.

It seems that "evaluation" is developing into a more or less regular component of innovatory projects in education and thus acquiring certain features of a professionalized activity. In this situation it is not enough to neutralize the unavoidable potential for conflict by reference to the differing standards obtaining in the professional systems of "science" and "education"; it is not enough for the evaluator to adopt ethical maxims without further ado from the ethics of research, which the social sciences have simply taken over, rather than developing them, in the course of their history; and it is not enough to reinterpret methodological principles, of whatever kind, in terms of the ethic of research. In the long-term view it will be indispensible to develop a code of behaviour for evaluators. Its formulation may be a matter for the (emergent) profession, but its testing and putting into operation will not be for evaluators alone: those whose work is to be evaluated (and for whom, significantly, evaluation theory has no simple designation) will also have to be heard. They will of course not only be listened to: they will have to make themselves heard. It is true that they know that evaluations touch upon their own interests, but they must seize (or create) opportunities to defend their interests and attitudes and rely more on themselves than on the evaluators. The aim should be a situation in which the potential and the limits of role definitions can be made transparent and to this extent negotiable. This may make evaluation more "democratic", and it can, as we have learnt, lead to results which in the end are more satisfactory for both sides – more satisfactory not because they are harder to achieve, but because more productive thought is invested in them, and hence more satisfactory for both sides even when no absolute consensus has been reached.

**Description and analysis of national "migrant education systems"**

The analysis and interpretative reconstruction of the "identity" of each of the pilot projects is situated, as it were, at one end of the scale of levels of analysis. At the other end is the analysis of the education provision which the individual societies organize for migrant children or which they variously deny them. This part of our programme was, at our instigation, expressly written into the terms of reference which we negotiated with the EC Commission. As a programme we considered it – and still consider it to be clearly necessary and in need of no further justification. As a concrete research project it was an adventure no less exciting than our collaboration with the pilot projects. Our initial knowledge of the political, legal, economic and social conditions under which ethnic minorities lived in the four countries involved in the pilot projects, as well as our knowledge of the children's educational problems, was rudimentary, being based on desultory reading and fortuitous personal experience. Yet the categories according to which the knowledge available in the specialist literature was to be selected, worked up and assimilated, insofar as it was relevant, seemed fully developed. The way in which education systems should be investigated seemed to us to present no problem of principle. We still had to learn from experience that the real difficulty lay not in learning what we still did not know, but to recognize what we still did not understand. Ethnocentricity was the key word, and immanent analysis the antidote.

Now it is almost axiomatic that the better the quality of the "indigenous" literature, written in the national language by members of a certain society for other members of the same society, the less likely it is to link explanation with description. The more highly developed and differentiated the educational debate is in a given country, the more self-referential the literature as a whole becomes, and the more hermetic the individual work is for anyone outside the debate. Hence, it seemed to us at times that we were less likely to acquire the vital structural knowledge we needed from the specialist literature than from competent informants, whether they were teachers or academics, parents or ministry officials, nationals of the host country .or members of the ethnic minorities. We sought out expert informants at all levels of the education systems in which the EC Commission had instituted pilot projects, sometimes pursuing our enquiries at some distance – even geographically – from the projects themselves. Those whom we came to regard as "experts on education systems" tended more and more to be people who, by conventional standards, would never have dreamt of describing themselves as such – in particular teachers and parents. As we became better acquainted with the structures of the different education systems and familiarized ourselves with the interpretations which dominated (and at the same time typified) the local debate on "migrant education", we had to alter our conversational strategies, being by now able to move away from general discussions and concentrate on drawing out our informants about their views on educational matters and the strategies they had evolved in their dealings with the system in order to put them into practice. Whenever we succeeded in this, the detailed knowledge we had acquired from our reading of the literature began to shape itself into a sometimes surprising and in any case sharper picture of the way in which the system functioned. We had to decide, on the basis of our knowledge of the literature, which educationist was most likely to give us informative answers to our questions and which senior official was likely to provide the best insight into the educational hierarchy. Although our journeys required long-term planning and careful timetabling – in other words, economical use of our own and other people's time – we continually had to allow time for a chance conversation – in the school playground or the canteen of a centre for in-service training, or in a staffroom that was positively humming with excitement after surviving a visit from an inspector. It is characteristic of the professionalized discourse which reflects the activity of educationists that the power relationships which structure their activity remain undiscussed, to make them accessible to analysis we therefore had to seek out and exploit conversational situations in which they were clearly in evidence.

Conversations with experts, combined with our own observations, could thus help us to organize the amorphous mass of knowledge we acquired from the literature. Conversely, the knowledge we needed in order to understand what they told us had to be sought in the literature, most of it written in the host country; for the comparative literature – insofar as it goes in for actual comparisons and is not confined to abstract arguments about comparative method – is all too liable to operate with striking antitheses which purport to explain much when most is still not understood. Categories like "centralism" and "local autonomy" are undoubtedly essential to an understanding of education systems, but anyone who wants to get a clear grasp, for instance, of what factors determine the degree of professional autonomy enjoyed by teachers in a given system, in order to understand what the "professional autonomy of teachers" means in that system, will have to ignore such categories if he is to have a chance of arriving at anything more than premature conclusions. Possibly the value of comparative studies is mainly heuristic, in the sense that they make the reader (and the author) aware of different ways of looking at his or her own system.

In fact we were at first less interested in the question of how systems differed or what they had in common than in the workings of the individual system, insofar as it helped us towards a more adequate understanding of the pilot project operating within it. Which of its problems were structurally conditioned? In what did its innovatory element consist? What difficulties would arise if the innovation were generalized? If we wanted answers to such wide-ranging questions, our first task was to assemble as accurate a picture as possible of the way in which the system functioned. Hence, we were often obliged to rely on talking to experts in order to plug the "systematic gap" between the comparative and the indigenous literature; this had the inevitable disadvantage that essential insights were occasionally not attested or hard to attest.

## Comparison and questions of transferability

In our analysis of the individual education systems we found it necessary to let ourselves be guided more by their specific structure than by preconceived categories and schemes of classification, because our investigations were intended to lead to an assessment of how far individual measures could be generalized within given systems or introduced into others.

The structures specific to individual systems make it impossible to set up uniform schemes for the achievement of identical objectives. Proposals along such lines would have to rely on abstract definitions of the problems, and such definitions would have at most a minimal chance of being recognized by those involved as adequate descriptions of the pressing problems they faced, and would therefore have scarcely any chance of being accepted as an appropriate means of dealing with them. Education systems "consist" not only of organizational structures and patterns of pedagogical activity: they also have their own language, which reflects this activity but is not universally transparent. But even if uniformly defined programmes were accepted and operated everywhere by the people on the spot, they would lead to disparate results within the complex structures of different systems, not only because the unintentional or unplanned side-effects would vary from system to system, but above all because the effectiveness of an innovation arises just as much from within itself as from its relation to marginal conditions. These marginal conditions · and hence the way in which the innovation is related to them - would be bound to vary from case to case.

This cannot mean, however, that a system-oriented analysis would have helped us to formulate our recommendations. One might conceive the attractive idea of taking certain measures that have proved successful in one context, and then identifying functional equivalents which could perform equivalent functions in each of a number of other contexts and which - at least in principle - could be formulated in the language of each of the systems and thus have a better chance of being accepted by those who would have to operate them. This, however, would require an analysis of extraordinary theoretical complexity, such as we could not have produced in the time available to us and with the means at our disposal. It is doubtful, moreover, whether such an analysis could be carried out successfully: there would be too great a risk that the scientific apparatus that would be necessary for carrying it out - and especially the administrative apparatus that would be necessary for the implementation of the results - would be smothered, as it were, by excessive complexity. If such a procedure were to be adopted, the basis for educational legitimation would become intolerably narrow, in the first place because the scientific and political outlay would quite probably outweigh whatever was gained in terms of educational innovation, and, in the second place, because viable pedagogical innovations can only be developed - or so we are convinced - in close contact with the day-to-day reality of school life.

Instead, we attempted to find an "intermediate level of abstraction", on which we could, on the one hand, discuss educational problems in reasonably concrete terms and, on the other, formulate meaningful statements which were independent of the specific contexts of particular systems. On this level, problem areas were defined in which it was possible to discern structurally similar pedagogical tasks. In selecting these problem areas we relied in the first place on classifications which have become established in the international debate on education; in the second place, the selection is the result of our own analysis and comparative study of the pilot projects It is the result of the individual analyses insofar as the findings of each of these reveals specific problems; it is the result of our comparative study insofar as it makes it possible to determine in terms of content, the "structural similarity" of problems which in the individual analyses appear devoid of content. What is proposed here in terms of further solutions or orientation for further experiments emerged from a process of discussion in which we confronted our own original positions with the insights we acquired while analysing and comparing the pilot projects; these were then discussed in the reciprocal context of situational conditions, the needs of those affected, the interests of

28

those taking part, and subject-specific aspects. This discursive approach implies a rejection both of the deductive application of our criteria to the states of affairs we found already existing and also of an inductive approach, the only objective of which would have been to add up the objectives that were discussed and aimed at in the various pilot projects and education systems, in order to declare the sum total of these objectives to be the yardstick for the whole.

This approach would have its justification in an "inductive implementation" of innovations which could rely on our proposals being independently discussed in the individual countries. Such an "inductive implementation" would have to go hand in hand with a strengthening of the role of teachers in the process of educational reform. In our evaluation of the pilot projects we endeavoured to follow a teacher-oriented procedure, not only because - to borrow Reich's bold formulation - we consider "the best instrument of evaluation to be the observant teacher who is able to form judgments and able to communicate" (Reich 1981, p 81), but also because we see the committed and well trained teacher as the person who ultimately has the decisive role to play where any innovation in educational policy is concerned - at any rate a role that is decisive if the innovation is to be effective and improve the situation of the pupils.

# Ethnic minority children in the Belgian education system

## The legal and social framework

Belgium has been a destination for migrant workers since before the First World War and saw several waves of immigration after each World War, the chief pull being exercised by the mining industry. At the end of the last century foreign nationals already made up 2.8% of the population, most of them coming from neighbouring countries (cf. Varzee 1980, p. 4). After the end of the First World War those who took up the mining jobs that Belgians found uncongenial were largely Italians and Poles. After the Second World War the mining industry set up recruiting centres for foreign labour, first in Milan (1946), then in Athens (1953), Madrid (1956), Casablanca (1962) and Ankara (1963). Towards the end of the fifties other branches of industry began to employ increasing numbers of migrant workers, and this resulted in a greater concentration of foreign nationals in the big towns outside the mining areas (Brussels, Antwerp. Ghent).

The economic boom of the sixties led to the arrival not only of workers who had official permission to enter the country, but of large numbers of others who entered clandestinely or as "tourists" and found employment without the necessary work or residence permits. Since the beginning of the seventies in particular, there has been, as a result of the fall in the indigenous population in certain parts of the country, an influx of dependants of migrant workers, a development which was not unwelcome and has been officially encouraged. However, the disproportionate rise in the number of non-working dependants from abroad has placed a growing social burden on the industrial conurbations. On 1 August 1974 the Council of Ministers for Economic Co-ordination finally resolved, in view of the progressive deterioration of the economic situation, to call a halt to further immigration except in the case of dependants from other member states of the EC and those of foreign nationals who had valid work and residence permits.

In 1980 the number of foreign nationals living in Belgium was estimated to be approximately 950,000 or about 10% of the total population (Warzee 1980, p. 8). In 1977 the proportion of foreign nationals in the Walloon region amounted to approximately 13%; in Flanders it was 4% and in Brussels 22%. The majority, i.e. about 61% come from member states of the EC. Some 12.2% of these are under twenty years of age, and of these roughly half were born in Belgium. The Italians constitute the largest group of foreign residents (33.8%), followed by the French (12.6%), the Moroccans (9.6%), the Dutch (8.3%), the Spaniards (7.6%), and the Turks (6.9%) (Rosiers-Pollain 1979, p. 10). In 1977 the number of children born to foreign nationals in the Brussels region represented 41.2% of all births; in the Walloon region the corresponding figure was 19.2% and in Flanders 8.2%; the figure for Belgium as a whole was 15% (Rosiers-Leonard/Pollain 1979, p. 16).

A foreign national wishing to work in Belgium requires a work permit and a residence permit. These were first introduced in 1936, and since then the regulations have been updated several times, i.e. adapted to the changing economic circumstances. Since 1968 no work permit has been required by citizens of EC countries, who now automatically receive a residence permit for a period of five years. In the case of other foreign workers the granting of a residence permit is dependent on their possessing a work permit. There are several forms of work permit:

- Card B, which is valid for only one year and for one specified employer, but may be extended after one year (Card B Sector); this new Card B allows the holder to work for another two years and to change employers, though not to move to another branch of employment;
- Card C, which is also valid for a limited period only, but is issued to workers who are employed by various employers (cleaning women, dock workers, etc)
- Card A, which is valid for an unlimited period and for all kinds of employment; this is issued according to criteria related to nationality, family status, and the length of time the holder has previously been employed in Belgium as a holder of either Card B or Card C.

Children of migrant families who have been resident in Belgium before attaining the age of fifteen are entitled to receive the same form of work permit as their fathers; those entering the country after this age have to apply for one separately.

Foreign nationals intending to remain in Belgium for longer than three months require a work permit before they can be granted a residence permit. There are two forms of residence permit:

- foreign workers who have a work permit valid for a limited period (Card B or C) are issued with a "white card" (CIRE) which entitles them to stay longer than three months, but must be renewed yearly;
- foreign workers who are in possession of a work permit in the form of Card A are issued with a "yellow card" entitling them to stay in Belgium for up to five years.

The wives and children of migrant workers who have regular employment in Belgium automatically receive a "white card".

The authority to grant residence permits and to extend the duration of their validity lies with the local aliens office, and in the last resort with the Ministry of Justice. A residence permit becomes invalid when its holder has not resided in Belgium for a period of more than six months; foreign nationals who have resided in Belgium for less than five years can have their residence permits withdrawn on grounds of public order or national security; those with more than five years' residence 'may lose their residence permits   only if they are found guilty of serious offences by the courts.

Foreign nationals in Belgium enjoy neither active nor passive voting rights. A growing number of advisory committees on aliens' affairs has however been set up since 1968, their members being elected by the aliens themselves. At national level there has been an advisory committee on immigration since 1965

Finding accommodation represents a serious problem for migrant workers. In the early days of immigration their employers often provided them with inadequate housing. Meanwhile ghetto-like conditions have developed in the industrial conurbations. Those who have lived in Belgium for some time and changed their place of abode frequently succeed in moving into residential areas favoured by the indigenous population. Today even the mining industry can provide its migrant labour not only with employment, but with job-linked accommodation of acceptable quality.

## Educational opportunities

Article 17 of the Belgian constitution of 1831 states: "Education is free; any measure which restricts this freedom is prohibited..." On the basis of this article an education system has evolved in Belgium in which education is provided by various school authorities or "networks" competing with one another. These networks comprise in principle all kinds of school and levels of schooling throughout the country. Educational freedom is thus understood as freedom of provision and freedom of choice. The state is obliged to maintain its own schools where the facilities offered by other bodies are insufficient to meet local needs. Beside these state schools we find independent schools (which are largely Catholic), community schools, and provincial schools; these last provide mainly secondary schooling. The independent Catholic schools are linked with one another at national level within the framework of the National Secretariat for Catholic Education (NSKO/ SNEC). There are very few independent schools belonging to other religious denominations or run by private bodies. State schools, community schools and provincial schools are denominationally neutral. The umbrella organization for community and provincial schools is the Permanent Commission for Official Neutral Subsidized Education (CEPONS). A large number of community schools are supported notably by those communities with large financial 'resources. Independent, community and provincial schools can receive state subsidies for buildings, equipment, administration and teaching staff if they satisfy certain conditions, which are constantly monitored by a state inspector of schools. The central umbrella organizations and the parents' associations affiliated to them exercise an important influence on the development of the Belgian education system. In view of this there tends as a rule to be a marked element of competition between schools belonging to the different networks; hence co-operation between them is exceptional, though it would be wrong to generalize.

A problem peculiar to the Belgian school system arises from the language controversy. The country contains four linguistic areas: a French-speaking area in the south (Wallonia), a Dutch-speaking area in the north (Flanders), a bilingual area in and around Brussels, and a German-speaking area around Eupen and Malmédy, which for administrative purposes belongs to the French-speaking area. The Dutch-speaking and French-speaking schools have separate education ministries. A law passed on 30 July 1963 lays down the linguistic priorities to be observed in schools: in Flanders the first foreign language is French, in Wallonia it is Dutch. Instruction in both begins in the fifth school year. In the bilingual region of Brussels heads of families can determine the linguistic medium in which their children are to be taught; here instruction in the first foreign language begins in the third school year. For this reason mother tongue teaching and the appointment of bilingual teachers are possible in the maintained sector only if the necessary order is issued to enable the existing language law to be bypassed. In other words both are virtually impossible because of political obstacles. Since, however, Islam became an officially recognized religion in Belgium in 1974, it has for some time been possible for instruction in the Islamic religion to be given by foreign teachers in Belgian schools. In the normal course, foreign teachers, who enjoy the status of consular staff, do their teaching outside the regular school hours.

Compulsory education begins at the age of five. Since 1965 schools have worked a five-day week. Many schools have lessons all day.

The Belgian school system is divided into three levels:

- elementary education and primary education, together constituting basic schooling;
- secondary levels I and II, i.e. lower school and upper school (here one must distinguish, according to a reform begun in 1969, between a traditional and a reformed type of secondary school);
- universities and institutions for higher or further education.

Pre-school education is an integral part of the general education system and is essentially subject to the organization and regulations laid down in school legislation. As a rule pre-school facilities are attached to primary schools and are often accommodated in or near the same buildings. Pre-school attendance is voluntary; children are admitted from the age of two and a half and may attend up to the age when compulsory schooling begins. No fees are payable. Approximately 85% of three-year-olds, 90% of four-year-olds, and 98% of five-year-olds attend kindergarten.

Few migrant children appear to take advantage of pre-school provision. Although there are at present no reliable figures to hand, what limited information we have suggests that migrant workers' families are unaware of the pre-school facilities available and hence make little use of them.

Until 1978 no special official provision was made for the pre-school education of migrant children. On 16 August 1978 a government order was issued affecting the whole of "basic" (pre-school and primary) education and establishing the rule that additional teaching staff could be taken on wherever the proportion of foreign pupils reached 50% or more. This was to be carried out according to a quota system, one teacher being appointed for the first twenty pupils and one more for every fifteen above twenty. Starting in the school year 1979/80 these norms applied also to pre-school institutions and to primary schools in which 30% of the pupils were of foreign origin; they applied also to reception classes, in which children newly arrived in Belgium were prepared for attendance at normal lessons. In view of the situation previously obtaining, this represented a considerable relief, since the average size of classes in "basic" education was 30, with a range extending from roughly 15 to 40. For the transition from pre-school to primary education migrant children benefited from the system of social and educational support that had been developed for Belgian children, there being no facilities or special provisions designed specifically for them.

The norms obtaining in pre-school education for the allocation of extra teaching posts to schools with a specially high proportion of foreign pupils applied equally to primary schools. Primary schooling extends over six years and comprises three levels. As a rule classes correspond to age groups, and a system of class teachers is operated. In the first two years the curriculum follows on from pre-school education, and at first there is no division into subjects. It builds upon the interests and experience of the children, the aim being to explore and observe the world in which they live. From the start, however, there is systematic instruction in the language of the relevant linguistic area, writing and arithmetic (basic skills) From the fifth school year on the teaching is divided to a greater extent into subjects.

Belgian children with learning problems can receive remedial teaching in primary schools up to a total of three lessons a week in small groups. This measure was introduced to relieve the burden on special educational institutions. On occasion migrant children have been admitted to these so-called "adaptation classes", though between 1973 and 1978 this was in principle not permitted. Another facility is specially aimed at migrant children who have attended primary school for less than three years: they can be taught in so-called "language classes" which take place three times a week and give them a special introduction to their second language. Such classes may be set up whenever there are at least ten children belonging to this target group. The success of this remedial measure has been hampered largely by organizational and timetabling difficulties. The special support facilities which are possible throughout the pre-school and primary sphere in schools with a high proportion of migrant children are provided through the appointment of teachers "for special duties"; these are appointed from the pool of fully qualified unemployed teachers, whose numbers have increased in Belgium as elsewhere, and their contracts are often part-time and short-term. This makes possible a considerable variety of teaching which is by no means confined to language instruction, but embraces support provision in all the subjects taught in the schools. Nevertheless, such teaching seems to suffer from the less than satisfactory situation of the teachers involved in it.

Apart from these regular support facilities, the Belgian system has put into practice a great variety of special forms of teaching, mainly *ad hoc* and, in individual cases, as officially recognized experiments. Among these are special classes for new arrivals, special classes to facilitate the transition from pre-school to primary school, tutorial programmes in which the Belgian pupils help the foreign pupils, classes designed solely for foreign pupils, etc. Because of the language legislation already mentioned, mother tongue teaching for migrant children is provided within the Belgian school system only in isolated experimental projects. For the rest it is arranged by the consulates of the migrants' countries of origin at their own expense and employing their own teachers, though accommodation is usually provided free in the schools outside normal school hours.

Secondary education at present embraces two co-existing types as a consequence of a reform initiated in the seventies: these are the reformed secondary school (Type I) and the traditional secondary school (Type II). Type I secondary education extends over six years and is divided into three stages, each of two years' duration. The "observation stage" consists of a first year taken by all pupils, and a second year in which they can choose between various subjects and combinations of subjects. The range of choice is enlarged at the "orientation stage", by the end of which technical subjects may be dropped. In the last two years, known as the "determination stage", the number of compulsory subjects is reduced to a third, all the rest being optional. Theoretically there are about 80 different options, though these are so disparate that for practical reasons no single school can ever offer them all. Secondary education of Type II likewise comprises six years, three spent in the lower school and three in the upper school. Three types of course are offered: a course of general education with a classical and a modern component, a vocational course with various subject combinations and specialisms, and an arts course. In the vocational branch the first or "orientation year" is common to all pupils. After three years they may either leave school without any qualification or stay on for a further year of practical specialized training for particular jobs. It is also possible, after the later stage of the vocational or technical course, to take a further year of specialized training leading to a vocational qualification. Some technical courses, while not leading to a vocational qualification, prepare the pupils for further study at a technical college or university. Entrance to the university is generally obtained through a central entrance examination.

Apart from individual projects there are no official support measures for ethnic minority pupils at secondary level. In consequence one finds only a few of them in the higher age-groups and the more demanding courses. Many ethnic minority pupils are already two or more years behind in their school progress when they leave primary school and hence not far off school leaving age. Rosiers-Leonard/Pollain 1979, p 60ff, draw attention to the fact that in this situation migrant students not only often opt for short-term training courses designed to prepare them for the transition from school to working life, but are also oriented towards jobs that have no significant career prospects (as tailors, hairdressers, shoemakers, etc). Thus the under-achievement of the pupils may be explained as due not only to the lack of specific support provision in secondary education, but also to the inadequate guidance given to parents and pupils, poor housing opportunities, switching schools during the school year, etc. Among the individual schemes which are operative in the secondary sphere one should mention the reception classes with intensive language teaching offered by one technical institute and a multinational reception class at a vocational school in Liège, special language teaching for foreign pupils in the technical departments of individual secondary schools in the province of Limburg, and a bridging class for foreign pupils aged ten to fifteen at a textile school in Ghent.

For the vocational training of migrant workers Further Education provision seems to have acquired special importance (cf. Warzee 1980, p. 21ff.) and arouses strong interest especially among the adult members of the migrant communities. There are language courses, courses in general education (e.g. in the mother tongue, mathematics and domestic economy), courses for further vocational training, literacy courses, etc. The success of such courses is admittedly somewhat limited, since only about 20% of migrants actually complete them. Migrant workers, like their Belgian colleagues, are entitled to paid educational leave provided that they are in full-time employment; if they are unemployed they have a right to free attendance at retraining courses. However, no figures are available to show how far migrant workers actually take advantage of these facilities.


## School achievement and vocational integration

It is only in the last few years that we have had statistics relating to ethnic minority children and young people in Belgium which may provide a basis – even if not a fully reliable one – for statements about their success or lack of success at school; many questions in this area still remain open.

For the academic year 1978/79 foreign pupils were distributed among the different levels of the education system as follows (the figures show them as percentages of the total numbers in education):

| Mainstream and | Languages | | | |
|---|---|---|---|---|
| special schools | French/German | | Dutch | |
| Level | Region | Brussels | Region | Brussels |
| Pre-school | 21.80 | 41.07 | 4.98 | 5.55 |
| Primary | 21.59 | 37.96 | 4.23 | 3.60 |
| Secondary | 15.90 | 23.05 | 2.79 | *) |
| Further/Higher | 16.73 | 18.43 | 1.40 | *) |

* = no figures available.
Source: Varzee 1980, p. 23, based on information supplied by the Statistics Department of the Ministry of Education.

A limited picture of the academic achievement of foreign pupils emerges from the following statistics for the year 1976/77. The data refer to proportions of primary pupils in mainstream classes who suffer from one or more years of "delay" in their academic careers.

| Nationality of pupils | Percentage of pupils with "delay" in year group | | | | | |
|---|---|---|---|---|---|---|
| | 1 | 2 | 3 | 4 | 5 | 6 |
| Belgian | 13.6 | 19.9 | 25.2 | 29.0 | 35.0 | 31.8 |
| Non-Belgian born in Belgium | 21.9 | 32.3 | 41.1 | 43.1 | 49.8 | 43.4 |
| Non-Belgian born outside Belgium | 40.9 | 56.5 | 60.4 | 69.6 | 73.4 | 71.6 |
| All non-Belgians | 26.0 | 37.0 | 45.6 | 50.3 | 52.9 | 52.0 |

Source: Varzee 1980, p. 39.

Note: These figures apply only to the French-speaking and German speaking regions, yet there is little reason to believe that the picture was substantially different in the Dutch-speaking region. Also, figures refer to *all* foreign pupils, not only to those from migrant workers' families. Thus it may be safely assumed that the relevant proportions would have been even higher among migrant pupils.

To appreciate this table one must bear in mind that in the Belgian education system (and, as we shall see later in the French education system) the "delay" (*retard*) of a pupil is regarded as the most powerful indicator of his or her academic achievement: a pupil whose performance is deemed inadequate at the end of a given academic year has to "repeat" the year with a class of pupils from the next lower age group. Thus, even though our table shows that up to 30% or more of pupils in any given class will suffer "delay", teachers tend to see this as a sign of low ability in individual pupils: they do not conform to the "norms", and the downward spiral is opened up. As the "delay" of pupils builds up, so do their chances of being considered "definitely a dunce": with a delay of two years, pupils are automatically screened for referral to an ESN school. This is why in the above table the number of pupils suffering from delay decreases between the fifth and sixth years of primary education: many pupils will now have accumulated two (or more) years of "delay", and are subsequently referred to ESN schools. Finally, this also explains why many migrant students enter secondary education with hardly any other prospect than that of being oriented towards the less demanding courses which lead to early – and more often than not unskilled – employment, or simply to unemployment.

Equally, it is this logic that ensures that the proportion of migrant students who stay on at school beyond the age of fifteen is lower than among their Belgian peers, and that the proportion of those in "working life" (including unemployment) is higher among young migrants than among young Belgians.

We may thus see that the proportion of young people aged between fifteen and nineteen who attend school is lower among migrants than among Belgians, and that a correspondingly higher proportion of them is to be found among young people who are in work or unemployed. Moreover, we find typical differences when we come to distinguish between types of employment. It is less common for young migrants to be self-employed or to work in white-collar jobs. These differences become even more obvious when one distinguishes between skilled and unskilled manual jobs (Rosiers-Leonard/Pollain 1979, p 22ff).

Data on unemployment in Belgium corroborate the following facts, which are also to be found in other countries that are subject to immigration: unemployment is higher among migrants than it is in the indigenous population, and young migrants are more often unemployed than young Belgians. In June 1978 the proportion of those out of work was 7.3% overall, whereas the corresponding proportion was twice as high among migrants. The fact that young people of foreign origin under the age of 25 were under-represented among the unemployed, however, is probably an indication of hidden unemployment: since many in this age group do not qualify for unemployment benefit, they see no point in registering as unemployed.

# The pilot project in Genk (Belgium)

## Approval and general conditions

In Hasselt, the capital of the Belgian province of Limburg, there has existed since 1964 a *Provinciale Dienst voor Onthaal van Gastarbeiders (POG)* ("provincial service for the reception of guest workers"). In 1974 a working party of the *POG*, the *werkgroep onderwijs* ("working party on education") began to consider ways of integrating the mother tongue education which was provided for the children of ethnic minorities outside normal school hours into the regular school curriculum. Early in 1976, on the basis of its deliberations, talks were initiated between the working party, the Ministry of Education (MNO), and the European Community on the setting up of a pilot project. The participants in these negotiations were the heads of the schools involved, representatives of the local educational authorities, the consulates of the interested countries, and the children's parents. What emerged was a plan for a three-year experiment.

The parties to the discussion had different expectations: some wanted to try out various forms of transition from pre-school to primary education or the children's acquisition of first-language competence; others wanted to explore collaboration between the state sector and the independent sector and between various nationalities (Greeks, Turks, Italians and Belgians), as well as ways of reducing the burdens placed on ethnic minority pupils and their teachers, of enabling these pupils to reach the learning standards required by the Belgian system while at the same time receiving mother tongue instruction, and of establishing comparability between experimental findings etc. In a government order of 25.08.1976 the project was approved by the Ministry of Education, in the first instance for one year. As a result of further applications for the school years 1977/78 and 1978/79 the government issued further orders authorizing the continuation of the pilot project, in each case for one year. At the same time it was extended to include new intakes of primary and pre-school pupils.

These government orders laid down the general and particular aims of the project, curricular, personal and organizational principles and measures, evaluation objectives, and the basic funding of the project. For the duration of the project and the area of the country in which it was to operate, the language law of 1963 was suspended so that mother tongue instruction could be integrated into the normal timetable. To facilitate the implementation of the project the Ministry laid down the following conditions: it should be implemented in both sectors, which were to be co-ordinated by the *POG*, and lead to identical and transferable structures; it should pay as much attention to Greeks and Turks as it did to Italians; the duration of the project should be limited to two to three years, but yearly applications should be made for its continuation; the schools should be free to decide upon the methods they employed.

On the recommendation of the responsible inspectors the schools selected to take part in the pilot project were the state primary school at Genk-Waterschlei and the two independent primary schools at Genk-Winterslag (one a boys' school and the other a girls' school). As is shown by the following statistics, the teaching of migrant pupils in the state school took place in particularly difficult circumstances:

| State school | Independent school |
|---|---|
| - 80% of the pupils are from migrant families and the proportion is increasing | - 50% of the pupils are from migrant families |
| - The migrant pupils have as a rule had no pre-school education | - Many of the migrant pupils have had a pre-school education |
| - Almost all the Belgian pupils come from miners' families and lack social motivation | - A fair proportion of the Belgian children are of lower middle-class origin |

Most of the foreign workers in Genk are employed in mining or metal-processing industries. Individual families, especially those of Polish and Italian descent, have lived in the area for three generations, yet often remain keenly aware of their origins and inherited culture. Foreign nationals make up a third of the population of Genk and account for roughly 50% of the birth rate in the area.


**Systematic description**

**Aims**

The aims of the pilot project in Genk were laid down in the Ministry of Education order of 1976. This stated that the general aim was the integration of immigrant children into pre-school and primary education; linked to this were the following specific aims:

-   to enable the immigrant children, through intensive instruction in Dutch, to take part successfully in regular primary classes;

-   to promote a knowledge of the language and culture of their countries of origin;

-   to integrate them into into the society of the host country;

41

-   to improve conditions for the acquisition of basic cultural
    techniques and the assimilation of the subject matter of lessons.

In an undated statement of principles issued by the *POG* the underlying
concept of the project is elucidated as "an agreed programme in which
teaching is conducted in the mother tongue for a certain number of
lessons, after the necessary agreement between the Belgian and the
bilingual staff, so that the children can acquire a good knowledge of
their own culture and mother tongue, while not missing any part of the
Belgian school curriculum".

Within this concept, reception teaching and mother tongue teaching are
closely related to the Belgian school system and its curriculum. Within
this concept of integrated teaching, instruction in the mother tongue
was assigned the following tasks:

-   It should keep open the possibility of the children's returning to
    their countries of origin;

-   it should help migrant families to overcome communication
    difficulties;

-   it should facilitate the children's reception into Belgian schools,
    help them overcome the difficulties they encounter at school and
    improve their understanding of the Belgian school curriculum;

-   it should help them in their social integration and living in a bi-
    cultural environment;

-   it must contribute to their integration into Belgian society and at
    the same time to their acquiring a cultural identity of their own;

-   it should serve to promote mutual contacts between the cultures,
    foster cultural exchanges and contribute to the enrichment of
    school life.

### School Organization

#### General

The three schools involved in the pilot project belonged to two
different sectors (the state sector and the independent sector). They
embraced years 1 to 3 of pre-school education and 1 to 6 of primary
education. Included in the project were the third pre-school year and
the first three years of primary school. The state school at Genk-
Waterschei was co-educational, while the independent Catholic schools
at Genk-Winterslag were single-sex establishments. Under the enabling
order all three schools were assigned the same aims and obligations.
The necessary co-ordination of measures was achieved through the

steering group and the *FOG*. This co-ordination was restricted, however, by the differing conditions under which the schools had to operate, by the absence of a common inspectorate, and by the fact that each sector had its own advisory and evaluative authorities. Hence, within the framework of the norms laid down by the Ministry of Education, the schools evolved their own relatively independent teaching and evaluation programmes.

## Class size and pupil-teacher ratios

A ruling by the Ministry of Education laid down that the number of pupils in the classes involved in the project should be fifteen. Starting in the third year, however, the project classes had to conform with normal class size. This led to improved staffing levels in the schools concerned. The state school was able to take on a new teacher for Italian, Greek and Turkish respectively, and the two independent schools between them took on two extra teachers for Italian, one for Greek and one for Turkish. The number of Belgian teachers was also increased in line with the rise in the pupil numbers. Moreover, the allocation of an extra teaching post made it possible for headteachers to be relieved of teaching duties (this being possible under normal circumstances only when the number of pupils increased to over 300). Starting in the second year of the project, an additional nursery school teacher was made available for the third pre-school class.

After the first year of the project, the classes moving up into the second year in all three schools were restructured on the basis of linguistic competence, being divided into groups according to their level of achievement. The independent schools set up two groups, the state school three. In its enabling order for the school year 1978/79 the Ministry of Education sought to prevent a situation in which differentiation between pupils on the basis of achievement led to classes consisting entirely of ethnic minority pupils, but in the state school this could not be avoided because of the small number of Belgian pupils attending it.

## The weekly timetable

In its enabling order the Ministry adopted in all essentials the weekly timetable that had been submitted for approval. Lessons were to be of 50 minutes' duration and cover the following subjects:

basic cultural techniques (reading, writing, arithmetic) (12 periods a week);

intensive instruction in Dutch (4 periods a week);

creative and expressive learning (2 periods a week);

43

games (1½ periods a week);

religious instruction (2 periods a week);

mother tongue teaching (maximum 4 periods a week).

The four lessons allocated to mother tongue teaching had to run concurrently so that the individual groups would not miss any of the normal lessons. In these periods both the mother tongue teaching and the teaching given to other pupils was to be devoted mainly to consolidating and revising what had been learnt. The mother tongue teaching was spread out over several days of the week. In the first year of the project the state school attempted to work in a fifth hour of mother tongue teaching in the form of a *belevingsles* ("experience lesson"), in which a Belgian teacher, in the presence of the bilingual teachers, introduced a new teaching unit. This extra lesson was abandoned in 1977/78 in order to avoid making excessive demands on the bilingual teachers' time.

## Special remedial measures

Thanks to the appointment of an additional nursery school teacher at the pre-school stage it was possible to divide the children involved into different groups. Despite differences between the activities pursued in the three schools taking part in the project, they all had similar grouping patterns: either the children were divided into two groups of the same size and the same age, or a small number of children were selected from the total class for special remedial teaching. In the latter case the nursery school teachers divided their time between the larger and the smaller group.

Even before the introduction of the pilot project the Belgian education system made provision for special remedial groups to help both migrant and Belgian children; such groups already existed in all three schools. The state school had a *taalklas* ("language class") in which small groups of ethnic minority pupils were taught Dutch as a foreign language, a specialist teacher being available for the purpose. Both the state school and the two independent schools had the services of a teacher for special duties (*taakleerkracht*), whose task it was to give intensive remedial tuition to small groups of pupils, especially Belgian pupils, who needed individual help in order to master the basic techniques of reading, writing and arithmetic; with the agreement of the class teachers, these pupils were allowed to miss about three regular lessons a week.

At the state school the language teacher taught each of three differing ability groups of ethnic minority children for four or five lessons a week. The aim was to limit the number of pupils in each group to seven, but this proved impossible because the number of pupils fluctuated. The groups were distinguished as follows:

- children with no knowledge of Dutch (illiterates and those who could read and write only in their mother tongues);

- children with a basic knowledge of Dutch vocabulary and simple sentence structure; these were taught by means of the Dutch teaching packs "Nou Jij" and "Mustafa";

- children who had lived in Belgium for about two years; in their case an attempt was made to use mother tongue methods to promote their oral and written proficiency.

## Pedagogical principles

The teachers taking part in the pilot project started from a particular educational tradition. This was naturally examined to see to what extent it could serve to justify the measures used for teaching ethnic minority pupils and for solving the educational problems arising from immigration, but it went broadly unquestioned. Faced with the new situation they sought guidance from the educational concepts which have been realised in the various reforms that have taken place in Belgian primary education from the sixties to the present day.

The educational principle underlying practice in the state school was *totaliteitsonderwijs* ("total education"). By this was meant a general education which took the children's inherited culture into account and, starting from their real situation, envisaged a continuous educational development from home to school, resulting in a harmonious and balanced personality. The content of the teaching was orientated towards the child, the family, the school, and society, and was given concrete form in such topics as "My father's job", "How to make a fruit salad", "The clothes we wear", "The parts of our body", "Mealtime", "Let's pretend we're shopping", etc. Each topic was introduced in an "experience lesson" given by a Belgian teacher. Starting from an experience common to all the pupils, the functions of speech, action, movement, perception and expression were practised, at first as a whole, and then with progressive differentiation. It was only gradually that the individual subjects on the syllabus took shape.

The teaching in the independent schools similarly took as its starting point major topics in the child's experience, but was geared to the subject known as *wereldoriëntatie* ("world orientation"). By this was meant a comprehensive form of teaching which was more strongly orientated towards practical subjects and aimed at a more precise and thorough presentation of the child's environment, resulting in a more rapid delineation of the individual subjects to be taught. The topics chosen centred upon the general concepts "other people", "nature", "culture", "modern civilization". These were agreed upon and worked out in detail by the staff, and then set out in the *afspraakboekjes* ("agreement booklets"). By following the *afspraakboekjes* it was possible to co-ordinate and structure the form and content of the teaching given by the Belgian and bilingual staff. The necessary arrangements were arrived at under the direction of the head teacher. Objectives, teaching content, working methods and teaching materials were integrated within the framework of these basic topics and designed to improve the motivation and activity of Belgian and foreign pupils alike.

## Learning areas

### Intensive instruction in Dutch

The intensive teaching of Dutch formed the core of the educational activities at the kindergarten and primary school stages, the starting point being the colloquial language and the children's first-hand experience. The intention was to provide regular teaching for both Belgian and non-Belgian children, and to this extent there was no express provision for the use of methods which involved the techniques of second-language teaching.

Superficially it seemed that all the schools taking part had the same understanding of the aims, content and function of such teaching. Its aim was to encourage linguistic activity in the children and promote a better active and passive command of colloquial Dutch (*allgemeen beschaafd Nederlands*). In principle it was geared to core topics which had been agreed by the teachers and laid down as binding upon them all. The central objective was to widen the children's vocabulary and promote oral competence. Nevertheless, the teachers seem to have had some difficulty in determining the function of this teaching in its relation to other educational provision. It was supposed to be differentiated from those lessons which were mainly devoted to the teaching of reading and writing; moreover, it was intended to serve primarily as an introduction to new central topics; finally, being designed as regular teaching for both Belgian and non-Belgian pupils, it could not rely on techniques appropriate to second-language instruction. Consequently, a central position came to be occupied by social and practical topics, the programme for these being worked out mainly by the Belgian staff. The independent schools had the following programme for the first and second years: vocabulary exercises, expression exercises, role-playing and dialogue games. The third year was concerned with inculcating the more subject-orientated notions. The colloquial language drills were aimed at enabling the pupils to understand and make contact with their fellow-pupils and helping them to express their thoughts and feelings, use terms correctly, state what they had learnt and give appropriate explanations. In order to be able to use the intensive teaching of Dutch as a basis for mother tongue instruction, an attempt was made to involve the bilingual teachers as guests in "experience lessons". However, these teachers could see little point in this. As an alternative it was later decided, at the independent schools, to introduce discussions between the bilingual teachers and the school heads; at the state school such discussions took place between the bilingual teachers and members of the evaluation team.

### Instruction in the mother tongue and the children's inherited culture

Because of the special legal problems posed by this kind of teaching within the Belgian education system, the Ministry of Education set out a list of fairly detailed rules and requests regarding its implementation. It should be integrated into the normal timetable so that it would not be an extra load on the children; the bilingual teachers should confine themselves to improving the children's colloquial use of the language; in addition it was suggested that the teaching given by Belgian and non-Belgian teachers should be co-ordinated in such a way as to enable the mother tongue instruction to be used as a means of revising and consolidating the knowledge acquired in the lessons given by Belgian class teacher. Accordingly the mother tongue instruction took place in withdrawal classes, and Greek, Italian and Turkish lessons ran concurrently. During this time the Belgian teacher had the chance to do revision work and consolidation exercises with the Belgian children and those ethnic minority pupils remaining in the class.

This concept of instruction in the mother tongue and the children's own culture was adopted in principle by the schools, though subject to certain modifications. There was a general acceptance of the aim that the mother tongue teaching should contribute to the consolidation of the knowledge and the practising of the abilities and skills that the children acquired in lessons given by the Belgian teacher. To this extent it was hoped that it would also provide some support for second-language teaching, and at the same time help the ethnic minority children by improving their knowledge of other subjects and contribute towards their social integration. In addition the children were meant to become sufficiently well acquainted with the language and culture of their country of origin to escape being faced with problems posed by generation gaps within the family, to avoid alienation from their cultural heritage, and to keep open the possibility of returning to their countries of origin.

Such substantial demands were not easy to meet. As early as 1977 it was pointed out that the quality of the instruction given in the mother tongue and the children's inherited culture could never match the standard of the teaching they would have received in their home countries. Above all the requirement that it should be confined to the spoken language seems to have put the bilingual teachers in something of a quandary. In November 1976, at the request of the Greek Embassy, the Greek teacher initiated a course in reading and writing. This lead was followed by the Turkish and, somewhat later, the Italian staff. On the Belgian side this move was defended with the argument that it had not been possible to construct a programme of mother tongue teaching on a solely oral basis. Success in the co-ordination of first and second language teaching was achieved in different ways in the schools taking part in the project. A considerable role in solving this difficulty was played by the ability of the Belgian and non-Belgian staff to co-operate with one another and by the opportunities for co-operation available to them. In the independent schools co-ordination was achieved partly with the help of the *afspraakboekjes*.

The *afspraakboekjes* of the independent schools were a kind of teachers' manual, in which the aims, subject-matter, procedures and teaching methods to be used for the different years involved in the project were grouped concentrically around certain basic topics. These topics were predominantly related to social situations and subject teaching. They acted as regulatory factors in the mother tongue teaching and linked it to the Belgian mainstream curriculum.

They were drawn up in the course of joint discussions with the bilingual teachers at the instigation of their Belgian colleagues. It was agreed that the function to be performed by mother tongue teaching in providing revision and exercises based on the regular Belgian instruction should not remain a pious hope, but be genuinely realised. This agreed intention gave rise to continuous co-operation which in this form was a novelty even to the Belgian staff. It led to a relatively precise terminology for designating the content of mother tongue teaching; this content was undoubtedly dominated by "Belgian" ideas, but it also led the Belgian staff to take cognizance of the ideas of their foreign colleagues and to appreciate the need to incorporate elements of the inherited culture into mother tongue teaching, and in some cases they were even prompted to incorporate some of these elements into their own regular teaching.


### Pre-school education

It was a special feature of the Belgian pilot project that the integration of ethnic minority children into the Belgian school system began as early as the final pre-school year. During this year the teaching was expressly geared to the pre-school syllabus for Belgian children and involved no mother tongue instruction. As in the primary school, it was understood that the aim of the teaching was to activate the children's knowledge of Dutch and to link it with the overall educational programme. The teaching started from the children's own experiences, viewed in their entirety, bringing in aspects of visual and auditory perception, movement, thought and language, encouraging musical expression, and attaching special importance to home-school liaison. The engagement of an additional kindergarten teacher to supplement the work of her permanent colleague made it possible to carry out a special programme designed to improve linguistic competence. The central topics chosen for teaching at the pre-school and primary stages were in large measure identical. The intention was to make the transition to primary education easier for ethnic minority children. However, since these children had not all attended kindergarten before starting primary school, it was impossible to make an adequate assessment of the success achieved by this pre-school provision.

**Persons and institutions taking part**

The enabling orders exempted the project from the law of 30 July 1963, which laid down what languages might be used in Belgian schools and ruled out the engagement of foreign teachers and the teaching of a foreign language as a first language. The regulations embodied in the orders were therefore largely concerned with the appointment of foreign teachers, a prerequisite for appointment being a knowledge of Dutch. The remuneration, social security contributions and legal responsibility for the bilingual teachers were assumed by their countries of origin, finance being provided from funds earmarked for the pilot project by the EC. The bilingual teachers did not become members of the Belgian teaching staff, though they were placed under the authority of the head teachers and required to co-operate with the Belgian class teachers. Their professional activity was restricted to giving instruction in their national languages and cultures within the framework of the lessons allocated to them in the timetable. The orders stipulated in addition that the *FOG* should co-ordinate the project between the state-sector schools and the independent schools. It was the inspectors from the two sectors, together with the head teachers, who applied for the project to be set up, and so to this extent they must be regarded as responsible for its implementation.

In the course of the pilot project the roles and functions assigned to the various participants were perceived and developed in very different ways. From the reports available and the interviews that were conducted the impression emerges that at the state school the main impetus came from the inspector and the employees of the evaluation and advisory service. At the two independent schools the head teachers undoubtedly provided an important stimulus, which did much to promote collaboration both within and between the groups of Belgian and non-Belgian teachers. There are many individual testimonies to the nature, intensity and scope of this collaboration, but no uniform picture emerges. After the project's initial phase (1976/77) co-operation between the two groups of teachers at the state school apparently slackened off or ceased entirely.

This was due partly to the fact that at the state school the project was unsuccessful because bilingual teachers could not be paid for a fifth hour a week, which would have given them an opportunity for

49

better collaboration with the Belgian staff and with one another. The independent school reported that this collaboration, which was at times intensive, took place at weekly meetings between members of staff in their free time and involved among other things discussions about teaching content, working methods and procedures, the keeping of class records, the preparation of lessons, evaluation; it involved also the attendance of the bilingual teachers at lessons given by their Belgian colleagues. Here too, however, there appear to have been some difficulties over collaboration between Belgian and bilingual teachers.

The tasks assigned to the *POG* consisted above all in co-ordinating the activities at the schools taking part in the project, administering the funds allocated to it, and carrying out joint schemes of further training. It must be assumed that, especially in the difficult initial phase, it was the *POG* that made it possible for the pilot project to continue. The *POG* often provided funds from its own resources for the acquisition of teaching materials etc; it also took an active part by carrying out its own investigations with parents and teachers.

## In-service training and counselling of the teaching staff

In the areas of support and in-service training, the pilot project represented a highly complex network of varied and interlocking procedures. The experience gained in the first year showed that for the project to be successful special measures were essential to qualify teachers to undertake the work involved. These included not only qualification measures in the narrow sense of the term, but also, linked with these, developments in curricula and teaching materials. Special in-service courses were put on (e.g. courses in Dutch as a foreign language for bilingual teachers), and various forms of systematic collaboration were organized within the schools between the staff and the head teachers. From time to time the *POG* arranged excursions, contact sessions, co-ordination sessions and training sessions in which the evaluation teams and the inspectors took part.

In both the state school and the independent schools a thoroughgoing in-service training programme was hampered by the fact that the bilingual teachers had so little free time, being obliged to support themselves by taking on other teaching commitments out of school hours. To judge by the reports, the bilingual teachers in the state school regarded their collaboration with Belgian colleagues as valuable. At this school, however, it was impeded by problems of space and a weak infrastructure. The bilingual teachers were accommodated outside the school building proper, and this made informal contacts difficult. The training provision included demonstration lessons, discussions about the co-ordination of teaching activities, and contact sessions of a more general nature, concerned with the exchange of cultural information and with aspects of the teaching methods employed in language classes and subject teaching.

The in-service training of staff at the independent schools was principally directed to aspects of teaching method, exchange of experiences and less systematic information about one another's cultural backgrounds. In both sectors the inspectors and the evaluation teams introduced a greater theoretical element into the training.

## The equipment in the schools

The bilingual teachers working on the project had their own teaching rooms, which they furnished with objects and teaching materials germane to their own language and culture. The state school, however, complained that because of its weak infrastructure the bilingual teachers had to be provided with rooms outside the main school building and that this was not conducive to communication with the Belgian staff. The independent schools reported on special measures they had taken to document the intercultural character of the project.

## Educational diagnostics

The evaluation of the pilot project set out not only to test the value of its results with a view to their general applicability, but also to inform the teachers about their pupils' achievements and the preconditions for successful learning. This aspect links the evaluation of the pilot project with educational diagnostics, which should contribute to an understanding of the children and their learning processes at school, so that measures can be devised to improve day-to-day teaching practice.

In both sectors, especially in the area of pre-school education, there was very close collaboration between teachers and educationists. The latter drew up dossiers of their observations on individual children, by means of which they were able to supply primary school teachers and evaluators with information about the characteristics of each child. In the state school the investigations into the children's learning process in language and reading provided most of the ideas for changes in teaching practice (e.g. splitting up classes into groups according to levels of competence). In the independent schools the absence of suitable tests led the teachers to develop their own observation and investigation machinery, geared in general to teaching aims and used in particular to test the children's abilities and achievements in the area of language learning. Teaching in the schools was also indirectly influenced by knowledge obtained by the evaluation team from studies of school-leavers and similar sources. The practical consequences drawn from such evidence in the independent school included the transfer of children to remedial groups, the intensified teaching of arithmetic, and measures aimed at differentiating and individualizing learning processes. Starting in 1977/78, differentiation according to linguistic ability (the introduction of equal ability groups) was carried out in all three schools.

## Home-school liaison

For some years Belgian schools have been required to allow parents a say in the life of the school. This obligation is binding upon state schools, but independent schools are allowed a transitional period in which to determine their policy. Parents have accordingly organized themselves into associations, which have set up umbrella organizations at national level. In practice, however, it has proved difficult to set up proper forms of representation for ethnic minority parents. As a rule, the migrant parents' associations deal with the school through representatives. The ways in which parents participate in school affairs vary according to local conditions. Those responsible for running the pilot project found that the ethnic minority parents were in the main favourably disposed to it, and Italian and Spanish parents' associations in particular expressed an interest in its implementation.

An initial opportunity for home-school liaison was provided at the start of the project by the need to inform parents about its aims and organization and to encourage them to take part and enrol their children. Both the state school and the independent schools did this by means of home visits. The POG organized parents' evenings, at which information was given about the nature of the project. All three schools consistently stressed the need for co-operation with parents of ethnic minority children. In spite of this, however, the parents seemed at first disinclined to attend parents' evenings at school. Accordingly in 1977/78 the state school set up a working party to discover new and more appropriate ways of conducting home-school liaison and supplying parents with relevant information. One opportunity for this was provided by the often irregular attendance record of migrant pupils. The Belgian authorities used home-school liaison as a means of getting to know the children's home background and discovering the reasons for the difficulties they experienced at school; in this way it was hoped to create a climate conducive to the children's integration into school life. In the third year of the project a scheme for home-school liaison was initiated in which an attempt was made to build up contacts between parents and school by means of weekly coffee evenings and neighbourhood visits. It became clear, however, that such activities out of school hours were an unacceptable burden on the teachers, since they could not find the necessary time. The independent schools sought to use home-school liaison to obtain information about the social life the children led at home, to provide their parents with information about the school and the pilot project, and in this way to create contacts between home and school. The head teacher took on the role of intermediary between the school and the parents. An important part in all this was played by social gatherings which were planned and conducted partly by the migrant parents, either individually or in groups. Otherwise contacts between the school and migrant parents arose either during home visits, which were made at the beginning of the school year to advertise school activities, or at school functions attended by parents. On such occasions the bilingual teachers helped their Belgian colleagues by acting as interpreters. The school was criticized for the relative lack of contacts between Belgian and non-Belgian parents, but it was unable to promote such contacts itself. It was also said that the contacts between the school and the children's homes concentrated too much on the exchange of information.


## Evaluation

### Planning and practice

The initial application to set up the pilot project envisaged an evaluation procedure, and a series of questions was formulated to which appropriate studies were meant to supply the answers. These questions were refined in the first enabling order for 1976/77, then adapted in subsequent orders to the latest stage in the progress of the project. As a whole they are to be seen as an attempt to establish the political and educational legitimation of the project, which was generally recognized as exceptional.

The planning and practice of the evaluation were made difficult, however, by the conditions under which the project was carried out. The fact that the state sector and the private sector operated independently meant that ultimately each school carried out its own evaluation, employing its own evaluation team brought in from outside and using its own evaluation machinery. A further obstacle to a thorough planning of the evaluation was the considerable time pressure under which the experiment was begun. It proved impossible, moreover, to find an evaluation team which was familiar with the development and monitoring of educational projects of this kind. In the event, the evaluation was entrusted to institutions which had been regularly employed within the Belgian education system, with differing remits, to carry out various psychological, pedagogical and sociological investigations in schools.

However, there were shortcomings in the concept of evaluation set out in the ministerial orders. On the one hand the approach was too rigid to allow of free experimentation in the development of evaluation techniques; on the other it was not sufficiently precise to help those taking part to formulate appropriate questions and objectives or to evolve the appropriate instruments. In addition, the evaluation process was impeded by a lack of suitable machinery for investigating the group under consideration, viz. ethnic minority pupils, and also by a certain degree of dissatisfaction on the part of the educationists with the facilities available for conducting psychological and sociological studies. The available records give no indication that any scientific discussion took place regarding the theoretical and methodological principles of the investigation, though in 1978 a colloquium was held which seems to have led to a higher degree of self-criticism and the introduction of a more formative element into what had at first been a merely summative approach to evaluation.

The independent schools, which took part in the project in the three years 1976/77, 1977/78 and 1978/79, included pupils from the third pre-school year and the first three primary-school years in the evaluation sample. It proved somewhat difficult, however, to find suitable control groups. As a rule, the control groups that were used were not comparable with the groups under investigation; moreover, they kept changing during the course of the project.

Altogether three types of test were carried out:

- the children's knowledge of Dutch was tested by means of *ad hoc* methods; at first the tests were confined to their command of the spoken language, but after the third year of primary school, and in each subsequent year, they were extended to the written language too;

- at the beginning of each year entrance tests and intelligence tests were carried out in pre-school classes and the first class of primary school;

- at the end of each academic year the customary Belgian tests were carried out to assess reading skills (comprehension and spelling), as well as arithmetical skills and linguistic competence.

At the state school too the classes involved in the pilot project were brought into the evaluation process, but here too it proved difficult to find suitable control groups. Those available had a different make-up from the sample group, and in the course of the project their number was increased. For the year 1978/79 there no longer seems have been a control group. The evaluation procedure can be gathered only indirectly from the minutes and reports, since these simply reflect the results. They reveal the following evaluation concept:

- At the beginning of the school year the usual entrance tests and intelligence tests were carried out on new entrants.

- At the beginning and end of each school year specially devised tests were conducted to assess the state of the children's knowledge of Dutch and their reading ability. In 1978/79 use was also made of reading tests developed outside the pilot project. In addition, teachers' assessments of the children's progress in linguistic competence and reading skills were brought into the evaluation.

- At the end of the school years 1977/78 and 1978/79 sociogrammes were devised by a social worker in the primary school classes involved in the project; these were evaluated for their bearing on the question of social integration.

At all three schools attempts were made to bring the mother tongue teaching into the evaluation. Accordingly, language tests in the children's mother tongues were carried out by the bilingual teachers at the independent schools, but the findings are not available. A similar procedure was adopted at the state school. The data for 1977/78 were exploited, but not those for 1978/79.

On the initiative of the *POG*, interviews were conducted with both the Belgian and the ethnic minority parents. A questionnaire was prepared jointly by both sectors, but the survey was carried out and evaluated by different teams. The survey, conducted in the spring of 1978, took the form of open or semi-standardized interviews. The ethnic minority parents were asked for information about their social situation, their views on the importance of bicultural teaching, the attitudes of their children, their contacts with the school, and how they saw the future of bicultural teaching. Similar but more varied and wide-ranging questions were put to the Belgian parents.

## Results and conclusions

The language tests carried out at the independent schools show that all the children made some linguistic progress, but that the pupils from ethnic minorities, while improving their school-related vocabulary, remained generally behind their Belgian peers when it came to formulating abstract ideas. In the course of the project, however, it was noted that individual migrant pupils caught up with and overtook the Belgians. This was attributed mainly to the intensive instruction they had received in Dutch. By the end of the three years, however, it was obvious that for most ethnic minority pupils this was too short a time in which to make up all the leeway. The tests designed to monitor school achievement, carried out partly in correlation with control groups, revealed no significant differences between the project groups and the control groups. The evaluators interpreted this as meaning that immigrant children were not disadvantaged by the incorporation of mother tongue teaching into the regular timetable. A significant difference appeared only in the case of the Belgian children who entered school in 1978/79. Because of the more intensive teaching of arithmetic, this group was found to have a higher degree of numeracy and a better command of arithmetical language.

In the state school too a more varied picture emerged from investigations carried out in the course of the project. A comparative study of first-year primary school children revealed that ethnic minority children who had attended kindergarten showed superior learning achievements. Progress in second-language learning was found to be greatest in those children who were farthest behind linguistically at the beginning of the period under consideration. The process of learning to read seemed to have been helped by earlier pre-school attendance. It became clear also in the last two years of the project that on average the Greek and Italian children performed better in the language and reading test than the few Belgian children in the project classes. Sociogrammes showed that the Belgian, Greek and Italian children (though not the Turkish children) tended to make choices which went beyond their own ethnic group. In the state school too the results of the evaluation were finally interpreted as showing that the migrant pupils were not disadvantaged in their learning of Dutch by the integration of mother tongue teaching into the regular Belgian timetable.

The conclusions drawn from the results of the investigation are only partly recorded in the reports on the pilot project. This reflects the character of the investigation, whose aims were educational rather than evaluative. In all three schools researchers and teachers collaborated in drawing concrete conclusions which would lead to a teaching programme geared to the achievement of the individual child or group of children. At the same time the state school placed great emphasis on the process of learning to read; on the basis of the results, it accelerated the pace and changed the content of the reading process, and for the second year of the project it also introduced a different teaching method. In all three schools the results of the investigation led to the selection of individual children for extra tuition and, starting in the second school year, to the division of classes into different groups according to achievement.


## Overall assessment

Despite the long preparatory phase, those involved in the pilot project finally found themselves working under considerable time pressure, because official approval of the project came only shortly before the beginning of the school year 1976/77. This time pressure made itself felt in all areas of planning. Lack of time and the need to act quickly worked in particular against free practical experimentation and adequate evaluation. One has the impression that, owing to the somewhat restrictive terms imposed by the Ministry, the schools taking part in the project had little scope for innovation. Even in those areas where the Ministry made no prescriptions, those working on the project were not always able to take advantage of the scope allowed them, presumably because they had insufficient help and guidance. This is one area of complaint in the interviews we conducted. At the same time it must be remembered that the incorporation of mother tongue teaching into the mainstream Belgian timetable could be regarded as a substantial innovation which both the Ministry and those charged with carrying out the project were obliged to justify.

The aims of the project were enunciated by those who applied for it to be set up; these aims were in all essentials adopted by the Ministry in its enabling order. The few modifications that were introduced seem to have been designed to bring it into line with government policy on immigration. These general aims were firmly adhered to throughout the three years of the project. One criticism of the way in which they were realized was that excessive reliance was placed on structural and organizational measures and that there was insufficient differentiation within the target group. The organizational consequences of these aims were clearly not thought out thoroughly enough to take account of the differing circumstances of the schools involved. The interest in keeping open the possibility of the children's returning to their countries of origin contrasts with the notion of making instruction in the pupils' mother tongues and inherited cultures ancillary to regular teaching and reception teaching. In the interviews this latter aim is generally applauded, though there are complaints that the measures arising from it cannot by themselves ensure equality of opportunity for children from ethnic minorities. Nor can it be said that the way in which the project was conceived and carried out, together with the findings that emerged from it, go very far towards meeting the interest expressed by the EC Commission in proposals for solving the problems involved in the transition from pre-school to primary education.

In evolving an educational method to meet the prescribed objectives the three schools were guided by differing principles. These derived from the educational traditions of the host country, though an attempt was made to ascertain whether they were adequate to the exigencies of the specific situation that had arisen in the schools as a result of immigration. It was above all the search for a teaching content with intercultural relevance that transcended the educational tradition.

For the benefit of the pilot project two special concessions were made which had a special effect on its organization: the first was the incorporation of mother tongue teaching into the regular teaching programme, and hence the involvement of bilingual teachers; the second was the reduction of the teacher-pupil ratio from the normal level to 1:15. The inclusion of mother-tongue instruction and remedial lessons in the timetable was in line with the principle that mother tongue teaching should help in the educational and social integration of the migrant pupils. From the point of view of organization and teaching content the greatest importance was attached to the intensive teaching of Dutch. Remedial classes for Belgian pupils were run in parallel with mother tongue teaching for ethnic minority pupils (this being understood also as a form of remedial and revision teaching), yet experiences in this area demonstrate that the learning load on ethnic minority pupils can be reduced, and their educational opportunities improved, only under very favourable circumstances (including the provision of counselling and in-service training for teachers, and the development of appropriate teaching materials). The success of such teaching can in no way be assured by merely organizational measures.

Moreover, while it is clear that the reduction of the staff-pupils ratio served to ease the burden on the teachers, such relief was largely offset by the additional work entailed in developing new teaching concepts and new materials. Further relief came from the opportunities for internal and external differentiation, e.g. the indtroduction of equal ability groups.

The schools taking part in the pilot project retained the right to determine the content of the various learning areas in the curriculum. In the state school this right was exercised by the evaluation team, in the independent schools by the head teachers. The Ministry's enabling order left the individual learning areas undefined as regards both their intrinsic content and their relation to other areas; in other words the tasks to be performed, the subject matter to be taught, and the media and materials to be used were not determined (at least not solely) by tradition. The didactic concept for linking the different learning areas, i.e. for relating major teaching units to central themes that had been worked out in greater or lesser detail, applied equally in the state sector and the independent sector. For the independent schools the work done in this area is recorded in the *afspraakboekjes*.

In the overall conception of the pilot project the intensive study of Dutch must be seen as the principal learning area, within which the basic teaching content of other learning areas was supposed to be developed. In practice, however, it became clear that it was too much to expect the schools to evolve a clear plan for this teaching area. Even the development of the *afspraakboekjes* brought only a small measure of relief. Ultimately the question of what linguistic demands could reasonably be made of the pupils, and what was the best way to help them meet these demands, had to remain open. Traditional teaching methods and traditional content were of only limited value when the language was being taught to mixed groups of Belgian and non-Belgian pupils.

The situation was similar in the area known as "acquisition of basic techniques". Here it was found that the language difficulties experienced by the ethnic minority children made it impossible for them to meet the demands that were made of them; for instance reading could be successfully taught only after they had been given a fairly thorough grounding in the colloquial language, and this was a task that fell chiefly within the scope of the intensive teaching of Dutch.

Difficulties of principle arose above all from the incorporation of mother tongue teaching into the regular timetable. In the interests of integration this was at first intended to be restricted to instruction in the spoken language, but this restriction could not be maintained: in the first place it became evident that to teach a language without resort to its written representation made excessive demands on teachers and pupils alike, and in the second place it appears that the ethnic minority parents and their national representatives intervened in the interest of preserving ties between the children and their countries of origin. This interest was never voiced in direct opposition to the notion of integration, but the modifications that were made in the teaching show that mother tongue teaching could not be restricted simply to supporting and consolidating the teaching content of the regular classes, but eventually took its place as an autonomous element in the children's education.

The greatest uncertainty attached to the function of the lessons which ran in parallel with the mother tongue teaching for the Belgian and non-Belgian pupils remaining in the regular class. In principle these were supposed only to extend and consolidate the basic knowledge the children had acquired from the intensive teaching in Dutch. However, as criticisms made during the pilot project showed, these lessons tended to work to the advantage of the pupils attending them and to the disadvantage of the pupils receiving mother tongue instruction.

The materials produced by the pilot project, such as the *afspraakboekjes*, related principally to matters connnected with the curriculum, the individual teachers being for the most part left to decide for themselves what form their lessons should take. In the case of the bilingual teachers this meant that they were largely exempt from external supervision. The teachers involved deplored above all the lack of learning materials for the remedial teaching in withdrawal groups.

The biggest problems seem to have beeen posed by the co-ordination of the various groups and interested parties involved in the pilot project. From the very beginning it was not clear what role the *FOG* was meant to play, and there was no authoritative body capable of developing and carrying through a conception of the project that had been jointly agreed between the state sector and the independent sector. In practical terms this could only have been achieved by the responsible inspectors in the three schools, but since they had only a limited amount of time at their disposal they could not assume the task of co-ordinating the project. In fact the responsibility for initiating and co-ordinating activities within the pilot project devolved upon the staff or the head teachers. Collaboration among members of staff and co-operation with parents seems to have been largely dependent on the commitment of the head teachers. This commitment may have been strengthened by the fact that the head teachers, having been relieved of their teaching obligations, could devote a good deal of their time to the project, but even they were unable to cope with all the work involved in planning the content of the new teaching programme. This becomes clear from their wish to have their own back-up facilities and in-service training.

The progress of the pilot project was not affected by the difficulties caused by occasional changes of staff. The one factor which lightened the teachers' load was the reduction of the staff-pupil ratio; however, no extra free time was allocated for additional work such as the preparation of teaching materials and the holding of staff discussions. The bilingual teachers were even more conscious than their Belgian colleagues of the lack of back-up, counselling and in-service training for their mother tongue teaching; moreover, in spite of a number of detailed job-descriptions, their status *vis-à-vis* the Belgian and foreign inspectorate was never adequately clarified. For those working in the state school especially there was the additional difficulty that after school they had to do a great deal of mother tongue teaching and so were unable to spare much extra time for the pilot project.

The situation of the evaluators is far from clear because so many different authorities were involved. The linking of their work to that of the teachers seems to have been only a limited success. This was due partly to the fact that they were overburdened, having other duties to perform apart from those connected with the pilot project, but partly also to a certain degree of resistance on the part of the schools, the head teachers and the staff. In addition to this, some evaluators felt that the scientific and practical tasks they were expected to carry out during the project made excessive demands on them.

In the course of the project the importance of back-up, counselling and in-service training for the teachers became increasingly clear. The school inspectorate and the *FOG* constantly tried to increase opportunities for in-service training, and the various schemes and activities in these areas added up to a quite respectable and successful programme.

Interest in encouraging co-operation with the Belgian and non-Belgian parents also became increasingly evident. New forms of home-school liaison were tried out, but experience showed that this put an excessive burden on the teachers - including the bilingual teachers, who often found themselves landed with this particular task. A way out of this particular difficulty would have been to give the teachers more free time and to provide them with a kind of counselling and in-service training which covered home-school liaison, or alternatively to bring in social workers.

Despite the relatively varied questions relating to evaluation in the enabling order, there was at first no clear evaluation concept; moreover, there was neither the time nor the personal expertise necessary for evolving such a concept. On the other hand, those responsible for running the pilot project had to justify it to outsiders, in particular to those who had commissioned it. Given the absence of such preconditions, the need for legitimation worked largely to the detriment of any innovatory developments within the project.

Since the project lacked more or less all the prerequisites for arriving at scientific results, there seems little point in a methodological or theoretical discussion of the procedures used and the results obtained. At best we may try to assess the plausibility of individual findings in relation to other findings resulting from the project. It is to be regretted that no advantage could be taken of the opportunity to compare different schools with differing ways of working (i.e. the two sectors represented). For the rest, the pilot project demonstrated that there is still no appropriate machinery for investigating the teaching of ethnic minority pupils. The instruments which were devised in the schools themselves were at best tests orientated towards learning objectives; they did not match up to scientific requirements, nor were they intended to. Nevertheless, because of the glaring lack of other suitable instruments, they were in fact used for scientific purposes.

# Ethnic minority children in the English education system

The legal and social framework

In the years immediately after the Second World War, British industry looked primarily to Irish immigrants and refugees from eastern Europe to supply the additional labour it required, but in the early 1950s immigrants began to arrive from the New Commonwealth. The first large influx was from the Caribbean; from the late fifties onwards there was a second influx from Asian countries, especially India and Pakistan.

The 1971 census revealed that out of a total population of 53,978,540 there were 3,088,110 inhabitants born outside Great Britain, 1,157,170 of these being from the New Commonwealth; these figures represent respectively 5.7% and 2.1% of the total (Campbell-Platt, p 2, Table 1, and CRE 1978a, p 10, Table 1). These demographic figures are inaccurate, however, for a number of reasons. Since respondents were asked to state simply their country of *birth*, the figures necessarily include British citizens of English, Welsh, Scottish or Irish ethnic origin who were born abroad. Conversely there is no indication of those members of ethnic minorities who were born in Great Britain; these include both "second and third generation children" and children born into long-established minority communities like those in Liverpool and Cardiff. Nor is there any record of the number of children of mixed parentage (CRE 1978a, p 7). Questions relating to ethnic origin were deliberately excluded from the census. Adjusted estimates for 1971 suggest an ethnic component from the New Commonwealth of 1,371,000; for 1976 the figure is 1,771,000 (including those from Pakistan) (COI 1977, p 4, Table 1).

Characteristically, public and official interest is concentrated on former inhabitants of the New Commonwealth and their descendants At the time of the 1971 census these accounted for just 38% of all inhabitants born outside Great Britain yet it is these who are being referred to when people speak of immigration, ethnic minorities, etc – and this necessarily applies in the present context also. The reason is obvious: they are dark-skinned. One of the versions of the ethnic question considered for inclusion in the 1981 census envisaged the following possible answers: "1. White (European descent), 2. West Indian, 3. African, 4. Arab, 5. Chinese, 6. Turkish, 7. Indian, Pakistani, Bangladeshi or Sri Lankan". This was to be followed by four questions relating to religion and an open "ethnic question for 'Others'" (CRE 1978a, p 8f.). This is nothing more than a classification by crass "popular" notions of "race", with little bearing upon ethnicity: only (5) and (6) are ethnic categories in any meaningful sense. In the end the "ethnic question" was once again dropped from the 1981 census form.

The principal countries of origin, in descending order of importance, were India, Jamaica, Germany, Pakistan, Poland and Italy (Campbell-Platt 1978, p 2, Table 1). The languages best represented were Punjabi, Urdu,

English Creole, Bengali, Gujarati, German, Polish, Italian, Greek, Spanish and Hakka (op. cit., p 1). The most important area of settlement is Greater London, where 41% of all New Commonwealth immigrants live, representing 6.4% of the total population; this is followed by the West Midlands, Outer London, the North-West, and finally Yorkshire and Humberside (CRE 1978a, p 10, Table 2). More than three quarters of the immigrants from the New Commonwealth live in these areas.

New Commonwealth immigrants appear to be fairly evenly distributed throughout the various branches of the economy (Cross 1978, p 38), although some branches show above-average proportions of ethnic minority workers: in the processing industries these are in particular engineering and the textile and clothing industry. A notorious case is public transport in London, whose employees come predominantly from the ethnic minorities. In addition to the hotel and service industries, one should also mention the special case of the nationalized sector of the health service, in which the ethnic minorities are clearly represented to a degree that is out of all proportion to their share of the total population (COI 1977, p 27). The reason why this is a special case is that otherwise members of the ethnic minorities are mainly found doing less skilled, lower paid and more strenuous work. Thus among men of Pakistani origin, for instance, the proportion of unskilled and semi-skilled workers was 58%, compared with 18% among the indigenous population. In the same group the proportion of men doing non-manual jobs was 8%, compared with 40% among the indigenous population (Smith 1976, p 110). Correspondingly the ethnic minorities are disproportionately affected by unemployment: in the city centres, where they constitute a higher percentage of the population than they do nationally, there are always substantially more of them out of work than would correspond to their proportion in the overall national workforce (Cross 1978, p 37, Table 6 - and these figures date from the period before the present crisis!)

The minorities live mostly in the big industrial conurbations, and there they occupy chiefly the inner-city areas. The housing shortage, which is a serious problem for Great Britain as a whole, is at its worst in these areas. Financial hardship, the above-average size of families (Cross 1978, p 65), together with the policy of building societies and local councils on mortgages (Rex/Moore 1967, pp 19-41, xiv), are all factors which put the minorities at a disadvantage: the percentage of minority families living in obsolete, ill-furnished and overcrowded accommodation is roughly twice as high as it is in the population as a whole, and among Pakistanis it is roughly three times as high (CRC 1976, p 10).

Thus in many respects the social situation of minorities in Great Britain does not differ structurally from that of minorities in the countries of continental Europe, yet there is one fact that must not be overlooked: insofar as their members are of New Commonwealth origin and entered the country before the Commonwealth Immigration Act of

1968 came into force, they enjoy the status of British subjects and hence unrestricted rights of citizenship. Any discussion of the "confused and confusing state" (Lester 1972, p 5) of the legal regulations pertaining to immigration must be conducted against this background.

The British Nationality Act of 1948, which became necessary with the beginning of the decolonization process, attempted to preserve, in the new era in which the British Empire was being superseded by the British Commonwealth of Nations, the uniform nationality that had been introduced by the Imperial Act of 1914 and had applied throughout the Empire. Both acts were of significance only in Great Britain, where every British subject had right of abode and was entitled to the same rights as a citizen of the United Kingdom, a status which he could himself acquire merely by being registered as one after a certain lapse of time. Neither in the Dominions nor later in the new countries of the Commonwealth were rights of movement recognized for British subjects (Prashar 1977, p 7). The act of 1948 introduced the status of Citizen of the United Kingdom and Colonies (CUKC), which was not entirely identical with that of citizens of the United Kingdom. This became clear in 1962 with the passing of the Commonwealth Immigrants Act, which made right of entry for Commonwealth citizens *and* for those CUKCs holding passports which had been issued not by the British government, but by a colonial government, dependent upon their having previously obtained an "employment voucher" – in other words the promise of a job (BIS 1977, p 1). These vouchers amounted to entry permits, and from 1965 onwards, as a consequence of the White Paper on "Immigration from the Commonwealth", the number of vouchers issued was progressively reduced from 30,130 in 1963 to 4,980 in 1967 (Rees 1979, p 77), with the result that for the first time Commonwealth citizens were faced with drastic restrictions on their right of entry.

A dramatic tightening of these restrictions was effected by the Commonwealth Immigrants Act of 1968, which was rushed through Parliament in three days and three nights, in flagrant breach of countless official promises and with the avowed intention of preventing the entry into the United Kingdom of Asian citizens from Kenya – and later from Uganda – who at the time of independence had been promised the right to exchange their colonial passports for passports issued by the British government. By its own admission the Labour government of the day decided on this step because it feared the effects that racialist agitation, inflamed by Enoch Powell, might have on the voting behaviour of its working class supporters (Lester 1972, pp 7–12). Under the new act CUKCs could now claim unimpeded right of entry if they themselves had been born, adopted, naturalized or registered in the United Kingdom or at least could show that one parent or grandparent satisfied these requirements (Prashar 1977, p 8). Finally, in 1971, a new Immigration Act introduced unrestricted right of entry and abode for so-called "patrials". In addition to the category of persons defined in the 1968 act, "patrials" now include:

64

- CUKCs who have resided in the United Kingdom for five years after having been admitted for an unlimited period,
- Commonwealth citizens who can show that one of their parents was born in the United Kingdom,

- female Commonwealth citizens or CUKCs who are or once were married to a man belonging to one of the three foregoing categories (BIS 1977, p 3f).

Coloured people thus have little chance of being recognized as "patrials". "The broadly racial distinction intended in the Act is not precise," remarks Dummett, "but its inexactitude is in practice corrected by the Immigration Rules ... and also by the manner in which the Rules are administered by the Home Office. In practice white non-patrials are often permitted to enter freely, while black patrials face difficulty in many cases" (Dummett 1978, p 38).

The foregoing paragraphs relate to the restrictions placed on rights of entry since 1962, but it must be emphasized that the rights of abode enjoyed by Commonwealth immigrants in the United Kingdom are incomparably more generous than those accorded to immigrants in other European countries.

Since 1971 all foreign nationals who fall outside the scope of these regulations and are not citizens of a member state of the European Community have needed a "work permit", for which the prospective employer has to apply and which is issued only if the prospective employee is to be taken on to perform a precisely specified activity which is necessary for the running of the firm and for which no suitable personnel can be found on the internal labour market (Rees 1979, p 78).

As if to counterbalance these restrictive and racially discriminatory immigration regulations, successive Race Relations Acts were passed in 1965, 1968 and 1976 to prevent discrimination in employment and housing, in the provision of public services, and (since 1976) in clubs and educational institutions. Until 1976 the monitoring of legislation was entrusted to the Race Relations Board and the Community Relations Commission; since then these bodies have been amalgamated in the Commission for Racial Equality, which is empowered to initiate formal enquiries, to introduce reconciliation procedures, to issue anti-discrimination orders, and to bring prosecutions before the criminal courts and industrial tribunals. In addition, the Commission for Racial Equality co-ordinates and supports the Community Relations Councils, of which there are roughly 100 operating at local level and playing a major role in the counselling of minority groups, the combating of discrimination, and the promotion of constructive contacts between various groups - including the indigenous majority (Home Office 1975; Home Office 1977)

## Special structural features of the English education system

It is not easy to give a concise account of the English education system. (No attempt will be made here to describe the education systems of Scotland and Northern Ireland, which are autonomous and have their own structures. The school system of England and Wales, on the other hand, is uniform, and in the interests of readability repeated references to Wales will be avoided. Nevertheless, all statements about the structure - though not necessarily the extent - of the education system apply equally to Wales. In any case the number of New Commonwealth immigrants in the principality is small: at the time of the 1971 census they numbered 13,730, i.e. approximately 1.2% of the New Commonwealth immigrants in the whole of the United Kingdom (see CRE 1978, p 10, Table 2).) The reason for this is that in decision-making there is a preference for consultative procedures and for solving problems on the basis of consensus, rather than by recourse to legal or bureaucratic means. In fact there is no central authority for administration and control, nor does the absence of such an authority typically seem to worry anyone but the outsider (e.g. OECD 1975). "The system of education in England is essentially dependent on the co-operative efforts of the central government, the local authorities, the churches, and the teaching profession" (Evans 1978, p 157). Another author puts it as follows: "It is this all-pervading partnership which makes the system work; were it to cease an entirely different - and in my view much less happy - system would emerge" (Dent 1977, p 163). Although such views of a happily co-operative English education system have increasingly come under attack in recent years (e.g. Kogan 1978), they were officially held at the time of our research and appeared to reflect the views of many, if not all, of our interlocutors. Our feeling was that for many it was not easy to draw the line between a rapidly changing reality and the myths which that reality had generated. The legal basis for this system is the Education Act of 1944, which gives wide powers to the Local Education Authorities (LEAs) (cf. Evans 1978, pp 95-115). Its proper functioning is ensured by an informal, almost "private" decision-making process which takes place through countless consultations in committees at all levels, often restricting the scope of the official, recorded consultations (Bell/Grant 1977, p 90) or pointing them in particular directions (Dent 1977, p 60). The decisive factor in the functioning of the system is not the power of any one body to regulate how things are to be done, but the effective exercise of influence in educational policy-making.

Two examples may serve to illustrate the extent of the autonomy enjoyed by the LEAs in England and Wales (of which there have been 104 since 1974) in matters of educational policy vis-à-vis the Department of Education and Science. In 1926, on the recommendation of the Consultative Committee of the then Board of Education, a two-tier structure of free, compulsory state education was introduced; this comprised elementary schooling for children aged between five and eleven, and secondary schooling for those aged between eleven and fourteen. Even in 1939 this system affected only a third of the children in the country, and it was not abolished nation-wide until 1965 (Blackie 1967, p 4f.). While many LEAs, immediately after the war, began to organize all newly built secondary schools as non-selective comprehensive schools (Burgess 1970, p 178), there were still, thirty years later, some LEAs in which the selection system of the forties was still in full force (Bell/Grant 1977, p 88). Characteristically, in both cases local action went ahead in advance of recommendations from central government.

What is characteristic about the second case is that Circular 10/65, issued by the then Labour government, which requested the LEAs to submit plans to the Minister for the introduction of comprehensive schools, was shelved in 1970 by the newly elected Conservative government, only to be renewed by the next Labour government in 1974. What is uncharacteristic here is the recourse to a circular: the case of the comprehensives is the only one since 1944 in which administrative measures have been taken to promote innovations which had obvious repercussions on the curriculum. True, "a Department circular can only acquaint the local authorities with the wishes of the central authority and has no statutory force, even though it is no light matter to ignore one" (Evans 1978, p 163). Both Conservative and Labour governments have used the most powerful weapon in their armory for pushing the LEAs in the desired direction, viz. the selective allocation of funds (ibid., p 113f). (Formerly the government bore 60% of the cost of the education service; since then its share has risen to a full two thirds. See OECD 1975, 27.) The decentralization of the education system admittedly goes even further: in practice the LEAs delegate their responsibility for the curriculum to the schools, especially to the head teachers, who decide what is to be taught and what teaching methods are to be employed (Dent 1977, p 65); the tradition of professional autonomy to which the teachers' organizations lay claim is hardly ever called into question (Bell/Grant 1977, p 16). In this connection at least some mention must be made of the Schools Council for the Curriculum and Examinations (usually called simply the Schools Council), founded in 1964. This is financed in equal measure by the DES and the LEAs, but on its committees (with the exception of the finance committee) the teachers' organizations have a statutorily guaranteed majority in order to ensure that the decisions it reaches — in particular the numerous and often costly projects for syllabus reform — are acceptable to the teachers in the schools (Evans 1978, p 292). The local Teachers' Centres, which are concerned with in-service training and syllabus development at school level and are attentive above all to local needs, often collaborate with the Schools Council. These too were the product of the movement for syllabus reform in the sixties: between 1967 and mid 1970 the number of Teachers' Centres rose from 140 to 400 (Brügelmann 1980, p 195). This efflorescence points to one of the strengths of the system, a strength which has its counterpart in the relative impotence of the DES, without necessarily resulting from this impotence: the lack of centralized control gives scope for educational reform that is teacher-oriented and teacher-led, and the opportunities it affords are confidently exploited by the profession - or at least by that section of the profession which is committed to reform and innovation. (It will be shown later that it can also be exploited to sabotage reforming initiatives.)

English education thus embraces a degree of variety and inconsistency that would be inconceivable in other education systems: since educational reform cannot be imposed from above - and in fact no attempt is made to impose it - the most progressive and the most conservative educational practices co-exist within the system, sometimes in close proximity; there is no way of obviating either the one or the other. Hence, in describing educational structures one must always make the proviso that there are possible exceptions. This is true especially of measures designed for the schooling of ethnic minority children. Tracing lines of development and identifying the forces for change and the forces that inhibit change will be found more fruitful than any attempt to present a synoptic view of the present state of English education.


### Mainstream provision

Pre-school provision is at present relatively undeveloped. Although a study written in 1972 lists nine different forms of pre-school facilities - ranging from the nursery schools provided by the LEAs to the play groups resulting from neighbourhood initiatives - which fall within the purview of a variety of different authorities, attendance among three- to four-year-olds is estimated to be no higher than 10% (Halsey 1972, p 80f). The official government aim of providing sufficient pre-school places by 1982 to cater for all children in this age-group whose parents wish them to attend (DES 1972 c) has not been achieved. In 1977, when more than half the children under the school age of five attended a pre-school institution, it was announced that because of diminishing resources further expansion would be restricted to areas that were especially in need, and that in any case, with the drop in the birth-rate, attendance rates would rise even if provision remained constant (DES 1977, p 14f).

Primary schooling takes up six of the eleven years of compulsory education, which runs from age five to age sixteen. For a long time it was customary to divide primary schools into infant departments (age five to seven) and junior departments (age seven to eleven), but more and more LEAs seem to be going over to a system comprising first or lower schools (age five to eight or nine) and middle schools (eight to twelve or nine to thirteen) (Dent 1977, p 73), thus blurring the borderline between primary and secondary education.

The progressive introduction of comprehensive schools, as a structural pre-requisite for the simultaneous abolition of the selective eleven-plus examination, was an institutional precondition for the triumphal progress of a child-centred educational philosophy, which carried the day in English primary schools in the sixties and seventies. Highly influential in this regard was the Plowden Report of the Central Advisory Council of Education (DES 1967), the recommendations of which relied on the results of developmental psychology and were adopted in a growing number of primary schools. The mere imparting of knowledge came to be regarded as less important than informal teaching and learning methods which aimed at developing and making full use of the children's spontaneity and initiative and their pleasure in discovering things for themselves. A pre-condition, and at the same time a consequence, of the move towards child-centred education was a new concept of the role of the teacher, together with the abandonment of traditional forms of school organization, in particular the replacement of rigid timetabling by the "integrated day" - which means allowing different groups of pupils in a class to engage in different activities for part of the day - and the intensification or introduction of co-operation between members of the teaching staff (cf. Blackie 1967, pp 37-55). Success can be achieved only through a concerted effort on the part of the staff. Many schools do achieve success, and we do not believe that Hopkins was exaggerating when he wrote that English primary schools today are "happy places" and remarked, "It is almost always a pleasure to go into one" (Hopkins 1978, p 51).

The variety to be found at secondary level will now come as no surprise. In the maintained sector, i.e. in schools that come under the LEAs, we find the following types of school (the percentages given in brackets indicate the proportion of the total school population attending maintained secondary schools in 1977, as stated in CSO 1978, p 74, Table 4.4): middle schools belonging to the secondary level (6.1%), modern schools (12.2%), grammar schools (6.3%), technical schools (0.3%), comprehensive schools (73.8%), and a residual number of schools which cannot be classified (1.2%). School fees are payable at the independent schools (which include the public schools) and the direct grant grammar schools, which are directly subsidized by the DES and reputedly have particularly high standards. In return, as it were, for their state subsidy the direct grant grammar schools are obliged to reserve a proportion of their places, fluctuating between 25% and 50%, for specially gifted pupils whose fees are paid by the LEAs (Dent 1977, p 114f). A bare 8% of all English children are educated at independent schools.

Grammar schools offer a traditional "academic" curriculum and see it as their principal task to prepare their pupils for university entrance. Their direct counterparts in the selective system are the modern schools, which confine their intake to pupils who fail to gain admission to grammar schools; their curricula are more practically orientated, though there is an observable trend to broaden them to include "academic" subjects. Technical schools, which are a kind of selective school for "gifted" children, were never very numerous and are now clearly dying out; the emphasis in their curricula lies in the commercial and technical sphere. Circular 10/65, which has already been mentioned, envisaged six different possibilities for the organization of comprehensive schools, which differ principally in their horizontal structuring, though provision for vertical structuring shortly before the end of compulsory schooling is not ruled out; in one case, viz. when middle schools are instituted, comprehensives may take pupils of eight or nine years of age. The commonest form is the "all through" comprehensive for pupils aged eleven to eighteen (Dent 1977, pp 80-86). The curricula of the comprehensive schools offer a broad coverage of subjects ranging from the academic to the practical; however, the pupils have the opportunity – at points in their school careers which vary from school to school, but seldom under the age of thirteen – of adding or dropping subjects, with the result that sometimes, towards the end of their compulsory schooling (and almost always afterwards), they take only those subjects which they intend to offer for examinations. Streaming, i.e. the division of pupils into groups with relatively homogeneous learning capacities, is widespread; in schools with a "setting" system, pupils can be allocated to different streams in the different subjects they are taking (Burgess 1970, pp 104-09).

Since the late seventies there have been lively discussions, though admittedly with no substantial upshot, about the definition of a minimal "core curriculum" that should be offered by all schools. It is for each school to decide what subjects it offers, and it is for the pupils and their parents to decide what subjects they take. The following is a characteristic statement by the DES:

> "English and religious education are in most schools a standard for all pupils up to the age of 16, and it is not true that many pupils drop mathematics at an early stage. But the offer of options and the freedom to choose do lead some boys and girls to abandon certain areas of study at an early stage.... Few, inside or outside the schools, would contest that alongside English and mathematics, science should find a secure place for all pupils at least to the age of 16, and that a modern language should do the same for as high a proportion as practicable" (DES 1977, p 11).

The teaching of the individual subjects is influenced to a certain extent by the leaving examinations, which are administered and supervised not by the teachers, but by the examination boards under the aegis of the Schools Council. Two different examinations are available: the Certificate of Secondary Education (CSE) and the more demanding General Certificate of Education (GCE). The latter has two levels, Ordinary (O) Level and Advanced (A) Level. Both examinations can be repeated an indefinite number of times, and there is no limit on the number of subjects the candidates may offer; there are no prescribed combinations of subjects. A Grade 1 in the CSE counts as equivalent to a GCE O level, while Grades D and E at O level are recognized as equivalent to Grades 2 to 4 in the CSE. An inadequate performance at A level can result in the award of an O level. The CSE is administered by fourteen Examination Boards with responsibility for certain regions of the country, whereas in the case of the GCE the schools may choose between eight Examination Boards which operate country-wide. There is nothing to prevent their putting in candidates for examination by different boards in different subjects. Finally, pupils may be examined in subjects which are not offered in their schools. Most pupils take their O levels at the end of their compulsory schooling, after which, if they do not leave school entirely, they concentrate on preparing for the A level examination (Dent 1977, pp 82 and 85; Burgess 1970, pp 111-16).

The following table below shows the distribution of school-leaving achievement in the various types of secondary school:

| School leavers in % | Maintained Sector | | | | Independent Schools | All Schools |
|---|---|---|---|---|---|---|
| | Comprehensive Schools | Grammar Schools | Other Schools | Direct Grant Schools | | |
| with 3 or more A levels | 5,6 | 29,9 | 0,9 | 50,4 | 35,6 | 8,6 |
| with up to 2 A levels | 6,3 | 22,0 | 1,8 | 20,7 | 19,9 | 7,3 |
| with 5 or more O levels | 8,3 | 20,6 | 6,1 | 12,8 | 18,3 | 9,2 |
| with up to 4 O levels 1) | 27,4 | 22,8 | 28,3 | 12,9 | 19,6 | 26,7 |
| without any O levels 2) | 35,6 | 3,1 | 43,4 | 2,2 | 5,2 | 33,0 |
| without any qualification | 16,9 | 1,5 | 17,5 | 1,1 | 2,4 | 15,5 |

1) O levels grades A to C; CSE grade 1
2) CSE grades 2-4; O levels grades D and E (E = fail)    Source DES 1979, p 7, Table D

The figures reveal that it is still an advantage to have parents who can find the fees for a direct grant or independent school. The comprehensives have not greatly changed the picture: although 94.2% of school leavers in 1977 came from maintained schools, only 71.6% of those who achieved three or more A levels came from these schools (DES 1979, p 6, Table D). And in practice three A levels are the requirement

71

for admission to academic courses at universities (Dent 1977, p 145). The picture becomes even clearer when we look at the subsequent careers of the school leavers: although 73.0% of first-year students taking academic courses come from maintained schools, 97.0% of school-leavers who go directly into employment - or unemployment - also come from these schools (DES 1979, p 6, Table C).

## Provision for the study of English as a Second Language

Figures for pre-school attendance of children from the ethnic minorities are not available, but a minor survey carried out at 33 day nurseries run by the DHSS in inner city residential areas with a high minority population shows that more than 50% of the children in these institutions came from ethnic minorities (CRE 1978b, p 15). (In view of the inadequate provision of pre-school facilities these figures should not be interpreted as meaning that in the districts investigated 50% of ethnic minority children attended pre-school institutions.) With one exception all the day nurseries included in the survey explicitly stated that one of their tasks was to promote the linguistic competence of the children in preparation for their primary schooling; the methods employed were essentially the same as those used with indigenous children - listening to stories, telling stories, singing songs, learning nursery rhymes, etc (ibid., pp 20-23).

In his by now somewhat dated study of 1971 Townsend lists the following ways in which the teaching of English as a Second Language to beginners is organized: full-time language centres in their own premises; part-time language centres in schools, which are also attended by children from other schools; full-time language classes and part-time language classes, which are attended only by pupils from the school in which they are conducted (Townsend 1971, p 123, Table A5). Since in every case classes were made up of ethnically mixed groups - usually for lack of any practicable alternative (it is reported that in one school no fewer than 37 different languages were represented, ibid. p 37) - the method generally employed was the direct method, sometimes supplemented by the use of a language laboratory (ibid., p 40). But even where the LEAs employed teachers from the New Commonwealth (which is unusual), they are more often placed in mainstream classes than in language centres or language classes, because there is too great a "risk" of their deviating from the direct method (ibid., p 94). Twelve of the 71 LEAs investigated took no measures to deal with children from the five to seven age-group, assuming that children of this age would learn English quite naturally as their mother tongue, and in general the number and extent of the measures taken increases with the age of the children involved: they are best developed and most varied where secondary pupils are concerned (ibid., p 38).

Attendance at language centres usually lasts one year, but it can sometimes be extended to three years. It may be surmised that these fluctuations are due to the variety of aims the language centres set themselves: some try to impart the broadest possible school experience to the pupils and hence provide not only instruction in English, but also subject teaching, in order to reduce the educational disadvantage of missing normal schooling; others, by contrast, aim at the rapid integration of their pupils into regular teaching. The decision to favour language classes rather than language centres is usually justified by the wish to avoid measures that lead to the segregation of certain groups. Moreover, the choice of language classes facilitates earlier transfer of pupils in easy stages, as well as co-operation between the English language teachers and the teachers running the regular classes (ibid., p 48). The setting up of remedial groups for children with learning problems who are temporarily withdrawn from their classes and then taught either by the head teacher or by some other available teacher is to some extent traditional in primary schools, and in many places this traditional model was applied to the teaching of children from ethnic minorities (ibid., p 44).

Such provision is often lacking, however, when pupils begin to be more or less capable of following normal lessons. None of the LEAs questioned envisaged continued support measures for children who had already been transferred to normal classes, and only occasional initiatives are reported from individual schools (ibid., p 47). The procedures employed to judge the language learning needs of the children are to a large extent subjective, being based on the teachers' assessments (Townsend/Brittan 1972, p 30). Townsend and Brittan hesitate to interpret the information given by schools about the placing of ethnic minority children with language difficulties in support classes because they say it is impossible to judge whether this represents a temporary - and hence a "genuinely" remedial measure - or whether it is a question of placing them permanently in classes for children with learning problems. Yet, according to these authors, "there seems little doubt that many immigrant pupils are placed with less able pupils because of language difficulties" (ibid., p 29).

In the same way it becomes clear that language difficulties are interpreted as an indication of more general learning problems when a large proportion of the LEAs that had a large percentage of ethnic minority children excluded Caribbean pupils from specific ESL provision (Townsend 1971, p 49f). If it is thought that English Creole is just another dialect of English and that therefore those who speak it are not labouring under any specifically linguistic difficulties, it may easily be concluded that the unsatisfactory performance of individual West Indian pupils is to be attributed to lack of "ability". Such a view is still widely held in English schools. Many authors (cf. for example Edwards 1979) see it as one of the reasons for the below-average school record of West Indian children (cf. on this point the studies of Rutter et al. 1974 and Little 1975). There are few indications that this situation has changed very much as a result of the development, under the aegis of the Schools Council, of a set of teaching materials specifically designed for West Indian children (Schools Council 1972). On a corresponding syllabus for children whose mother tongues were not related to English (Schools Council 1969ff), we were told in schools and language centres that, while they had provided themselves with the course, they preferred in many cases not to introduce it, but to work with more flexible "home-made" teaching materials.


## Mother tongue teaching

Mother tongue teaching, whatever form it takes and whatever its aims, is regarded by the vast majority of LEAs and schools as an activity in which the English education system is not called upon to engage. Admittedly, Townsend reports a few cases of pupils preparing themselves outside school hours and at their own expense for GCE examinations in their own languages (Townsend 1971, p 60), a possibility existing in principle for twenty-two languages (Schools Council 1975). Moreover, Saifullah Khan reports (Saifullah Khan 1976, p 46) that a few schools offer languages such as Punjabi and Urdu as optional subjects at O and A level, and the Bullock Report on the teaching of English recommends that the bilingual competence of many immigrant children should be seen as a potential to be developed (DES 1975, p 294). Nevertheless, such provision as exists for mother tongue teaching is exceptional and far to seek, and the recommendations of the otherwise influential Bullock Report are in any case not very precise and have had little or no concrete effect. The universal habit of subsuming pupils (and their languages) from the Indian sub-continent under the term "Asian" and not differentiating any further throws into sharp focus the rudimentary awareness many teachers have of the linguistic variety that exists in their schools. compared with the degree of bilingualism possessed by their pupils. Teachers are often unable to state what are the mother tongues of the pupils they teach (Rosen/Burgess 1980).

Finally, it must be stated that in the period under review, except for the Bedford Project, which was promoted by the EC Commission, and another project in Bradford, financed by the DES, in which half the teaching given to new pupils took place in the medium of the mother tongue as a transitional measure of one year's duration (cf. Rees/ Fitzpatrick 1980), there was quite simply no mother tongue teaching in English primary schools, even where there were linguistically homogeneous groups of sufficient size and enough teachers available with the necessary linguistic qualifications to make it a viable proposition without any serious organizational difficulties.

On the other hand there have been numerous initiatives on the part of the communities themselves, using their own resources, to organize mother tongue teaching outside the normal school system. The scant information available on these was collected by Saifullah Khan (1976);

since 1979 a research project, financed by the DES, has been running in the University of London, one of the aims of which is to study this community-based provision (LMP 1980). The spectrum ranges from flourishing full-time schools such as those run by the Jewish community in London, which have their own premises and employ permanent, fully trained staff, to the overcrowded mother tongue classes which are conducted in private houses in the evenings or at weekends by unpaid and untrained teachers. Additional mother tongue teaching is financed, organized and supervised by some of the European countries from which immigrants come, such as Italy, Spain and Portugal, through their consulates. The poor countries of the Third World, especially those of the Indian sub-continent, are either unable or unwilling to do the same; in this case the local communities are obliged to rely on self-help. However, some LEAs make school premises available for afternoon lessons at no cost, while others let rooms out; but the great majority do nothing at all. Some schools confine themselves solely to language teaching, while others incorporate into the curriculum elements of the immigrants' native culture. Religious instruction often plays an important part, and in the case of the Muslim communities, for instance, this leads to Arabic being taught in addition to the mother tongue. We may surmise that the community schools do more - and at the same time less - than what is associated with mother tongue teaching in the present context: they are centres of cultural life, and this is how they see themselves, often quite explicitly - as an expression of the communities' will to assert their individuality. Whether, under existing circumstances, there is any long-term prospect of their pursuing the educational aims of mother tongue teaching in a more technical sense must remain an open question.

## Concepts of education in a multiracial society: assimilation or pluralism

As will by now have become obvious, statistics relating to pupils from ethnic minorities do not play a large part in English discussions. Although one not infrequently hears references to the high proportion of children from ethnic minorities in the school populations of inner city areas, one looks in vain for statistically based analyses of the overall situation. The emergence of this state of affairs, and the state of affairs itself, may serve to throw light on certain characteristics of the English education system and certain current trends which have been prompted by the presence of ethnic minorities.

From 1966 to 1973 the DES collected data from the LEAs regarding immigrant pupils, using Form 7(i). For this purpose the term "immigrant" applied to children whose parents were born outside the British Isles and who were not born in the country themselves, as well as to children born in the United Kingdom whose parents entered the country not more than ten years before the date for which the return was made (Townsend 1971, p 13). Here we are concerned with *one* implication of these problem-orientated statistics: what was perceived as a problem was the short time the child might have spent in the country, together with what was generally regarded as consequential upon a short period of residence, viz. an inadequate command of English. This perception of the problem in its turn corresponded to a particular view of the ideal course that events should take: a knowledge of English is essential "if the immigrant child is to develop self-confidence in his new social relationships, to grow culturally in his new environment, to become part of his new community" (DES 1971, p 9). "The ten-year rule was based on the assumption that when immigrant parents have been in this country for ten years there will have been a degree of integration which should mitigate both the children's language problems and their problems of adjustment to a new society" (ibid., p 25).

In the sixties the educational objective had been "assimilation", and when the concept of "integration" gained currency in the early seventies it was coloured by the idea of assimilation; the process of integration was seen as leading in one direction – to the integration of minorities into the majority society. What was novel about the shift towards "integration" was that interest was now directed to the cultural pre-conditioning of the immigrant communities, or, more precisely, to their inherited cultures, even though in the first instance this interest was not linked with any desire for the positive recognition of cultural diversity. The desired objective – a culturally homogeneous society – remained at first unchanged. A genuine shift of emphasis in progressive educational (and political) thinking – from integration dependent on assimilation to integration involving cultural pluralism – did not occur until it was recognized that processes of integration were not as straightforward as had at first been assumed, that the aspirations of immigrants – and especially those of the second generation – to equality of opportunity did not necessarily presuppose a complete break with their inherited culture, and that viable and relatively autonomous minority cultures were beginning to develop "on British soil" (Bolton 1979, p 4f). It was now recognized that education in a multiracial and multicultural society should not be directed solely to the removal of whatever impeded adaptation to the majority culture, but also to the consistent development of the potential inherent in all individual cultural groups.

Admittedly educational concepts of this kind are singularly at variance with the tradition of "racial inexplicitness" (Kirp 1979, pp 30-68), which seeks to justify specific measures of positive discrimination not on specifically ethnic or racial grounds, but on narrower – yet at the same time more general – grounds such as inadequate knowledge of English or social disadvantage (Jones 1977, p 177). In this connection it is important to mention Section 11 of the Local Government Act of 1966, which guaranteed funding for extra teaching posts in schools with a high proportion of recent immigrants, and also the Urban Aid Programme of 1968 (ibid., pp 179-83). The attempt made by a Labour government to separate the provisions of Section 11 from the "ten-year rule" and to allocate special funds for measures designed to benefit ethnic minorities which had suffered long-term disadvantage (Home Office 1978) was not followed up by the Thatcher government which came to power shortly afterwards.

The educational option for cultural diversity (and hence for "explicitness") meets with resistance, not least from the teachers themselves. A strategy whose aim is "for the extant regular curriculum during the years of statutory schooling, or, to put it more broadly, for what happens to children at school in that period, to be permeated with an infusion of multiracialism and multiculturalism" (Jeffecoate 1975, p 7) cannot be realized without making the relations between ethnic or racial groups into a real issue. In 1972 a materials pack on "race" which was developed within the framework of the Humanities Project, financed by the Schools Council, was rejected by the representatives of the Teachers' unions in the programme committee of the Schools Council. Six years later the project on "Multiracial Education: Curriculum and Content 5-13", also promoted by the Schools Council, was likewise rejected. In neither case was the outcome published (Hodges 1978). The controversial nature of the issue is dramatically highlighted by these and similar events, and it is clear too that the influence of the teaching profession need not in all cases be used to bring about educational change. Hence Bolton (1979, p 4) seems to be quite right in observing that the three stages of educational thinking outlined above should not be seen as reflecting the chronology of these developments, first of all because the three approaches are not necessarily mutually exclusive, but also because all three had their supporters at the same time. Nevertheless it is undeniable that proposals for future development such as those made by Jeffecoate are today finding increasing support, and that practical results can be observed in the schools. In the medium term they will lead to further curricular reforms of a more systematic kind - at first only in some LEAs - but it is conceivable that in the long term they may even establish the pre-conditions for the introduction of mother tongue teaching. Of course such developments cannot be expected to proceed with any greater consistency, uniformity and rapidity than other major reforms in the English education system.

# The pilot project in Bedford (England)

## Approval and general conditions

The initial negotiations between the European Commission and the Bedfordshire LEA were conducted in mid May 1976. Thanks in no small measure to pressure from the Adviser for Multi-Racial Education, the LEA declared itself willing to set up a pilot product on "Mother Tongue and Culture Teaching" at the beginning of the academic year 1976/77, i.e. fourteen weeks later. It was at first decided that the project should run for three years, although funding could be allocated only on a yearly basis. In the event it ran for four years, until July 1980.

No specific aims were laid down by the Commission; instead, the LEA was referred to an internal document (European Communities XII/226/76) in the hope that this would help "to clarify the priorities which the Commission has in mind at this stage".

With the summer holidays beginning in July, only a very short time was available in which to plan the content and organization of the pilot project. Schools, teachers and accommodation for the project had been found and the ethnic groups selected by September. The original plan was to involve pupils whose mother tongues were Italian, Punjabi and Hindi, but this had to be modified, since there were not enough Hindi-speaking pupils to make up sufficiently large learning groups; this left only Italian and Punjabi. Two mother tongue learning groups consisting of pupils aged five and six were formed at each of four primary schools. Apart from parental consent (which was refused in only one case), a pre-condition for admission to these groups was very recent entry into the country (a condition which nearly all the Italian and most of the Indian children failed to satisfy). Each group received one mother tongue lesson a day; this was held in the afternoon to minimize the amount of teaching the children would miss in the central subjects of the curriculum, which were taught in the morning. The teachers involved in the project thus had the mornings free to develop teaching concepts, devise teaching materials and produce some of these materials themselves, and to prepare individual teaching modules or lessons. For this purpose they shared an office which was put at their disposal in one of the schools taking part in the project.

Teachers whose mother tongue was Punjabi or Italian worked in the LEA's mainstream classes and could be seconded for the duration of the project. The one exception was the Project Co-ordinator, who originally had the same teaching obligations as his colleagues in addition to the tasks of co-ordination, planning, organization and internal evaluation. This post had to be advertised in the national press and could not be filled until November 1976, i.e. two months after the start of the project. This meant that there were originally two teachers for each of the two languages. However, one of the Italian teachers left after the first year, and his post was filled by ·advertising in the national press. Since the tasks with which the Project Co-ordinator was originally charged could not be performed by one person alone, he was relieved of a large part of his teaching duties and organizational tasks in spring 1979 by the appointment of another Italian teacher and an "operations organizer", so that he could devote more of his attention to the internal linguistic evaluation. The two Punjabi teachers remained on the project throughout its duration, except that one of them took maternity leave in the final year. This teacher was temporarily replaced by a male teacher who was already working for the LEA and had the necessary qualifications.

The planning and implementation of an external evaluation was first discussed four months after the start of the project in talks with members of the University of London Institute of Education, though no contract was concluded. From September to December 1977 a preliminary study was carried out by an Australian researcher. From January 1978 to July 1979 the evaluation was in the hands of a member of the Cambridge Institute of Education; she withdrew from the project at the time when it was originally due to end, and the task of evaluation was then assigned to a member of the National Foundation for Educational Research in England and Wales (NFER). All the evaluators had roughly ten days each term available for field research on the project.

The experiment with mother tongue instruction during the pilot project represented a complete innovation in the English education system, for despite the large number of ethnic minority children in English schools there had been no previous attempts to incorporate their mother tongues into the primary school curriculum. It is true that, under the influence of the EC directive, but not least under the pressure of demands from the minorities themselves, the subject had become a matter of lively controversy in those sections of the public with a direct interest in educational policy, but these same professionally interested parties seem to have shown little more than a detached though benevolent interest in the initiative of the Bedfordshire LEA. The DES maintained the stance of an interested observer and gave no official support to the pilot project outside the international colloquium.

Roughly 30% of the inhabitants of Bedford belong to ethnic and linguistic minorities, and it is estimated that more than fifty languages are spoken in the town. The most important groups are the Italians, the Asians (Indians and Pakistanis), the West Indians, the Poles and other Eastern Europeans. The Italians, Indians and Pakistanis work mainly in the local brickworks.

Schools in the town centre had a high proportion of pupils from ethnic minorities, in two cases nearing 80%. Of the schools involved in the project two were situated in areas inhabited mainly by ethnic minorities. Outside the pilot project mother tongue teaching was organized by the communities themselves (in the case of Italian with the support of the Italian consulate and partly on school premises made available by the LEA free of charge). Pupils of secondary school age were taught English as a Second Language in language centres, while younger children were taken out of the regular classes for support teaching given by specially trained teachers. In some regular classes teachers were employed who themselves came from ethnic minorities and had a teaching diploma recognized by the DES. This entitled them to work anywhere in England as normal teachers, enjoying the same legal and financial status as indigenous teachers. At some secondary schools Italian teachers with Italian teaching diplomas were employed as teaching assistants for Italian as a foreign language.


## Systematic description

### Objectives

Up to the time of the talks with the potential evaluators from the University of London Institute of Education, no firm objectives had been laid down. Since at about that time requests for information about the project were being received by the LEA from all over England, an information brochure was drawn up containing the following information:

"Originally, the expected results which the EEC wished to monitor independently were:
  (a) an enhancement of the self-image of the immigrant concerned,
  (b) a carefully controlled integration into the English education system,
  (c) an increase in esteem for the immigrants on the part of the indigenous children in the school,
  (d) a greater understanding on the part of the immigrants of the host country's language, culture and education,
  (e) general educational interest on the part of both indigenous and immigrant groups,
  (f) an opportunity to found, in Bedford, a resources bank for Italian language and culture which is likely to be of interest to other authorities as well as Bedfordshire."
What are tentatively described here as "expected results" were later upgraded and came to be spoken of as "objectives" by those working on the project, although there was all-round agreement at an early stage that these objectives, while presenting a general picture of the overall aims of the pilot project, did not provide an adequate practical structure for the running of the project – and in particular for the work of the teachers. Perhaps the very formulation quoted above, which initiated the debate on the aims of the project, is symptomatic of the uncertainty of approach to the problems to which it gave rise. Although the word "originally" might induce readers to assume that these aims or results were revised at some later stage, this was never the case: the above statement was reiterated unchanged in all formal project documents.

80

Among members of the project team, at any rate for the first three years, these aims remained a matter for discussion and occasional controversy, though they were never properly clarified. To this extent it is logical that they were unable to give any identifiable profile to the work done by the teachers on the project. The contradiction between the supposedly binding character of the aims, which was in no way diminished by the continuing debate, and the vagueness of their formulation, was resolved by only one teacher on the project – privately as it were – when she dismissed the debate as irrelevant and let herself be guided by her own ideas, which were "both more modest and more general". For the other teachers this contradiction remained a constant source of uncertainty.

The one exception to all this is the last of the stated objectives, the setting up of a resources centre; this assumed increasing importance during the course of the pilot project and in its last year came to dominate a large part of the teachers' activities. In the end it also proved possible to incorporate the teaching materials produced by the Punjabi teachers.

## School organization

The mother tongue groups comprised pupils taken from up to seven different mainstream classes. The following table shows the size of the learning groups. (Figures for the year 1979/80 are not available; moreover, in this final year considerable changes were made in the organization of the project, as some of the pupils who had moved into the middle school were given mother tongue instruction by teachers working on the project.)

| School | Italian | | | Punjabi | | |
|---|---|---|---|---|---|---|
| | 76/77 | 77/78 | 78/79 | 76/77 | 77/78 | 78/79 |
| Livingstone | – | – | – | 14 | 20 | 20 |
| Marlborough | 8 | 12 | 11 | 33 | 24 | 24 |
| Queen's Park | 7 | 6 | 4 | 19 | 19 | 21 |
| Castle | 12 | 15 | 20 | – | – | – |

The children at Livingstone and Castle could be taught at their own schools in classrooms which were made available for the duration of the project. The pupils from Marlborough and Queen's Park, however, had to be taken for their mother tongue lessons to an empty school building situated halfway between the two schools. In order not to waste time the mother tongue teachers usually collected the children from the playground a few minutes before the end of break.

With the exception of the Indian woman teacher, who taught at only one school until the end of the academic year 1978/79, all the teachers taught at various schools throughout the project. This fact, in addition to the concentration of the teaching in the afternoon, made it necessary for the teachers to rush from school to school, so that they were left with little opportunity to liaise with their colleagues at any of the schools and reach agreement with them on how to link the content of their own lessons with that of their colleagues' lessons. Only the Indian woman teacher regularly spent one afternoon a week in the academic year 1978/79 in "her" school in order to seek contact with her colleagues.

There are reports from all the schools of attempts to give the teachers on the project the chance to take part as guests in mainstream classes. Since they had no teaching duties in the mornings this would have been easy to organize. However, very little use was made of this opportunity. The mainstream class teachers, on the other hand, were only rarely able to attend mother tongue classes, since it was difficult to arrange for them to be replaced during their absence. Such attendance was often possible only when the headmistresses stepped in and took their classes for them.

Many pupils complained about the fact that mother tongue teaching took place in the afternoon, since this meant that they often missed parts of the play and creative activities they specially enjoyed. There is for instance a report about a girl from Queen's Park who attended Italian lessons only with reluctance because it meant regularly missing a drama session that took place in a normal afternoon class. When it was realized that this was the reason for the girl's reluctance to attend mother tongue teaching, the class teacher managed to make the necessary alteration to her timetable. Here it must be remarked that with the high degree of flexibility in the structuring of the timetable, which often remained the sole responsibility of the class teacher, such individual solutions were in principle possible in other cases, though this would have required a willingness on the part of the staff to deviate from established practice.

The mother tongue teachers had corresponding, though different, difficulties to contend with. They were faced with exceptional demands on their ability to make internal differentiations in their teaching in two respects: as already stated, the children in the mother tongue groups all came from several different mainstream classes; moreover, the state of their linguistic competence varied greatly at the start of the project. Some could speak fluently, at least in their own dialect; others understood the language, though without being fluent in it;

others had comprehension difficulties even in their own dialect. In large measure this was true of both groups, though it seemed that the Italians - the "older" of the two immigrant groups - had lost their command of their native language to a greater extent than the Indians, and that its predominant use in the Italian families was no longer unrestricted. Observations during lessons increasingly gave rise to the impression that those teachers who had worked in English mainstream classes at primary level before the start of the project were relatively better equipped to meet the demands arising from this situation. Here the informal co-operative style that one observes in many English primary school classes may have made it possible for some teachers virtually to abandon formal teaching and to encourage various activities involving completely different teaching contents simultaneously in the same classroom, thus pursuing a variety of goals with a variety of children in a complex learning situation, yet never losing sight of what was going on in the class as a whole. Thus even in lessons which appeared at first sight to be strongly geared to learning goals the children could be given opportunities for independent spontaneous communication. In the classes taken by the two Indian teachers there was a lively linguistic exchange both within the groups and between them and the teacher, with the result that it was possible for the achievement of learning goals to be continuously monitored by the teachers and for new material to be brought in where necessary either for purposes of consolidation and practice or in order to introduce the next item in the learning programme.

**Pedagogical and didactic principles**

The experimental syllabus for mother tongue teaching submitted by the Adviser for Multi-Racial Education in summer 1978 underlined in the first place the need to respect the language spoken by the child on entering the school. It then went on to refer to two functions of language: as a means of communication and as a means of structuring and handling external reality:

> "If a child does not encounter situations in which he has to explore, recall, predict, plan, explain and analyse, he cannot be expected to bring to school a ready-made facility for such uses. But that is not the same thing as saying that the ability is beyond him. We have to create the contexts and situations in which the ability can develop."

In particular the following activities were recommended for the use of the mother tongue:

> "reporting on present and recalled experiences;
> collaborating towards agreed ends;
> projecting into the future: anticipating and predicting;
> projecting and comparing possible alternatives;

perceiving causal and dependent relationships;
giving explanations of how and why things happen;
expressing and recognizing tentativeness;
dealing with problems in the imagination and seeing possible
solutions;
creating experiences through the use of the imagination;
justifying behaviour;
reflecting on feelings, their own and other people's."

The express aim of these exercises was to foster the linguistic skills
of all the children in the class. Special importance was to be placed,
by means of emphasis, revision and repetition, on the consolidation of
the knowledge acquired and on a gradation in the learning process,
which in principle should follow the sequence of hearing and
comprehending, speaking, reading and writing. On the assumption that
the children would have no opportunity to use their mother tongue
outside the mother tongue lessons, the lessons were to be carefully
structured and organized. There should be an informal atmosphere
allowing scope for games, songs, counting rhymes, etc.

These guidelines were understood to be no more than recommendations
and only partially observed in the lessons of the individual teachers.
This was due in part to the fact that the teachers, on the basis of
their disparate experience and training, attached varying degrees of
importance to different aspects which did not necessarily harmonize
with each other (for instance the demand for carefully structured
lessons and for an informal atmosphere), but also partly to the fact
that there was no lack of sound arguments relating to the particular
situation they faced, though admittedly these were not usually voiced.
One teacher, for instance, decided to adhere only to a limited extent to
the open and informal style of teaching that is customary in English
primary schools. He justified this decision on two grounds: in the first
place he did not want to disappoint the parents, whose expectations
derived from notions of more rigid models of efficient learning, and in
the second place the possibility could not be ruled out that after the
pilot project was over the children would be taught Punjabi again at
the *gurdwara* (the Sikh temple), by inadequately qualified teachers and
in excessively large classes. He saw it as his task to pitch his style
of teaching "somewhere in the middle", between the *gurdwara* and the
English primary school. The view of his female colleague, on the other
hand, was that she could and should form her own judgment, on the
basis of her own qualifications, as to what style of teaching was
appropriate to the children, and that she must not allow the parents to
pre-empt this decision. A further reason was that the syllabus took no
account of various special features of the mother tongue groups
involved in the project: since for instance it had clearly been drawn
up on the model of English syllabuses for English mother tongue
teaching, it overlooked the differences in the children's initial
competence which have already been mentioned. A high degree of internal
differentiation was required of the teachers, as well as the ability to

combine methods of foreign language and mother tongue instruction and to switch rapidly from the one to the other. This seemed scarcely possible to the teachers: while one teacher oriented her lessons to the methods of second language teaching, the others used chiefly those of first language teaching.

Problems arising from all this were occasionally neglected in favour of "solutions" that were only superficially convincing: so long as the children in a single class come to it with such disparate knowledge of the language, the rigorous insistence on using only one language in the mother tongue groups is bound to appear questionable, since it probably makes it more difficult for some children to catch up with the others or to be brought on at an equal pace. The use of games, songs, dramatization etc, as recommended in the syllabus, could be observed only in the lessons given by the Indian woman teacher, who was also the only one to give the children fairly regular opportunities to communicate entirely spontaneously in their mother tongue (when painting pictures or decorating the classroom together etc). In classes given by the other teachers, of course, the children had a chance to talk and tell stories freely.

The Co-ordinator adopted a position that was sharply at variance with that of the Adviser. His intentions were most clearly expressed in a paper which he submitted to the LEA early in 1979, i.e. after the Project Organizer had joined the project team. Starting from a six-stage analysis of the language learning capacities of the Italian children, a course based on the method of guided transfer should be developed for standard Italian in primary schools and an extensive set of materials should be compiled consisting of exercise books, textbooks, structure modules, tapes with structure drills and stories, together with a teacher's manual. (The method of guided transfer from dialect to standard language essentially means a progression from identical structures via similar structures to ones that are markedly dissimilar. For a full account of this concept - and also of the Co-ordinator's overall view of the project - see his recent book (Tosi 1984), which also provides a detailed picture of the socio-linguistic situation of the Italian community in Bedford.) For the linguistic analysis he envisaged the following steps:

- to analyse "the position of Standard Italian in the Mother Tongue project";
- to identify and examine "the learning conditions of dialectophone Italian children learning Standard Italian in a foreign context";
- to produce a "comprehensive contrastive analysis of phonetic and morphological structures between Standard Italian and Campano dialect";
- to produce "guidelines for the classroom use of a method of guided transfer from dialect to Standard Italian";
- to conduct a "survey of parents' attitudes towards bilingualism";

- to conduct a "study of variables determining children's motivation in learning Standard Italian".

The Co-ordinator was not able to realize this programme: the LEA instructed him to carry out a rather less ambitious research programme relating directly to the progress of the project.

It is true that the paper just quoted had a different status from the Adviser's syllabus in that it was not intended as a direct guide to teaching practice, but in the first instance as an attempt to describe the path that should be followed in order to develop pedagogical and didactic principles for the mother tongue teaching of the particular pupils involved, yet all the same it contains by implication an alternative to the scheme proposed by the Adviser. The proposals set out in the two schemes differ in the first place as regards their general application or their applicability to a specific learning situation: whereas the Adviser was clearly concerned primarily with what English educationists customarily call "good primary school practice" - in particular an informal, co-operative approach on the part of pupils and teachers alike, leading to lively communication between teachers and learners - the Co-ordinator began from the other end of the scale, considering it of vital importance first to establish systematically the conditions for language learning. Nevertheless the demand for strictly thought-out progressions of learning goals seemed at the same time to imply a demand for a style of teaching that was rigorously orientated to learning goals and gave preference to cognitive teaching strategies. Common to both positions was the fact that each emphasized *one* of several functions of mother tongue instruction at the cost of neglecting other dimensions which were no less important. Throughout the course of the project no accommodation was reached between the two positions.


## Learning areas

Apart from mother tongue teaching it was originally intended to bring in elements relating to the history, geography and society of the pupils' countries of origin. However, this intention was given up in view of the age of the children, the limited teaching time available (five lessons a week), and the inadequate linguistic competence of many of the children. Instead it was decided to introduce games, songs and stories from these countries, as well as individual cultural *topoi* into the language teaching whenever it was possible and likely to be successful.

All the teachers gave priority to the acquisition of language skills over cultural teaching. It was only in the teaching plan of the Co-ordinator and the Indian woman teacher that an increase in the cultural content was to be observed, corresponding to the progress the pupils were expected to make in their learning. While from the third year onwards the Co-ordinator dealt only with "Italian" themes, his Indian colleague endeavoured to incorporate the real life the children led in England in the list of themes treated in her lessons. Among other things she systematically brought in aspects of school life (an excursion to the Transport Museum and a visit by a transport expert) and of the children's experiences outside school. The other teachers were only occasionally observed to link their teaching with topical events in this way.

All the teachers endeavoured, to various degrees, to relate their teaching to the life led by the children in the specific context of the immigrant sub-culture. Not all, however, were seen to link their treatment of the circumstances of the immigrants with acceptance of the specific form of language that was used by them, which had often diverged considerably from that spoken in their countries of origin. Only the Indian male teacher tolerated the use of English in the oral and written usage of the children. He justified this by saying that even in the Punjabi spoken in India there were no native equivalents for a number of objects and ideas. A further reason was that the language of the parents living in England – even those who spoke no English – contained a large number of English words and expressions. These concepts admittedly often had equivalents in Punjabi, but these were unknown to many speakers since, by reason of the socio-cultural conditions obtaining in India, they performed no function there.

Such reflections show how precise one's knowledge of the immigrants' living conditions has to be if one is to understand their linguistic situation. They also show how unwise it is to talk of cultural learning so long as no analysis of such complex states of affairs is undertaken. And finally they show that, given the fact that quite plausible reasons can be advanced in defence of diametrically opposed decisions, it is indispensable to have an informed language policy in order to ensure the consistency of educational practice that is desirable in the interests of the children. In developing such a policy – or, to put it another way, in developing learning goals which would take account of the specific linguistic and social learning conditions of the children – the teachers found no support whatever. Reflections such as those of the Indian teacher quoted above remained isolated in two senses: they depended on chance discoveries, and they were not passed on to his colleagues on the project.

In the course of time, as a result of the methodical and didactic principles recommended in the Adviser's syllabus, all the teachers found themselves involved in an increasing amount of paper work. The structure of initial teaching in reading and writing relied on a variety of teaching manuals that had been introduced in English schools. There was considerable variation from teacher to teacher in the length and intensity of the preparatory phase preceding the introduction of writing.

## The development of teaching and learning materials

Materials from the pupils' countries of origin were hardly ever used by any of the teachers. Various reasons were given for this. Whereas the Italian teachers agreed that materials imported from Italy and designed for mother tongue instruction in Italy were inappropriate to the learning situation of the children and could therefore not be used with success, the Indian teachers were not faced with having to make such a judgment: with the exception of a few booklets brought back by one of them after a visit to India, they had no Punjabi materials.

It was clear from the whole organization of the project, with the large allocation of time to the development and production of teaching materials, that this was considered to be one of its most important tasks where both languages were concerned. In view of the fact that this was the first time in the history of English education that mother tongue teaching had been introduced into the primary school curriculum, this decision has to be seen as unavoidable. The materials compiled in the course of the project may be divided into two groups:

- Adaptations of English-language materials:

  All the teachers developed large collections of letter and word charts which were composed on the model of English initial reading methods or adapted directly from these (by substituting the corresponding letters and words). Among others the models used were "Touch and Tell", "Sound Sense", "Breakthrough". These methods permit of a large measure of individualization in the rhythms of learning and variability in the designing of lessons.

- Independently designed materials:

  These are less numerous than those in the former group. Three teachers produced series of small duplicated primers, each containing several ten- or twelve-page fascicles. The materials of the two Indian teachers are similar in structure, though they did not co-operate to produce them. Both begin with exercises on the identification of letters and words, accompanied by drawings which are either linked with them or which the children are expected to link with them. The materials produced by the Indian woman teacher are strictly monolingual, whereas her male colleague, in the first fascicle of his series, frequently attaches terms from both languages to the drawings and does not work monolingually until the next stage. This procedure probably accounts for the fact that this teacher's material does not progress beyond the copying of single words, while that of his female colleague is constructed in such a way that in the last fascicle the pupils have reached the stage of reading and answering questions on their own in writing. Comparable exercises were designed by the male teacher in the form of worksheets with a progression from copying individual words, via texts containing gaps to be filled in, to the reproduction of little stories. Both teachers used these self-designed materials in class, paying due regard to the children's degree of linguistic competence, so that the children were all able to cover the same ground at their own speed.

The Italian primers devised by the Co-ordinator were used only in reading lessons and were designed for pupils with a fairly high degree of linguistic competence, operating from the start with complete sentences grouped thematically around certain topics and linguistically around certain areas of phonetics and grammar.

**Persons and institutions taking part: their status, roles and relations**

The overall running of the pilot project was the responsibility of the Chief Education Officer, though his role was largely confined to mediating between the project and the European Commission and occasionally intervening when disagreements arose. Much more directly involved was a Senior Assistant Education Officer (SAEO) and the General Adviser for Multi-Racial Education, who was responsible for the day-to-day running of the project; eventually, in the fourth year, the LEA's Modern Language Adviser took on an increased advisory role in the project. For all three the project represented an extra burden in addition to their normal professional duties.

From January 1979 onwards all the members of the project team and the heads of the schools at which the project groups were taught took part, at irregular intervals, in discussions about the project. Previously these discussions had involved a smaller number of people (the SAEO, the Adviser and the Co-ordinator). Their purpose was to discuss current developments in the project and plan future developments, to confer on questions of evaluation, to settle whatever disagreements might arise, and generally to ensure that all members of the group were kept properly informed. Heads and teachers alike, however, complained that the content of these sessions was often of a very general nature and that they often tended to lose touch with the day-to-day reality of the project. Moreover, the discussions – which one teacher described as "occasionally stormy" – often did not lead to decisions being made, and even those decisions that were made failed to be implemented on more than one occasion.

Throughout the project it proved impossible to organize satisfactory co-operation between the project teachers and the teachers of mainstream classes. Visits by project teachers to mainstream classes and by the teachers of mainstream classes to mother tongue groups were organized only sporadically and only rarely led to mutual agreements on learning content, when the project teachers took up themes from the mainstream teaching. One teacher on the project reported that colleagues at her school repeatedly asked her what she actually did in her class, even though she had regularly made a point of informing them about the content of her teaching at the beginning of every term. The peripheral position occupied by the project teachers was difficult to remedy because all of them except her taught in more than one school. This led one head-mistress to conclude that she could recommend the continuance of mother tongue teaching after the end of the project only if the mother tongue teacher worked solely at her school.

On the other hand it became clear that attempts at practical co-operation were possible only in those cases where satisfactory personal relations existed between a project teacher and the headmistress. In some cases the project teachers felt isolated from the rest of the staff. The class teachers denied that the mother tongue teachers occupied a marginal position or were willing to admit it only in an indirect way. They did so in particular by complaining about there being insufficient information about the aims, content and background of the pilot project. Some of them expressed the view that the project had initially been "sold" to them, but that subsequently they had not been adequately involved in helping to run it.

Such problems of co-operation existed not only between project teachers and class teachers, but within the project team itself. In spite of the comparatively favourable conditions - in particular the provision of a large shared office (to which a second was added in September 1978), which enabled the teachers to meet daily to exchange ideas - there was hardly any co-operation on such crucial questions as the development of teaching concepts, the preparation of lessons and the devising of materials, and to the existing disagreements over how the teaching should be designed and carried out were added conflicts of a personal nature.

These conflicts existed between the very people who, in view of the tasks to be performed, ought to have been the first to collaborate. The Project Co-ordinator and the Adviser had almost diametrically opposed views about the tasks to which the project should address itself: for the Adviser the principal aims were the social integration and mental development of the children, whereas the Co-ordinator placed his main emphasis on the development of linguistically based progressions of learning goals. This conflict, which was in large measure the outcome of the training, background and professional experience of the parties involved and could not be resolved by recourse to the ill-defined objectives of the project, led first to a conflict of status as to who was actually in charge of the project, and then to personal resentments, the reasons for which were not always clear. These disagreements were not mitigated by interventions on the part of the LEA, who tried to strengthen the position of the Adviser, since the implementation of decisions was either not monitored at all or the monitoring was placed in the hands of the conflicting parties. The lines of responsibility thus became more and more tangled. This conflict placed a strain not only on the persons directly involved, but on the rest of the team. There was a lack of guidance and direction as to teaching content, with the result that in the conduct of their lessons the teachers went their own separate ways, letting themselves be guided by their own training and experience. The conflicts described here, which were no doubt partly due to the excessive workload borne by both the Adviser and the Co-ordinator, consumed a great deal of energy which was consequently not available for evolving the teaching content of the project.

Eventually this conflict – which, it must be repeated, arose from a concrete disagreement – played its part in creating disagreements between others: as confusion grew about where the decision-making authority lay, as more and more contradictory instructions were issued, and as information percolated through to those involved in the project in an increasingly unreliable and apparently haphazard fashion, rivalries between the individual teachers increased. In the growing atmosphere of uncertainty they partly believed that they had to compete with one another for the well-paid and prestigious posts as mother tongue teachers which the LEA might establish upon the conclusion of the project. Alliances (of an unstable character) between individuals who were in dispute with one another began to loom large, and in the end practical differences of opinion assumed the character of personal shortcomings in the eyes of those affected by them.

At a certain point in the project, co-operation between all those involved – school inspectors, the Co-ordinator, the project teachers, headteachers and class teachers – became an overriding problem and remained so until the summer term of 1979, when the first effects of the appointment of the Project Organizer became clear: the lightening of the workload on various members of the team and the clearer view that then emerged of the differences between the various tasks to be performed brought a measure of relief, making it possible for some degree of co-operation to begin and for some of the parties in dispute to steer clear of conflict in future. The skill shown by the Organizer in setting aside hitherto existing conflicts, though not necessarily solving them – a pre-condition for this being the authority to make decisions – together with the prospect of the International Colloquium, finally brought the members of the team closer together.

(This attempt to characterize the conflicts – not to describe them – is one possible interpretation. It has been carefully considered, but we are aware that other interpretations are possible. This one rests on the weighing up of contradictory and in part unverifiable information. It is quite possible that it would not gain the assent of any of the persons involved. Some areas of conflict have not been mentioned, nor have some of the identifiable causes, while others are indicated at the appropriate point in the systematic account of the project.

These conflicts made the work of the project considerably more difficult, but they had to be mentioned so that an impartial view might be taken of the successes that were achieved in spite of them.)

## Pedagogical diagnostics and the monitoring of learning achievement

The question of the development and application of tests was a matter of controversy throughout almost the whole duration of the project. Because of lack of time - and a lack of suitable instruments - no tests were carried out on the pupils' linguistic competence at the inception of the project, and there ensued an inconclusive debate as to whether the first year should be left out of account in this respect so that it might at least be possible to measure the learning achievements of subsequent years.

The task of monitoring learning achievements was written into the job descriptions of all the members of the team, and the majority of the project teachers - and some of the headmistresses - regarded this task as indispensable. The LEA vacillated on this point: the measurement of learning progress was described alternately as a subject for internal evaluation - a task that fell primarily to the Co-ordinator - and as the aim of external evaluation. Whereas in the discussions with members of the University of London Institute of Education "the development of competence in schoolbased skills, particularly linguistic competence" was identified as a possible area for external evaluation, not long afterwards the Co-ordinator was charged with developing an "evaluation programme on 'language'", which was to pursue two objectives:

1. to establish a baseline from which the children's progress could be further monitored;
2. to devise appropriate tests to measure progress in the pupils' mother tongue and interference with the acquisition of English.

The Co-ordinator's submissions, including a lengthy paper entitled "Guidelines for a structured method of literacy development in Standard Italian for bilingual children (English and Italian Dialect) at primary school level", however, were dismissed as "too academic" and "irrelevant for classroom teachers", and a later test devised by him to measure interferences between dialect and standard in Italian was rejected as too difficult. Instead he was expected to translate or adapt a standardized test for English as a second language, though this too was never used.

Since no authoritative line was agreed upon for the use of tests to monitor learning achievement, the teachers used various methods more or less of their own devising to assess the progress of the pupils. The results arrived at in this way are naturally "not comparable with anything else"; yet even they confirm the impression, which was not given - at least to the same 'extent - by any of the other pilot projects in the programme, that the children made considerable progress in learning their mother tongues; this was due partly to the comparatively large number of lessons (five a week), but above all to the teaching abilities of the teachers engaged in the project.


## Home-school liaison

Although the members of ethnic minorities have the same rights in school affairs as the English parents, they generally took no part in school life. This was changed by the project. The communities' reaction to the project ranged from approval to enthusiasm. More than two hundred Indian parents signed a petition - admittedly to no avail - which demanded the incorporation of mother tongue instruction into the curricula of other Bedford schools.

Despite difficulties of this kind, it proved possible to develop the contacts that the mother tongue teachers had made with the parents when they visited them in their homes at the start of the project to seek permission for their children to join the mother tongue groups. Thanks to the intensive home-school liaison carried out by the teachers - mostly in their free time - the project came to enjoy high regard in the ethnic groups involved. In most cases the conversations between the project teachers and the parents soon lost any official or formal overtones, and there was a consequent overall improvement in relations between the parents and the English teachers, especially as the project teachers were often present to support the class teachers in their meetings with the Indian or Italian parents, acting as interpreters and providing explanations when necessary. The English teachers came more and more to value the help of the project teachers in identifying family and health problems among the children. At a parents' evening held at one school it was observed that all the parents of the pupils in the Italian group came along to learn about their children's progress, to leaf through the textbooks and teaching materials, to talk to the teacher and seek her support in their conversations with the English staff. The connection with the mother tongue teaching was obvious: although the school had pupils from various other ethnic groups only Italian and English parents were present. Everyone involved - including the teachers of the mainstream classes and the school heads - was agreed that these successes, which they felt to be spectacular, were due to the devotion of the mother tongue teachers, and they saw this as one of the most obvious benefits of the project.


## Evaluation

The external evaluation of the pilot project, as Simons puts it succinctly, "had a diverse history" (Simons 1979b, p. 21). Although altogether six scholars were involved in it, only Simons (1979a, 1979b) and Tansley (1981), who had contracts for five and three terms respectively, were able to submit fairly detailed studies. As already stated, both had about ten days per term to carry out field studies; both worked on a part-time basis.

As Simons explained in a paper submitted at an early stage, she feels herself to be methodically committed to the (relatively recent) tradition of "illuminative/responsive" evaluation (for the "birth certificate" of this approach cf. Hamilton et al. 1977). According to her paper, this approach is "less concerned with identifying statistically significant differences in pre-specified variables ... and more concerned with responding to how the innovation develops and informing all the interested parties of the process and outcomes" (Simons 1979a, Appendix 1). Tansley also pursued a similar approach – for general methodological reasons and in order to preserve a certain continuity of approach. It is true that there are great similarities between the two studies in the details reported and the narrative presentation, but Simons, unlike Tansley, refrains from any explicit criticism or expression of opinion and tries as far as possible to let the facts speak for themselves.

For both evaluators the most important means of arriving at an assessment were interviews and conversations (preserved on tape) with those taking part in the project (teachers, heads, inspectors) and to a lesser extent with parents and children. In addition to these – and in principle of equal weight – there were observations (of teaching), analyses of documents and contributions to discussions. Information disclosed in conversations was treated in confidence at the request of those who were interviewed, and if there was a possibility that it might be cited it was submitted again to the informant for checking and approval. However, at least Simons' work became a matter of controversy during the project: while those in charge of the project and the headmistresses testify to the fairness, accuracy and correctness of her reports, these were not approved by the LEA. This disapproval expressed itself not least in the LEA's attempt – which eventually failed after long arguments – to gain control over their dissemination, presumably in order to restrict it. The reason for this seems to have been the relatively critical tenor of the reports. It is true that the criticism is not explicit, but the facts presented are apt to lead the reader to critical conclusions, especially as regards the planning and running of the project. The LEA seems to have made up its mind on the question of whether the causes of such (imagined) critical conclusions reached by imagined readers were to be sought in the reported facts or in the report as such. (Tansley's report is obtainable only from the LEA.)

The findings of both reports agree for the most part with our own; this also applies to most of Tansley's assessments. In our view both may be regarded as reliable sources for further study of the pilot project.

The controversy that has already been mentioned relating to the value of tests of linguistic competence and measurements of learning progress did not escape the notice of the external evaluators. Simons stressed at an early stage that the developing or carrying out of language tests was outside her professional competence, and in addition she later emphasized that in view of the absence of appropriate instruments the development, rather than the application, of tests must be regarded as one of the real tasks of the project, since it had been necessary at first to gain a broader and more varied knowledge of the problems these particular children had in language learning in order to be able to identify significant test items. Even the LEA – after rejecting the tests which were at first expected from the Co-ordinator and which were in fact developed by him – finally came close to adopting this position, though in its report to the International Colloquium it went a step further, declaring that the development and validation of adequate tests could have been achieved only by means of a project specially designed for the purpose. Thus towards the end of the pilot project it seems that something like unanimity was achieved on this point.

Many of the results of the external evaluation were embodied in this report, though this is not expressly indicated on every occasion. Observations on aspects of the development of the curriculum and teaching materials are scattered throughout the reports, and it will be useful to summarize them here. At an early stage the LEA perceived that this was inevitably a central task of the project if results were to be arrived at which could be applied outside it and if these results were to facilitate the integration of mother tongue teaching into the curricula of primary schools outside the LEA. The absence of models to which the mother tongue teachers could orientate their teaching, their total – and unavoidable – lack of experience of such teaching, and finally the schools' lack of experience in creating the necessary organizational conditions, made this task seem a matter of urgency even within the horizon of the project itself.

Yet at first, in the rush to get the project off the ground, no attention was given to the problem, and it was not until the first term of 1978 that a serious start was made on developing a syllabus. In May 1978, after a draft submitted by the Co-ordinator had been rejected, the Adviser for Multi-Racial Education developed his own definitive version of a further draft submitted by the teachers, which embodied his conception of the aims of primary education. He himself described his text as experimental, one of the reasons probably being that it did not go beyond an enunciation of principles which are recommended by modern English thinking on mother tongue teaching. The one reference to the special learning situation of ethnic minority children – viz. the assumption that they would hardly have any opportunity to use their mother tongue outside school – represents a misapprehension about their socio-linguistic background. Nor does the text take account of the wider aims the pilot project set itself. If therefore the draft had little impact on the actual teaching practice of the mother tongue

teachers, it must nevertheless be borne in mind that it would have
served perfectly well as a starting point for further reflections and
efforts on the part of the teachers. This was prevented by the
difficulties that have already been mentioned regarding the definition
of objectives, and by lack of co-operation within the team itself; as a
result this conceptual lead was not followed up. If, therefore, the
impression arises that the devising of the syllabus was no more than
an obligatory exercise, it must also be stressed that the teachers
endeavoured individually and with different degrees of success to
tailor their language teaching strategies to the situation of the
children. The most systematic approach was that of the Co-ordinator,
though the strong emphasis it placed on the standard language seems
rather inappropriate to the aim of helping children from dialect-
speaking workers' families to identify with their ethnic milieu.

Collaboration between mother tongue teachers and class teachers -
which was of central importance for the integration of mother tongue
teaching into the curriculum - was always perceived as problematic,
though as a rule it was no more than a source of dissatisfaction to the
project teachers. It was not explicitly mentioned in the syllabus or
elsewhere. This meant not only that in the schools involved the project
remained a more or less tolerated foreign body which only occasionally
received active support, but also above all that there were no
systematic efforts to develop possible forms of co-operation; it was
therefore not possible to deal systematically with the organizational
and educational problems that inevitably arise when children are
withdrawn from various mainstream classes to form mother tongue groups
within the framework of the normal timetable.

The members of the project team devoted enormous energy to the
development of concrete teaching materials. We did not have the time to
reconstruct, from the differences between the materials developed by
the teachers and the English-language models they used, their efforts
to take into account the specific language learning situation of the
children; all the same we can concur with Tansley when she emphasizes
that the authors highlighted the project through the wealth and variety
of their materials (Tansley 1981, p 48). By setting up the resources
centre within the framework of the pilot project the LEA in principle
created the possibility for itself to support committed and imaginative
teachers who give mother tongue teaching in Punjabi or Italian anywhere
in England.

Attempts to use the interim results of the external evaluation in order
to draw conclusions for the further development of the project seem
largely to have come to nothing. Occasional complaints from
representatives of the LEA that the external evaluation was limited to
reflecting the discussions that went on within the project team and
hence made no constructive contribution miss the point to the extent
that Simons, at the start of her work, expressly declared that she
would not take on an advisory role. Since no reference could be made to

similar experiences in the English school system, the project was to
some extent bound to take on a highly exploratory character. This seems
to have disappointed the expectations of many participants who were
hoping for demonstrable "successes". The pilot project raised more
questions than it was able to answer. In this situation the aim of the
external evaluation could only be to work through these questions and
make them available for others who might attempt similar innovations.

## Critical assessment of certain aspects

Those working on the pilot project team cannot be blamed for the fact
that it was mounted in haste. In the circumstances that developed while
the project was running it proved extremely difficult and in part
impossible to make up for the inadequate conceptual planning, which it
had not been possible to complete during the preparatory phase. Apart
from the disagreements between those taking part, which overshadowed
the project during its first three years, further difficulties probably
arose from the fact that the members of the team had to be constantly
active - they all had to give ten lessons a week. The contractual
framework created further problems: since the Commission could give
definitive undertakings regarding funding only on a year-to-year basis,
there were recurrent doubts, especially on the part of the headmistresses, as to the educational legitimacy of an experiment whose
institutional basis was so inadequately secured. The headmistresses
also had misgivings about the fact that the pilot project was
originally meant to run for only three years and would therefore not
coincide with the whole of the children's primary school career To
this extent the decision to prolong it for a fourth year came too late,
however fruitful its results may have been.

The vagueness of the objectives, which has already been mentioned, can
also be attributed to the hectic rush of the first phase. However, one
should not lose sight of the fact that the formulations in the
catalogue of objectives derive from descriptions of expected results
which the EC Commission wished to have monitored. It was to some
extent inevitable that these descriptions should fail to provide
effective guidance for practical action; the results of this were seen
in the teaching practice adopted by the individual teachers, which
continued to be determined by their disparate training and professional
experience. When the conflicts within the project team became more
pronounced it was impossible to solve them by arguing from the aims of
the project, since these afforded no basis on which social and
professional integration might be achieved within the project team.

The pilot project did not give itself the means to attain all its
objectives. The fourth aim - to bring about "a greater understanding on
the part of the immigrants of the host country's language, culture and
education" - can hardly be achieved by mother tongue instruction as it
was organized in the project. Only the Indian woman teacher took steps

in this direction by sometimes choosing events from the pupils' immediate school – such as the visit of the traffic expert – as topics for lessons. The reason she gave for doing this was that it was necessary to provide the children, even when teaching them their mother tongue, with access to specifically "English" ideas and practices. Her aim in doing this was to show the children that their own language too could help them to get to grips with their predominantly English surroundings. We do not know to what extent these reflections were discussed within the project team; at all events they produced no echo in the lessons given by the other teachers. The possibility of intercultural teaching being given jointly by class teachers and mother tongue teachers does not seem to have been considered at any point during the project. Such teaching could have afforded an approach not only to the objective in question, but also to the third objective, viz. "an increase in esteem for the immigrants on the part of the indigenous children in the school"; it would finally have been bound to lead the project team to address itself afresh to the question of co-operation with the class teachers – and to pose it in a quite different way, viz. as a question about the integration of the pilot project into the schools involved in it.

In criticizing the objectives, however, we must not overlook the possibility that their formulation was due to a misunderstanding between the LEA and the EC Commission. The LEA, faced with the need to come up with an independent statement of aims while not acting contrary to the intentions of the body that had commissioned the project, seems to have relied on its own ability to interpret Document XXII/226/76, forwarded to it by the Commission, and some of the formulations used in the initial negotiations. A more precise statement of aims was promised by Brussels, but never materialized. If on the other hand one can presume that the Commission, for its part, intended to make it possible for the LEA to design the project in conformity with local educational policy and in the light of the specific debate that had developed in England, then this might be the explanation of the dilemma: the offer made by the Commission (which is being supposed here) was not taken up by the LEA. However, a more energetic and purposeful exploitation of the room for manoeuvre (which was actually available), would have been not just desirable, but necessary.

The above-average academic qualifications and the above-average remuneration of the teachers reflect the LEA's desire to appoint only highly qualified teachers. In this it undoubtedly succeeded, and it proved to have been right to give preference to this policy rather than the alternative, which would have been not to require above-average qualifications in the teachers and to go for the creation of conditions which were as "normal" and "generally applicable" as possible. Naturally one must ask whether the professional achievement of the teachers can of itself be rated as a success in a project whose tasks were primarily innovatory and exploratory; naturally the extraordinary commitment of the teachers was partly due to their hope – which could not be shaken by denials from the LEA – that they might retain their privileged position as mother tongue teachers when the pilot project came to an end: yet there is no doubt in our minds that the results achieved in the areas of home-school liaison, the development of materials and, not least, in the mother tongue teaching itself, were due in substantial measure to the skill and devotion of these teachers. Precisely for the reason that problems existed in other areas we ought not to overlook the results that were achieved.

# Ethnic minority children in the French education system

Immigration into France had already reached substantial proportions before the Second World War: in 1931 France had 2.7m foreign residents, representing 6.6% of the population. Admittedly the character of the immigration has changed in the course of time, from a population drift which had its source for the most part in the other countries of Europe to an influx of migrants in search of work or prompted by political motives, most of them coming from the Mediterranean area; moreover the immigrants tend increasingly to be concentrated in certain areas (the Paris region or Rhône-Alpes). It may be said, however, that France has more experience of immigration than other continental countries.

In 1975 the number of foreign residents in France was 3,442,000. Of these the most important groups were the Portuguese (1975: 758,925 = 22% of the total foreign population), the Algerians (710,690 = 20.6%) the Moroccans (260,025 = 7%), the Tunisians (139,735 = 4.1%), the Poles (93,655 = 2.7%) and the Yugoslavs (70,280 = 2.1%). By 31 December 1978 the number of foreign nationals resident in France had risen to 4,170,353.

Most of the migrant workers employed in the processing industries, the building industry, in trade and the service industries have relatively low qualifications. Their social situation, like that of migrants in other comparable countries, is characterized by a disproportionate level of unemployment, poor living conditions, and insecurity with regard to their legal status.

From the end of the Second World War until immigration was halted on 4 July 1974 there existed a relatively stable system of graded residence and work permits; it was also possible for illegal entry to be regularized retrospectively and for families to be reunited without restriction. This was followed, from 1974 onwards, by a policy of consolidation, and in 1977 a policy of repatriation began to be openly pursued, with the result that the legal standing of migrants has progressively worsened. This process is characterized by political, parliamentary and administrative wrangling about numerous details of the law relating to aliens: changes in the system of work and residence permits, the blocking of retrospective regularization of unauthorized entry, the halting of family reunification, the simplification of deportation procedures, the temporary payment of repatriation grants, the fixing of maximum quotas for work permits issued to foreign nationals. Officially, of course, one speaks of a "policy of exclusively voluntary repatriation", yet at the same time the argument involves calculations relating to quite considerable repatriation quotas intended to ease the burden on the French labour market.

In the academic year 1978/79, according to official statistics, 882,400 migrant pupils attended French schools (including pre-school institutions); this represents 7.2% of the total school population. The trend is upwards: the proportion for the *premier degré* is 9.4%, for the *second degré* 5.9%. The overwhelming majority of migrant children (94.4%) attend public sector schools. There is a disproportionate representation of foreign pupils in special classes at schools belonging to the *premier degré* (14.1% of the total) and in the practical vocational classes of the *second degré* (CPPN: 8.5% of the total, CPA: 11.2%); they are under-represented in the longer courses at secondary schools of Type II (3.4%). Information about the number of foreign pupils who obtain a school leaving qualification is not available.

## The social integration of migrant families and pre-school education

Almost all the studies so far available relating to the problems of migrant families in France regarding social integration deal with the period after pre-school age and contain for the most part informed reflections by experts which, in nearly every case, relate to the identity crisis of adolescence. Common to nearly all these investigations is the conclusion that the migrants are "socially handicapped" (Berthelier 1976, p 33) owing to the severing of the link with their cultural heritage and inadequate socio-cultural integration. This low degree of integration, hypothesized by the authors of these theoretically orientated studies, is confirmed by empirical investigations, especially for Maghrebian and Portuguese families. Beside these studies, which concentrate on the cultural situation of the migrants and largely typify the French view of the question, there are the arguments which insist that in principle the position of migrant workers is identical with that of French workers (e.g. Gokalp 1976) and go on to postulate educational requirements consequential upon such identity. It is striking that hardly any attention is paid to the idea that the French working class has acquired a substratum made up of migrant workers, an idea which would lead logically to a differentiated assessment of their social and educational situation. There is a lack of empirical studies and theoretical discussions of the processes of socialization that such hypotheses imply.

Although no precise figures are available, it seems reasonable to suppose that a very high proportion of ethnic minority children attend pre-school classes. For 1978/79 it is recorded that 202,042 migrant children (i.e. 9.3% of the total pre-school population) attended pre-school institutions in the public sector. There is no doubt that this widespread pre-school attendance, which is a specifically French feature of the situation of migrants in general, serves to reduce the rate of under-achievement among children from all social backgrounds. Yet at the same time the concomitant integration of migrant children into French culture brings with it a potential source of strain in the relations between the children and their parents.

**Admission of ethnic minority children to primary and secondary schools**

Attendance at primary school begins at the age of five. As a rule foreign children have by this stage acquired a sufficient knowledge of French while at kindergarten to start attending mainstream classes immediately, and they have the same right to support teaching as French children. Such teaching, however, is not geared to their specific needs, and many teachers refuse to take part in it because it is only marginally effective and because they have had no special training for it.

Since 1979, migrant children newly arrived in France and unable to speak French have had the opportunity to attend a *classe d'initiation* *(Cl. In)* designed exclusively for the teaching of French. There are three types of *Cl. In*: those which extend over the whole school year, those lasting six months or a term (depending on the time of the child's arrival), and an integrated crash course *(CRI = Cours de rattrapage intégré)*, in which the migrant children receive seven or eight special language lessons a week, but otherwise attend the same lessons as their French classmates. In pursuance of a recommendation contained in a government order, these integrated crash courses are due to be integrated into the *tiers temps pédagogique* introduced in 1969. The *tiers temps pédagogique* essentially provides for a tripartite division of the school week into the teaching of basic subjects (French and arithmetic), *activités d'éveil* (practical subjects) and games. It cannot be said, however, that the intended parity of the three teaching areas has been achieved; this is clear for instance from the fact that in common parlance the terms *activités d'éveil* and *tiers temps* are used synonymously. It is because of this assumption that the *activités d'éveil* are of lesser importance that the crash courses have been moved into this section of the curriculum. It is nevertheless doubtful whether the attendance of non-francophone children at mainstream classes on reading, writing and arithmetic - in which no distinction is made between them and the other children - is particularly effective, and certainly the absence of the ethnic minority children from lessons which form part of the *activités d'éveil* and stress spontaneity and creativity, is unlikely to promote their integration into the class as a whole. The schools have therefore in the main opted for the one-year type of *classe d'initiation*. In the *Cl. In.* a conscious effort is made to integrate the migrant children into a French culture, this being considered the precondition for further meaningful schooling - an attitude which is based on the abstract supposition that, so to speak, "all learners are equal".

Migrant children who enter the country after the age of twelve are placed in a *classe d'adaptation (Cl. Ad.)* in the type of secondary school that provides a general education or, if they are fourteen or over, in the type that offers vocational training or work preparation; attendance at these is compulsory for one or two years. In these *classes d'adaptation* they learn everyday French together with the specialized language of the branch of employment for which they opt; in addition they have a chance to study their own language, which is treated as their first foreign language. However, Hamburger 1978, p. 55, is probably right to describe the *Cl. Ad.* as an "educational holding institution for those children...who from the start are considered to have no prospect of gaining a school-leaving qualification or joining a mainstream class". No figures are given in the Ministry's published statistics for the number of *classes d'adaptation* in operation, but for 1980 the number of *classes d'initiation* was estimated at about 1,000.

**Mainstream and specific educational provision at primary level**

Apart from introducing the *tiers temps pédagogique*, the 1969 reform of primary education brought in a new structuring according to age:

- Cours préparatoire (CP), first school year
- Cours élémentaire 1, 2 (CE 1 and CE 2), second and third school years
- Cours moyen 1, 2 (CM 1 and CM 2), fourth and fifth school years.

The timetables are the same for all five years: ten periods a week allocated to French, five to arithmetic, six to *activités d'éveil*, and six to physical education.

The aim of the reform was to democratize education and at the same time introduce modern psychological and pedagogical thinking, but it led neither to appropriate opportunities for teachers to receive further training nor to better equipped schools. As a result, "the primary school remains for the time being first and foremost an institution for learning the mother tongue and arithmetic" (Doll 1976, p 42).

At secondary level two educational subsystems co-exist, one leading to a university education and the more prestigious types of employment, the other providing vocational training and work preparation for the great mass of pupils and leading to skilled and semi-skilled employment. In view of this it is one of the functions of the primary schools to select pupils for the next phase of their education and orientate them towards it (Baudelot and Establet 1971). It follows that children from ethnic minorities, upon entering the French mainstream classes, move into a climate which is geared to learning achievement and competition and which places a considerable burden even on their French peers, especially those from less privileged backgrounds. Pupils frequently have to "repeat" a year, so that "delay" in their school career (*retard scolaire*) may almost be regarded as a "normal" phenomenon. The earlier the children experience "delay", the less likely they are to reach secondary level. At primary level the CP and the CM 2 constitute particularly demanding hurdles (with 12.6% and 15.6% respectively having to repeat the year, compared with roughly 9% in the other years). The background-linked effect of this selection process is

unmistakable: at the end of the primary school period in 1974/75, 45.9%
of the children of industrial workers had experienced "delay", whereas
the corresponding figure for children of executives and professional
people is 12.9% (Ministry of Education 1976, p 26). It is clear that all
this has an effect on the careers of migrant workers' children, though
there are no representative studies on the subject. The much-quoted
study by Gratiot-Alphandéry and Lambiotte comes to the following
conclusion on this question:

> "...the obstacles the child encounters cannot be attributed solely to
> a greater or lesser lack of linguistic competence, but to the
> difficulties they have in overcoming the whole range of socio-
> cultural handicaps, difficulties which increase as schooling
> progresses and the standards demanded become higher" (1974, p 69).

It is true that in the debate on the findings of this study one
encounters a kind of interpretation which differs from that of the
writers, concentrating less on the children's handicaps and more on the
"failure of educational institutions to adapt" (Charlot et al. 1978, p
11) - in other words demanding adaptability on the part of the schools
rather than on the part of the children. This point of view rests upon
a tradition which is peculiar to the French debate on education policy
and might, if pursued in a positive manner, provide a starting point
for constructive solutions of the problem in future.

A first step in this direction was taken by the Ministry of Education
in 1973/74, when provision was made, first in the case of Portuguese
and then of Italian children, for three weekly lessons of mother tongue
teaching to be incorporated into the *activités d'éveil*; these were to be
given by teachers responsible to the Portuguese and Italian consulates
and were intended to help new arrivals to adapt themselves to their
new surroundings, as well as to enable children who had been in France
for some time already "to feel more self-confident in exercising their
bilingual skills". Gradually this scheme came to include mother tongue
courses for Tunisian, Spanish, Moroccan, Yugoslav and Turkish pupils.
Beside these integrated courses there exist also the so-called
"parallel" (i.e. supplementary) mother tongue courses; these were set up
following a government order of 12 July 1939, which was replaced by a
new order issued on 30 June 1976. These courses usually take place on
Wednesday afternoons (when there is no school in France) or on
Saturday mornings. According to information supplied by the countries
of origin, the number of pupils attending mother tongue courses, both
integrated and supplementary, is about 139,000, i.e. about 40% of all
possible takers; according to the Ministry of Education the figure is
65,658, i.e. about 20%. The integrated courses seem at first sight to
offer considerable advantages: the pupils are not subjected to the
burden of additional afternoon lessons, and the bilingual teachers are
integrated into the staff of the host school, thus making it possible
for the teaching methods employed by the indigenous and the bilingual
teachers to be co-ordinated and for the content of their lessons to be

linked. They also have the effect of enhancing the status of the migrants' languages in the minds of both the French and the immigrant children, as well as in the minds of the French teachers. Yet the potential inherent in such courses often fails to be realized, either because there are various practical obstacles to co-operation or because the teachers themselves are unused to co-operation; other reasons for their lack of success are the heterogeneous nature of the groups that make up the classes, competition between *activités d'éveil* (which are popular with the pupils) and mother tongue teaching – such competition being a burden on the pupils – and the limited room for manoeuvre available to the bilingual teachers. The fact is that, despite all the obvious difficulties connected with them, it is often the parallel courses that lead to better learning achievements.

The few facilities offered for intercultural teaching have not yet progressed beyond the stage of pilot projects. One example is the pilot project in Paris, which will be described in the next chapter.

## Orientation to or within secondary education

A special feature of the French school system is the elaborate provision it makes for orientation and guidance, which at one time was employed primarily for the allocation of primary school leavers to the different branches of the secondary system, but which now, since the Haby reform, is directed mainly to pupils at secondary level I, in order to influence their subsequent school career and guide them towards appropriate vocational choices. The chief instruments designed for this purpose are information brochures, personal counselling sessions with pupils and parents, and institutionalized collaboration in the orientation decisions that are taken at the end of the *cycle d'observation* (i.e. in the seventh year of schooling) and the *cycle d'orientation* (in the ninth year of schooling), both of which take place at secondary school.

The system as a whole works effectively. However, there are no studies available on how and to what extent ethnic minority pupils and their families take advantage of the guidance provided. Nor do we know of any attempts being made to develop forms of guidance adapted to the cultural traditions of the migrants or to cater in any way to their specific needs. This is probably an area of French education where important steps need to be taken in the provision for migrant children.

## Mainstream and specific educational provision at secondary level

By the Haby reform, which became law in 1975 and began to come into force by stages in the academic year 1977/78, the earlier tripartite secondary system was transformed into one which was organized along comprehensive lines. The residual effects of the old system are still very much in evidence, however, so that it is not possible here to describe a single uniform system of secondary education.

Secondary level I is divided into a *cycle d'observation* and a *cycle d'orientation*, each lasting two years. The former now has a uniform timetable for what are in principle supposed to be mixed-ability classes; the overt differentiation between pupils begins officially in the *cycle d'orientation*, which looks forward to the school leaving qualification, intermediate qualifications, or actual employment. Stream III classes lead directly to the so-called *classes préprofessionelles de niveau (CPPN)*, which provide a general preparation for working life or - if the pupils have already reached the age of fifteen by the end of the *cycle d'observation* - to the *classes préparatoires à l'apprentissage (CPA)*, which prepare them directly for particular jobs and embody a high degree of practical training. Classes of this latter type may also be attended by pupils who have completed the *CPPN*. It is in these two types of class, which were not abolished under the Haby reform, that migrant workers' children are most over-represented; only here is the selection function of secondary level I seen to be manifestly in operation.

Upon admission to secondary level II, on the other hand, all pupils are definitively allocated to different branches of the school system. The short courses of two or three years' duration (*deuxième cycle court*), which are provided at the *lycées d'éducation professionnelle (LEP)*, offer vocational training leading to a recognized leaving certificate which constitutes a vocational qualification. Another type of course, with an inferior rating, leads to the *certificat d'aptitude professionnelle (CAP)*, with approximately 250 possible specialisms. Attendance at courses of the latter type is regarded by many French educationists as evidence of under-achievement. Even the more highly rated leaving certificate, the *brevet d'études professionnelles (BEP)*, enjoys relatively little prestige, even though it certifies that the holder has undergone a substantial specialist training with a considerable theoretical component - a training, moreover, for which there is an economic demand. The *BEP* involves about 40 specialisms in three areas of employment (industry, trade and administration, and medical and social work). The qualifications that enjoy real prestige are those which are obtained after three years of study at secondary level II (*deuxième cycle long*); these involve a great variety of courses in arts, science and vocational subjects. These are offered by the *lycées*, and the drop-out rate is high.

Mother tongue teaching for ethnic minority pupils takes two forms: it is either a mainstream provision or an optional extra. At French secondary schools a total of twelve modern foreign languages may be studied - or could, at the time of the present investigation. These are, in descending order of demand, English, German, Spanish, Italian, Russian, Arabic, Portuguese, Hebrew, Chinese, Polish, Dutch and Japanese. The prescribed minimum size of learning groups is sometimes eight and sometimes fifteen pupils. While in 1978/79 Spanish and Italian were still relatively well represented, with 520,685 and 96,550 pupils respectively, the other two languages which concern us here, viz. Arabic and Portuguese, were poorly represented, with 3,876 and 4,628 pupils respectively. Even supposing that these languages are chosen only by native speakers, the figures still show that not more than 4.15% of the children from North African countries study their mother tongue at secondary school, while on the same reckoning the corresponding figure for Portuguese children is 8.27% (Boulot/Clévy/Fradet 1980a, p 34). It would be pointless to make a similar calculation for Spanish and Italian, since it must be assumed that these languages are studied by a substantial number of French pupils as well.

There is the additional possibility, not only at primary, but also at secondary level, of attending mother tongue courses run by the consulates of the migrants' countries of origin (cours parallèles). In an order issued in September 1977 the Ministry of Education emphasized that before such courses were set up there would have to be a careful examination and maximal exploitation of the possibilities for providing teaching of this kind within the framework of mainstream foreign language provision, the specific implication being that there had to be a possibility of bringing pupils of different age groups together in one class. Nevertheless, even where no such possibility exists - as is to be expected with languages like Modern Greek, Turkish, and the various languages of Yugoslavia, as well as with other languages for which there is even less demand - it is laid down that a pedagogically realizable link should be established with mainstream teaching and school life generally, viz. through the acquisition of the relevant books for the school library and the communication of the bilingual teachers' "assessments" (though not their actual marks) to the French teachers.

## Academic achievement

Statements about academic achievement can be made only to a very limited extent, since the official statistics do not provide the precise distinctions required and there are few relevant studies available.

In the first place we should mention the work of Clévy et al. (1976), who investigated the school achievement of migrant children in six French towns. They found that, of the migrant children aged fourteen whom they studied,

- 20% could not read French;

- 40% had only reached the standard of the third year of primary school (CE 2, normal age eight years);

- 20% had reached the standard required for school leaving, though without gaining a school leaving qualification;

- 20% had been successful at school and were attending secondary modern or technical schools.

The authors compare these findings with those of a later study made after the introduction of *classes d'initiation*. This involved 1,600 foreign pupils aged between six and twelve who had completed a one-year *classe d'initiation*:

- 70% of the children aged between six and eight had been taught in a mainstream class without suffering any "delay" apart from the inevitable preparatory year;

- 60% of all the children were (*a*) either in a primary school class with not more than two years' delay, i.e. with some prospect of being admitted to a secondary modern or grammar school (both of which are now integrated into comprehensives) or (*b*) already in one of these two streams, this being regarded as an indication of educational success.

From these data Clévy and his co-authors (1976, p 43) conclude that the *classes d'initiation* have been a "limited but...indisputable success". The limits of this success are demonstrated above all by the proportion (about 25%) of pupils in the age-group nine to twelve who are three or more years behind in their schooling and have thus reached a "point of no return", i.e. a point beyond which they can continue only in one direction, with no chance of having any benefit to show from their schooling.

The much-quoted study by Gratiot-Alphandéry and Lambiotte provides data on the *retard scolaire* of foreign primary school pupils in the Paris suburb of Aubervilliers. The proportion of foreign pupils attending the local primary schools was 23%, which was about average for the Paris region. The ethnic groups best represented in the suburb present the following picture:

|  | normal age | 1 year's delay | 2 years' delay |
|---|---|---|---|
| Algerians | 45% | 31% | 21% |
| Spaniards | 56% | 28% | 14% |
| Portuguese | 39% | 28% | 32% |

Source: Gratiot-Alphandéry/Lambiotte 1974, p 69.

These are average figures for primary schooling as a whole. An analysis according to age shows that from *CP* to *CM 2* the proportion of children of normal age ranges from 63% to 35% for Algerians, from 81% to 37% for Spaniards, and from 47% to 23% for Portuguese.

At secondary level II the proportion of pupils attending the *classes préprofessionnelles de niveau* and the *classes préparatoire à l'apprentissage* may be taken to indicate a lack of school achievement. In public sector schools of this type the figure for French pupils is 6.6%; for foreign pupils it is 12.6%.

For secondary level II we only have figures showing the numbers of students attending short courses and of those attending long courses: short courses at public sector schools are attended by 42.1% of French pupils and 65.3% of foreign pupils. A more detailed analysis is not possible, since the statistics do not distinguish between the courses leading to the *BEP* and those leading to the *CAP*; and where the long course is concerned there is no distinction between the general education stream and the vocational stream. Finally, there is no evidence for determining the proportion of students who fail to complete these courses.

# The pilot project in Paris

## The general framework

The pilot project involved ten different schools in Paris and its suburbs. It is not possible here to give a full account of the movement of immigrant workers to Paris, or even to describe the social structure of all ten districts where the schools are situated. We will therefore take as examples three districts which contrast markedly with one another and will thus serve to illustrate the wide variety of social conditions with which the project was concerned.

The first example is the primary school in the rue Keller in La Roquette, a residential district in the XIth *arrondissement*. This in fact consists of two co-educational schools housed in the same building and having between them about 225 pupils, 120 of whom are of foreign nationality. The school took part in the pilot project from its inception by running Portuguese and Spanish courses. In addition, it mounted integrated courses for Moroccan and Tunisian pupils, as well as a preparatory course in French for new arrivals from abroad. The school is situated in a busy, but decidedly poor part of Paris, with many old houses which are due for redevelopment and occupied mainly by working-class families. Redevelopment is in fact already under way; hence one finds, side by side with such obsolete housing, recently erected buildings which are in stark contrast with the old, but no less unattractive. Only the local boulevard is lined with handsome houses from an earlier period; these are inhabited by people of a higher social class - civil servants, teachers, and other salary-earners. The high proportion of migrant residents determines the character of the neighbourhood, both visibly and audibly, with its many ethnic restaurants and food stores and its semi-oriental street life. The immigration of Italians and Spaniards to the area is already a thing of the past, but in recent years they have been joined by Portuguese, Arabs and Yugoslavs. There are also political refugees from Asia and Latin America, and a well established Jewish community with its synagogues and kosher restaurants. The barriers between the French and migrant communities, whose members belong largely to the same or similar social strata, seem to be less rigid here than elsewhere.

A quite different picture is presented by the neighbourhood of the school in the rue Hamelin in the XVIth *arrondissement*. This too is a co-educational school, with a widely fluctuating population: in 1977/78 the number of pupils rose from 146 at the beginning of the school year to 169 by the end. The proportion of ethnic minority pupils is almost exactly 50%, made up of 18 nationalities, the largest groups being the Spaniards, with 30 pupils, and the Portuguese, with 20. In the second and third years of the project the school put on Spanish and Portuguese courses. A decisive factor in ensuring that the school joined in the project was the commitment of one inspector, in whose area the school is situated. The XVIth *arrondissement* is the smartest and most expensive residential area in Paris. Here one finds fine old upper-class houses side by side with tall, well-appointed, modern apartment blocks. There are two reasons for the high proportion of foreign residents in the area (about 30%): first, a large number of diplomats and their families, of various nationalities, live in the area, and many of the diplomats work at the numerous embassies situated here; secondly, many prosperous French and foreign families employ migrant domestic staff. Hence the mothers of many of the foreign children are *concierges*, while the fathers are workers or – to a lesser extent – domestic servants themselves. These families often live in the cramped servants' quarters or basements of the large houses. In the evening the fathers can be seen frequenting the few modest or run-down cafés of the area, while the French population remains, as it were, discreetly out of sight. There is hardly any street life.

Our third example is the suburban primary school of Villejuif. This again is a co-educational school with about 300 pupils, some 50 of whom are of foreign origin – Italian, Portuguese, Spanish, Algerian, Chilean and African. The Italians and Portuguese form the two largest groups, with 18 and 12 pupils respectively. In addition to the integrated Italian courses which form part of the pilot project, the school runs a parallel course in Portuguese. Villejuif is a suburb with a small-town atmosphere in which the social strata tend to mix. Roughly 40% of the population is made up of workers, 25% of salaried employees, and 20% of *cadres moyens*, i.e. technicians, foremen, supervisory staff, etc; this mixture is reflected in the variety of housing one finds in the suburb. There is a clear social stratification in the immigrant population of Villejuif: owing to the fairly long tradition of Italian immigration, some of the Italian children at the local school belong to the third generation, which has almost abandoned its Italian roots and its Italian "mother tongue". Some of the parents have become skilled workers, occupying the better jobs and hence constituting an "upper" stratum among the immigrant population *vis-à-vis* the North African and Portuguese parents, who do the more unpleasant and poorly paid work.

### The pilot project

The pilot project covered the three school years from 1976/77 to 1978/79. At the beginning of the first year there were some organizational difficulties to be overcome at the schools, and certain problems relating to the integration of the bilingual teachers had to be solved, but by the beginning of 1977 all four bilingual teachers were working with seventeen groups of ethnic minority pupils at altogether eight schools. The second year of the project brought a number of changes. There were replacements in the Spanish and Portuguese staff. Of the eight schools taking part in the first year, four withdrew from the project, while two new schools joined it, sc that it continued at six schools, with altogether ten groups of foreign pupils. Teacher counselling was entrusted to CEFISEM Paris, an institution which provides in-service training for teachers working with foreign children, while the expert back-up was provided by CREDIF, an institute for educational research attached to the *Ecole Normale Supérieure* at Saint-Cloud. CREDIF reported annually on the progress of the project, which concluded with a colloquium held in Paris in October 1978.

## Development of objectives

On 6 September 1976 the department of the Ministry of Education with responsibility for primary education published an order laying down the outlines of the project:

the EC would bear the cost of employing four mother tongue teachers and of the running and evaluation of the pilot project:

the aims of the project were: to carry out an integrated programme of mother tongue teaching involving three lessons a week, to promote an awareness in French schools (among teachers, pupils and parents) of the cultures of the ethnic minority pupils, and to provide these pupils with general support designed to facilitate their possible return home and improve their chances of making contacts in France by giving them access to the French language and to the values of French society;

the pilot project was to be carried out in Paris and the surrounding area at primary schools which had a high concentration of ethnic minority pupils;

the schools were called upon to make the necessary arrangements, in particular to make accommodation available and to inform the French and migrant parents about the project.

This order placed the mother tongue teaching connected with the pilot project within the framework of the "integrated courses" introduced in 1975; it was emphasized, moreover, that several thousand migrant pupils in France already received such teaching. The Ministry thus regarded the project as an opportunity to intensify and continue a policy that was already being implemented. This view of the project was not without its consequences. It anchored it fairly and squarely within the regular education system. On the one hand it offered the possibility of finding solutions to "normal" problems in "normal" circumstances, solutions which might have applications outside the project itself; on the other hand, it brought with it the problem that in "normal" circumstances it is usually difficult to find novel solutions. The innovatory character of the project was seen to lie primarily in the attempt to integrate instruction in the language and culture of the children's countries of origin, as far as possible, into the French school system. In this context integration is not to be understood solely in an organizational sense; it also involves promoting a general sensitivity in French schools to the presence of pupils of different nationalities. In this connection it was pointed out that there were ample opportunities for opening up "entirely new possibilities of evaluation".

In this statement of aims it is possible to discern differing interests which are not always compatible. Thus the repeated references to the contribution the pilot project should make to the possible re-integration of the migrant children into the school systems of their own countries is more in line with the idea of repatriation, which was strongly emphasized in French immigration policy at the time, than with the aim of creating a multicultural society in France. And, in fact, the setting up of the pilot project did arouse apprehensions, at least among some migrant parents, that it might be used as a way of putting pressure on them to return home. Less clearly emphasized is the tendency towards the harmonizing of differing interests. It is stated that the pilot project should give the migrant pupils "freer access to the French language and the values of French society, simply by virtue of the fact that their own language and their own values, which are linked with these, are fully recognized and appreciated". Such a formulation may serve to reconcile the interest that French schools have in assimilating their migrant pupils with the aims of the pilot project, which are orientated towards linguistic and cultural diversity and towards ministerial policy on the education of migrant children.

Within the pilot project an attempt was made also to take account of the interests of the official representatives of the children's countries of origin. This was done by involving them in the project from its inception - at first in the selection of the bilingual teachers and then, during the second and third years, in the evaluation process. Naturally their chief interest is the propagation of their own languages and cultures, quite independently of whether or not their governments pursue an open repatriation policy. They are thus natural allies, as it were, in any educational policy that is orientated towards linguistic and cultural diversity, rather than simply partners responding to considerations of foreign policy. This does not mean, however, that there was automatic agreement on matters of practical organization and educational objectives. In this area different positions are taken up by the different nationalities, and even among representatives of one nationality there can be substantial differences of opinion. It emerged, for instance, from a conversation with a representative of the Yugoslav embassy in Paris in July 1977, that the embassy placed total reliance on its own efforts, i.e. on the supplementary courses it provided. He viewed the pilot project - and integrated courses as a whole - with benevolent indifference, drawing attention to the problems of timetabling. He did not believe that the integrated courses were really more economical than the supplementary courses, stating that in the view of his embassy everything necessary had been done for the teaching of Serbo-Croat (and the other languages of Yugoslavia) in France; there were guidelines; there would be textbooks; there was adequate provision for teachers; the interests of the parents and their wishes with regard to repatriation were in accord with the measures taken by the Yugoslav government. His successor, on the other hand, speaking at a colloquium held in October 1985, declared herself to be in full agreement with the aims of the pilot project.

The basic principles laid down by the Ministry remained in force throughout the duration of the project. A reformulation contained in the second interim report introduced only a minor modification by adding two further general aims: the "development of the child's personality" and "access to a multicultural society". In the course of the project, however, its aims were subject to two kinds of interpretation, one on an intellectual and the other on a practical plane.

In discussing the legitimation of the project its defenders refer, in very general terms, to the opening up of the French school system to differing cultures, with the result that the postulated educational processes appear possible at the same time and to the same extent, these processes being: the strengthening of the migrant pupils' cultural self-assurance, the creation of a degree of sensitivity among French pupils to the cultures of their ethnic minority classmates, and the facilitation of the migrant pupils' access to the culture of the host country (cf. for instance Clévy, in CREDIF 1979, p 36). Porcher included all these processes in his programmatic concept of intercultural education (cf. op. cit., p 26f).

The CREDIF experts, however, arrived at a critical, even pessimistic view of the aims of the project (CREDIF 1979/80, vol 1, pp 71-80), starting from the problems arising from the relations between language, culture and social class. They were critical of the seeming compatibility of integration with language acquisition and cultural teaching, maintaining that such a combination of aims could in fact be pursued only to the detriment of each individually:

> "Is not practice in the mother tongue, which is offered to the children by the institution (in three lessons a week!) one way of depriving them of it? Does not the learning of the mother tongue in fact *conflict* with everything else?" (Pelfrene, CREDIF 1978, p 76)

But they are critical above all of the notion of inherited culture, maintaining that it is alien to the real world in which the migrants live and hence can only serve to alienate them further; in their view it should be replaced by an analysis of the concept of immigrant culture:

> "Is it possible, in France today, to speak of cultural exchange? The immigrant is the object of a functional integration which creates social isolation. One cannot speak of a living culture since the immigrant has in fact neither the right nor the means to express

114

himself. How can one speak of cultural exchange if one starts out
from the immigrant's real situation? (Perotti, op. cit., p 75).

Gokalp expresses the same view in lapidary form when he writes:

"Les émigrés ne sont pas échangistes" (op. cit., p 76).

Perotti recognizes two sources of identity, though from a different
point of view from that contained in the official formulations of the
aims of the project:

"The immigrants cannot become aware of their cultural identity
unless they become aware of belonging to a particular ethnic/
national or social group. These are the two collective dimensions
in which the immigrants live, the only ones that can give them a
notion of a shared history which does not represent a defensive
recourse to an idealization of their national culture and does not
force them to remain a more or less amorphous aggregate of
individuals" (op. cit., p 85)

The practical interpretation of the aims of the project is on a quite
different level and has been the subject of far fewer official
pronouncements and public discussion.

The didactic interpretation, that is to say the formulation of aims for
mother tongue teaching, intercultural teaching and home-school liaison
was primarily a matter for the bilingual teachers and those of their
French colleagues who took part in the intercultural activities.
Uniformity was neither sought nor achieved. The diversity of
interpretation is clearly illustrated by the comments of two teachers
attending the colloquium:

"One must set a priority: is it not better to start by giving the
child the greatest possible chance of integration (insertion) and
success in the French school system? A child who has acquired a
good command of the language and a good knowledge of the culture
has every prospect of success wherever he goes. Since the means
available for instruction in the mother tongue and the child's
inherited culture are limited, is it not preferable to ensure that
he acquires a good knowledge of the language of the host country?"
(CREDIF 1979, p 58f).

"It is the aim of the Yugoslav representatives to enable the
children to act as ambassadors of Yugoslav culture, which rests
upon the Serbo-Croat, Slovenian, Albanian and Macedonian languages."
(ibid., p 53).

Responsibility for promoting an awareness of foreign cultures in the
French schools and among the French parents rested with the head
teachers, yet this aim was not formulated in concrete terms, any more

115

than were those of improving the migrant pupils' access to the French language and culture or of developing closer contacts with their family backgrounds. Nor were there many further statements about the aim of keeping open the possibility of the children's re-entering the school systems of their home countries. At the colloquium the representatives of Portugal, Spain and Yugoslavia explained briefly how their governments regulated teaching abroad, what possibilities there were for gaining national qualifications, and what support facilities existed for any children who might return home. There was no specific reference to the pilot project in connection with any of these points: no attempt was made within the project itself to create better opportunities for children returning home, nor did the representatives of the countries concerned consider the possibility of introducing procedures which would make it any easier for pupils taking part in the project to have their educational achievements recognized.

On two important points, however, the gap between the theoretical and the practical interpretations of the aims of the project was bridged: the Spanish teacher took up the "intellectual" problems arising from the concept of culture; she argued that priority should be given to school achievement in France and hence that more importance should be attached to the acquisition of French than to mother tongue teaching. From this she drew conclusions relative to her own teaching – conclusions which clearly deviated from the line that had otherwise been pursued in the project. The second matter on which an attempt was made to link theory with practice in a way that would be conducive to new solutions, was the devising of a curricular framework for intercultural activities and the structuring of these activities in the form of a number of teaching units. These proposals too were clearly at variance with the practice that had previously been adopted in the pilot project, in that they subordinated the task of preserving or inculcating the children's inherited culture to more general pedagogical objectives (summed up as "developing the child's personality").

Collaboration between French and bilingual teachers

The differences between the educational principles followed by the bilingual teachers and those of "the French school" gave rise to a number of difficulties in the course of the project. Despite certain notable exceptions, it may be said (admittedly at the risk of over-generalizing) that the bilingual teachers were observed to have a more authoritarian style of teaching, to set greater store by factual knowledge, and to favour purely verbal communication in class. This earned them a certain amount of criticism from their French colleagues. The French instructors responsible for in-service training advised them, for instance, to make more extensive use of audio-visual materials in their mother tongue classes and to experiment with methods of learning through play, but this advice was not always sufficiently heeded. Nor had all those who were recruited as teachers undergone a full course of teacher training, and so it was not always possible to build upon the necessary foundation of educational knowledge and teaching skills. However, as Clévy rightly points out, the choice of traditional methods of language teaching did not result solely from a personal decision on the part of the foreign teacher: it was prompted partly by demands from the parents and from the representatives of their countries of origin (CREDIF 1979, p 42). The bilingual teachers were thus caught between the French expectation - which they tried to meet, with at least partial success - that they would adapt themselves to the French system, and the expectation of the parents, whose general approval of their mother tongue teaching they could on no account risk losing.

The French staff were greatly influenced by the far-reaching changes in educational thinking that found expression in the school reform of 1969. Here we will consider only three points. In the first place there is the very general notion of a kind of primary school teaching which is fairer to the child, that is to say a kind of teaching which, instead of trying to satisfy normative requirements, pays greater attention to the children's differing aptitudes and learning capacities, and insists that the function of the school is to be supportive rather than selective. This was one of the basic ideas underlying the pilot project; without it there would have been no possibility of taking ethnic and linguistic diversity into account within the French school system. This basic idea continues to be applied in the reweighting and restructuring of the curriculum. Whereas traditionally the main emphasis was placed on the basic subjects, i.e. French (especially standard written French - with concentration on spelling, grammar and composition) and mathematics, a higher value is now placed on artistic subjects and games, and above all on practical lessons orientated towards the children's environment (the so-called *activités d'éveil*). It was only by incorporating intercultural activities into this form of practical teaching and linking it with mother tongue instruction that a fairly concrete form could be given to the principle of taking the special characteristics of the ethnic minority pupils into account while still operating within the integral framework of normal school activities The revival of notions of comprehensive teaching which was associated with the school reform undoubtedly encouraged the ·demand - which was made repeatedly and insistently by the theorists involved in the project - that the teaching of children from ethnic minorities should combine language and culture.

French primary schools are firmly wedded to the principle of the class teacher, the only "specialist teachers" being those responsible for art and craft and physical education. This supplied a good basis for the pilot project, since a single class teacher is in a better position to take cultural differences into account in his/her teaching than a number of subject teachers would be, and since the more progressive French teachers could be expected to be familiar, from their normal work, with the linking of linguistic and practical teaching. It was a

117

disadvantage insofar as co-operation among teachers is not regarded as particularly necessary under the French system and does not take place to any great extent. The "specialist teachers" for art and craft and physical education generally play a marginal role and have little contact with the class teachers. There was thus a danger that the bilingual teachers might be placed in a similar position and become "specialist teachers for mother tongue instruction". Since all the bilingual teachers worked at various schools during the course of the week and no provision was made for them to be in regular contact with the head teachers or their French colleagues, their "official" affiliation to the French school remained problematic. Their professional "marginality" is indicated in a number of ways: there were gaps in the information they received, they were not sufficiently informed about the teaching given in regular classes, they seldom attended teachers' conferences, and they had virtually no say in the running of the school.

There are reports of successful communication, especially at the schools in Villejuif and the rue Hamelin. Both schools felt fully involved in the project. In neither case was co-operation between the French and the foreign teachers achieved automatically. In Villejuif it was largely to the credit of the headmaster and the headmistress that the Italian teacher was particularly well integrated into the school and that the aims of the project could be pursued on a broad basis. At the school in the rue Hamelin there were additional factors: the local inspector was actively committed to the project, and CREDIF concentrated much of its development work on the school. Similarly encouraging results were initially achieved at the school in the rue Keller, as long as the local inspector was actively involved in the progress of the pilot project there. In general it may be said that successful co-operation in one form or another depended on additional support and encouragement from a higher quarter.


**Mother tongue teaching**

**Linguistic pre-conditions**

A few of the children in the courses were recent immigrants, but the overwhelming majority had been born in France; some knew their "mother tongue" only from talking to their grandparents. This applied especially to the Italian children in Villejuif. According to the teachers, however, most of the children still used the everyday colloquial form of their mother tongue at home. The problem of dialects was often mentioned by the teachers in connection with the Yugoslav and Italian children, and occasionally in connection with the Spanish children. Some of the Spanish and Italian children were said to have a better command of French than of their own language. There was the additional difficulty that the language spoken at home differed from the national standard taught in schools. This problem affected the Italian children, who spoke

118

various dialects, but it was particularly acute in the case of the "Yugoslav" course at Ivry; this was attended by Serbian children (one of whom had French as his mother tongue), a group of children whose mother tongue was Albanian (though one had a colloquial knowledge of Serbo-Croat), and a group of gypsy children.

What was bound to strike a German visitor was the high value that all the children placed on French, much higher than that placed on German by ethnic minority pupils in the Federal Republic. Thus, though the children in the Serbo-Croat class at the school in the avenue de la République spoke Serbo-Croat to the teacher, they spoke French to one another. Two of them said that they would rather talk Serbo-Croat than French, yet they used French in informal conversations in class with their Yugoslav classmates. Sitting in at Spanish classes at the rue Etienne Marcel, one heard the children talking to one another in Spanish, but not always: one group of children was heard arguing in French about the ownership of an item of property, and one child was heard to ask another in French about the meaning of a certain Spanish word. Another two were heard deliberating in French about the answer to a certain question, but they then wrote down the result of their deliberation in Spanish. The Italian children in Villejuif used French not only in informal conversations with one another, but also during "official" Italian lessons. Whatever they said about the lessons was couched in French, and they even pronounced their own names more often in the French manner than in the Italian. Their Italian vocabulary seemed on the whole somewhat limited, and they were often uncertain about points of Italian grammar. French interference in their Italian was also a frequent phenomenon.

The groups were made up of children of different ages, though it was only in the Yugoslav group at the school in Aubervilliers that one found an age-range extending from the first to the fifth school year. In all the other schools pupils from the first three or the last two primary years were taught in one class. Normally the groups were composed of pupils from regular classes, though the courses were also attended by some children from *classes d'initiation*.

## The timetable

We now come to the chief organizational problem facing the pilot project. One of its central aims was the integration of mother tongue teaching into the normal timetable, and this was a matter which was inevitably raised by the head teacher and the staff at virtually every school that was visited. Yet the findings of the project contain no comprehensive discussion of the models that were used in solving the problem. What we do find, however, is a relatively uniform appreciation of the difficulties, a certain consensus about the best model to adopt, and a fair degree of variation in the way it was realized at individual schools.

For periods of mother tongue teaching the migrant pupils were withdrawn from various classes to form a special teaching group. The main problem was then to minimize the amount of "normal" teaching that the migrant pupils inevitably lost as a result. The chief fear of the head teachers and their staff - a fear which they knew to be shared by many of the migrant parents - was that the children were not getting enough teaching in the basic subjects, viz. mathematics and French.

A second fear of the French teachers was that the children might suffer more general psychological damage. One said in an interview:

"After all it's quite a wrench for the children to have to leave their class. You know, the classroom community is of enormous importance to the children and the teacher. It's a separation - something is being taken away from them - and so sometimes they leave a bit regretfully."

From the children's point of view the loss is seen rather differently. To quote again from the same interview:

"... but not drawing or games, which are the things the children are especially fond of. We didn't want to deprive the children of the subjects they like in order to give them Spanish or Portuguese lessons; that really would be the best way of putting them off mother tongue teaching."

The consensus is that the best solution (or at any rate the least harmful one) is to devote those lessons which run concurrently with mother tongue teaching to *activités d'éveil*. Consequently most of the mother tongue courses are put on in the afternoon, which is usually reserved for *activités d'éveil*. The French teachers were generally unwilling to rearrange their timetables still further to allow mother tongue instruction to be given in the morning. A survey conducted among the teachers revealed that, at least during the first year of the project, the number of French teachers who would have preferred mother tongue teaching to be put on outside the normal timetable was distinctly larger than the number who were in favour of its integration (CREDIF 1977, p 212). Even so, 15 of the 84 French teachers questioned said that their classes had French or mathematics lessons while mother tongue instruction was being given (ibid.).

## Pedagogical problems

Undoubtedly the bilingual teachers and the migrant parents, as well as the majority of the French staff, imagined that the institution of mother tongue courses would make it possible for the pupils to acquire a full command of their mother tongues and hence ultimately to become fully bilingual. However, in view of the linguistic prerequisites for the achievement of such a result, and given the external conditions prevailing, this objective was bound to prove illusory. In CREDIF's final report it is pointed out that the introduction of mother tongue courses, like any other change in the teaching system, aroused a certain amount of initial opposition, and that institutional factors such as the number of lessons available, fluctuations in pupils' attendance, staff changes, and contradictions arising between the teaching given in the mainstream classes and that given in the mother tongue classes, made any such success unlikely from the start (CREDIF 1979/80, vol 1, p 6f).

As a result, the bilingual teachers progressively scaled down their objectives and to some extent modified the content of their teaching, as may be seen from the following excerpt from an interview:

"I think the aim of the project is that the children should learn the language, that they should acquire a solid grounding in it. I would even say that the parents could be certain, were such teaching available, that if they went back to Italy their children could be integrated into the Italian system. Now that's too big an aim for the project when you look at what you've got, the material conditions, the reality of the situation we find ourselves in. We do our job, but it's very hard... I can't do much, but then it depends on what one is aiming at. So if it's a question of teaching them Italian, of giving them a real basic course in Italian, it's obvious that that's not possible... If it's a question of giving the children a bit of encouragement to try a little - I'm only saying 'try', because that would be an enormous job too, and unfortunately we simply haven't got the right conditions for it - to try to make them aware of this language, which is their parents' language, to make them aware too of certain values, which are their parents' values, of Italian culture, certain aspects of which they are familiar with - through their parents. If we've succeeded in doing this then perhaps we've achieved a minimum."

This turning away from linguistic teaching objectives, which are to some extent quantifiable, towards aims which are less easily quantifiable, such as inculcating cultural values, developing the child's personality, and possibly - as a long-term goal - improving his/her chance of success in the French education system, is typical of most bilingual teachers on the pilot project. Whereas at first their ideas were in the main strongly influenced by their embassies, in other words geared to the standards of language acquisition existing in their own countries, contact with the real teaching conditions in the schools during the pilot project brought significant changes of attitude. And it was not least the educational advisers from CREDIF who encouraged them to draw educational conclusions from their revised assessments.

The governments of Yugoslavia, Italy and Portugal worked out their own programmes for the teaching of the languages of their countries; these programmes essentially amounted to a somewhat reduced or generalized model of the mother tongue teaching given in the home countries, but

121

required the teachers to exercise a high degree of initiative in putting them into practice. The teachers on the project were familiar with these programmes, but they obviously found them of little help in defining their objectives.

In these circumstances the teaching aims (in the more restricted sense), as formulated by the bilingual teachers, were inevitably rough and ready, having no obvious systematic structure or sequence. The following aims were listed: promotion of written and oral expression, introduction to reading and writing, widening of vocabulary, removal of grammatical uncertainty, dealing with the most important linguistic interferences in the areas of syntax, morphology and spelling.

One question which was argued about more among the experts than among the teachers was that of which form of the mother tongue to teach. The experts saw this as a dilemma:

"The bilingual teachers were nominated by their consulates and are paid to teach the standard languages of their countries, so that if necessary the children can be integrated into the school curriculum of their home countries. We, however, consider it essential to bring into the language courses the languages that are actually spoken in the migrant communities so as not to undermine the children's respect for their parents... But at present it is not possible to impose new norms on the bilingual teachers, who are supervised by their own consulates." (Clévy, in CREDIF 1979/80, vol 1, p 131)

At first this question hardly posed any problem for the bilingual teachers: they were quite clear that what they had to teach was the standard language. They were quite aware of how the language spoken in the children's homes deviated from the standard, causing difficulties in class; it was a source of error that had to be plugged, an impediment that had to be overcome or, as far as possible, removed in order to eliminate obstacles to the attainment of the teaching aims. In exceptional cases, which admittedly became more numerous as the project progressed, intermediate forms of the language were used, forms which lay somewhere between the standard and what was spoken in the children's homes, or sometimes linguistic variations were discussed in class. During the last year of the project three Italian teachers in particular made systematic efforts in this direction (cf. Perotti, in CREDIF 1980 a, pp 37-45).

The teachers geared their instruction less to the systematic study of the language than to certain topics or texts; this seems entirely appropriate for language teaching at primary level, especially in view of the wide range of linguistic competence they had to deal with. The methods that were chosen varied from case to case.

The Italian teacher who was employed during the first two years of the pilot project, faced with the fact that most of her pupils had only a limited command of the language, was advised by CEFISEM to teach Italian as a second language. Accordingly she worked with sets of transparencies taken from a textbook on French as a second language; these were admittedly not furnished with accompanying dialogue or narrative texts. The stories were worked out by the teacher and the children in conversation, then dramatized with cut-out figures, and finally written down by the older pupils. Throughout this process she helped the pupils by teaching them vocabulary and correcting their grammar. The themes represented in the transparencies were, so to speak, culturally neutral and in any case somewhat remote from the world of the children's experience (e.g. "The Crocodile and the Jackal", "The Girl and the Little Bird"). However, another teaching unit used by the same teacher, this time without transparencies, took as its starting point the children's own experience; its theme was "The Flat". The children described their own experiences; these descriptions were corrected from the point of view of grammar and vocabulary, then written down and read out to the class.

The Italian teachers who were employed in the third year worked mainly with a flannel board; in doing so they too experienced the difficulties presented by the kind of teaching that centres upon artificial dialogues. The evaluator's criticism (Perotti, in CREDIF 1979/80, vol 3, pp 68-74) comes down clearly in favour of texts which relate to the pupils' everyday lives or school experience. One interesting and novel idea, though one which was not pursued, was an attempt to discuss and exploit methodically the situational use - even in the classroom situation - of different linguistic registers in Italian (dialect vs. standard) and of French-Italian bilingualism.

The Portuguese teacher who was employed in the first year, however, pursued a method which was distinctly orientated towards the mother tongue, choosing topics relating to Portugal (e.g. "Typical Animals of Portugal", "Fishing in Portugal"), taken from Portuguese textbooks. These topics were discussed almost wholly in conversational form, with occasional use of the blackboard, after which the pupils wrote about them. The teacher saw it as her main function to provide factual and grammatical information relating to the text under discussion. The Portuguese teacher who took over from her in the second and third years did not continue this style of teaching exactly, being more aware than his predecessor that teaching Portuguese in France cannot be exactly equated with teaching Portuguese in Portugal, and that it would not do justice to his pupils' linguistic situation merely to scale down the objectives of the teaching. His solution was to gear the choice of topics principally to the interests of the pupils, though the Portuguese orientation was basically maintained (typical topics being "The Great Discoveries" and "Our Holidays in Portugal"). He too centred his teaching on texts, largely based on a Portuguese textbook for the teaching of practical subjects.

Also oriented to the pupils' country of origin, though in a rather different way, were the lessons given by the Spanish teacher in the first year of the pilot project. Whereas concentration on themes specific to the culture of the home country has to be seen as a way of exploring the emigrants' situation, this particular teacher behaved in class as though she were teaching in a primary school in Spain. Underlying her lessons was no doubt some concept of comprehensive teaching which laid stress on the creation of an emotionally satisfying learning climate, in which the topics chosen for lessons are taken from the child's narrow, undisturbed social and "natural" environment (e.g. "The Family", "Christmas", "The Months", "The Parts of the Head") in such a way as to combine language teaching directly with subject teaching and to facilitate a free interchange of themes and teaching methods (conversation with the pupils, explanations by the teacher, use of the blackboard and exercise books, singing songs, parading round the classroom, etc). This teacher's successor did not take over her mode of teaching. She attempted, at least in one of her four teaching groups, to draw the logical conclusions from her conviction that success in the French school must take precedence over all other objectives. At first she orientated the content of her Spanish teaching directly towards that of the mainstream (French) lessons, thus using the mother tongue as an aid to mastering the subject matter discussed in the regular lessons. This attempt failed, as it proved impossible to relate three hours of mother tongue instruction in any meaningful way to the entire programme of two or sometimes more mainstream "feeder" classes. She then tried taking a French text used in a French lesson, analysing and commenting on it in Spanish. This experiment failed at once on two counts: first, because the pupils refused to read French texts in Spanish lessons, and secondly because there was no possibility of co-ordination. At the third attempt, however, she succeeded in making a breakthrough by combining mother tongue teaching with the school's intercultural activities. The evaluators rightly remarked that "from then on the Spanish lessons shed the character they had previously had, viz. that of casual and random learning, and acquired a function, that of contributing towards the understanding and explication of a subject on which the pupils had been working" (Boulot/Fradet/Obispo, in CREDIF 1981 b, p 132).

What is known about the Serbo-Croat teaching indicates that it was partly geared to the mother tongue (with resultant failures in the case of pupils whose mother tongue was not Serbo-Croat), using Yugoslav materials and giving preference to culture-specific subject matter, but it also employed the methods of foreign language teaching, with a "free" use of slides taken from French teaching material. A large part of the teaching was taken up with grammar and vocabulary exercises.

In the pilot project, then, we initially find attempts to carry over into the teaching given in the host country the methods of instruction used in primary schools in the pupils countries of origin, though with some modifications in the choice of subject matter and the standards aimed at. Side by side with these go attempts at working with the methods of foreign language teaching, though modified in the direction of greater flexibility; this approach was adopted particularly in the case of children who were in danger of losing their mother tongue. Neither approach led to any significant successes in language learning. At this point a certain amount of methodological rethinking was done, leading at first to an attempt to turn mother tongue instruction virtually into a variant of reception teaching or remedial teaching, in the sense of its being designed to provide direct support for the mainstream teaching. A similar experiment was tried out in the Belgian pilot project; in Paris it was a failure. The other new approach involved combining mother tongue teaching with intercultural activities. This may be illustrated by the following account given by an Italian teacher who worked on the pilot project during its third year:

"I discovered, as I've already said, that it wasn't possible to give the children a solid grounding in the mother tongue - let's just admit it - but because I wanted to do something jointly with the French teachers and get the children to tackle certain problems with their classmates, I was able to organize the language courses like this... The joint activities are set up and, starting from these, from the stimulus we've got from them, we work separately in the language course. It's language teaching, but it's always linked to what we've been doing in the French class... For instance I taught the very small children about the Italian masks of the *Commedia dell'Arte*. I structured the teaching in a certain way. At first the aim was to tell the children about a certain aspect of culture which they could grasp, an aspect of Italian culture, while at the same time letting the whole school share this knowledge, and then to do a linguistic exercise related to it in the language course. So the ultimate aim was to get the children to invent a play, which was to be acted in Italian, with Italian dialogue. All this led to their going into the different classes to show off the Italian masks - it was the children who were presenting this knowledge they had acquired to their French schoolmates - to let them share in it by for instance asking them to make masks and costumes themselves."

This combination of language teaching and intercultural activities may be regarded as the outstanding didactic achievement of the pilot project.


Intercultural teaching

The general objectives have already been mentioned: creating a degree of sensitivity in the French school to the presence of the ethnic minority pupils, recognition of the cultural values of the societies they came from, and strengthening the children's self-confidence. These aims were adopted directly by the French and the bilingual teachers

125

involved in the project and linked with their teaching activities. There was an absence, at least in the initial stages, of a recognizable structuring and ordering of more specific aims. By contrast with the mother tongue teaching, there was also an almost complete lack of educational models and previous experience, except for the pilot project at Fontenay-sous-Bois (cf. IRFED 1978), which shows certain parallels with these elements in the Paris project. The objectives were thus at first given concrete shape through a relatively arbitrary choice of themes. As a rule it was the bilingual teacher who proposed a theme; one or more French colleagues would then show interest in treating the theme in their French classes in collaboration with the bilingual teacher. Characteristic of this initial period was the choice of what might be called classic culture-specific themes which could then be illustrated in the form of individual performances in the French classes: tales, legends, fairy stories and songs from the children's home countries; special features of their history and geography; monuments and works of art; customs, festivals, national costumes and cooking recipes.

In the second and third years of the project an attempt was made to bring more cohesion into the intercultural teaching and to discover more solid forms of collaboration: one of the bilingual teachers might agree to collaborate with a French colleague for a certain length of time, during which they would work on various themes, or a French and a bilingual teacher might join forces to carry out a certain project. An example of the former kind is the collaboration between the Portuguese teacher and a French art teacher at the school in the rue Keller. In the course of one school year they worked together on the following themes:

a Portuguese legend from the age of the voyages of discovery about a fish that changed shape: the legend was told, with each pupil taking part of the story and producing a pictorial representation of it on a slide; tape recordings were also made for it, and the whole composition could be shown to the French classes as a show combining music and pictures;

the discoveries of Portuguese and French explorers;

the revolution in Portugal, with a discussion of wall-inscriptions and graffiti;

Portuguese and French houses, illustrated by photographs and stories told by the pupils;

festivals in Portugal and France;

fishing in Portugal;

126

clothes: the children brought typical clothes from home, dressed up in them, and made drawings of them;

recipes of Portuguese dishes, supplied by the mother of one of the pupils and given to all the children to take home and try out;

coins from all over the world, from which the children made rubbings.

The themes were to a large extent suggested by the pupils. Each theme took up roughly two to three double lessons. It would be agreed upon between the two teachers, but they would do the preparation independently. The Portuguese teacher saw his role to be mainly to supply factual information and, where his Portuguese pupils were concerned, linguistic information (and in fact it turned out that the other pupils too were interested in being given linguistic information). The French teacher saw it as her role to stimulate the pupils to treat the factual information they were given in pictorial form, to discuss their work with them, and to get them to write down what they had learnt. She clearly regarded "exposure to the environment" as more important than simply teaching art – an attitude which brought her a good deal of criticism from colleagues.

A more advanced stage in intercultural activities is represented by the projects on "The Italian *Commedia dell'arte*", "Reading of excerpts from *Les Ritals* by Cavanna" (Ivry), "Napoleon", "Guernica" and "The age of the great discoveries" (rue Hamelin). Characteristic of these are the wider thematic range, their incorporation into the regular curriculum, the active involvement of pupils of all nationalities (instead of performances organized by individual bilingual teachers), and the conception of intercultural teaching as a link between mother tongue teaching and the mainstream teaching that took place in the school.

As an example we will take the project entitled "Napoleon: the conquest of Spain or the War of Liberation" (CREDIF 1980b, vol 2): it was carried out in the second half of the fourth school year, which already had "Napoleon" as a subject on the syllabus. It was decided, at the instigation of CREDIF and with the support of the inspector, to incorporate this theme into the intercultural teaching, placing particular emphasis on Napoleon's Spanish campaigns.

The first step was to question the parents, through their children, about their view of Napoleon; the results were then compared in the mainstream class. The subject was introduced by a short text entitled "Napoleon in Spain", available in both a French and a Spanish version (which were read by the French and the Spanish children respectively). To place the subject in its historical context – indeed to build up a sense of historical periods in general – the notion of "generations" was explained to the Spanish group (first with the help of the children's own family trees and then with reference to that of the

Spanish royal family). In the mainstream lessons the pupils' family trees were treated mathematically in order to express the historical gap between the present and the age of Napoleon in terms of generations. With the Spanish group this abstract notion was given concrete shape by comparing Goya's painting "The Family of Charles IV" with two pictures of the *Grupo Crónica* which present Goya's royal family through the alienating device of a modern middle-class context; the French teacher worked out a similar exercise, using David's "Coronation of Napoleon". In the Spanish group the next stage was the reading of a Spanish comic dealing with the events of May 1808, accompanied by elucidations of the terms "occupation", "uprising" and "independence"; the French teacher later conducted a parallel analysis of a French comic treating the conquest of Spain. In the regular class the children were presented with contrasting notions of the events as seen from a French and a Spanish viewpoint. In this way an initial awareness of historical relativity was created. One French teacher said in an interview:

"One person's defeat is another person's victory. The reaction to a historical phenomenon – if you like, to a historical fact. What one side sees as an invasion the other side sees as victory, as progress; on the one hand there were the imperial conquests, the extension of Napoleon's empire, on the other there was the Spanish people, rebelling against the occupation and wanting to free themselves... And the children grasped this; there were no problems whatever. No, I didn't have the impression that they resisted the idea."

In the Spanish classes the children then read excerpts from Galdos' *Episodios Nacionales* dealing with the uprising of 1808 (a tabulated exposition of the text) and compared Goya's pictures "The Second of May" and "The Third of May" with Vernet's "Napoleon before Madrid".

"We worked at this picture very seriously, but in a way this gave the children a lot of fun. We didn't say. 'Here you see this. and there you see that', but discovered everything step by step. In the first place there was the artistic aspect, the composition of the picture, etc. Then there was the historical side – why the picture was painted, when it was painted. They were actually very receptive, both the French and the Spanish children. It really was a great success. The fact that the children were able to make aesthetic discoveries, that they learned something from an artistic point of view, provided an additional medium for the approach to history, and it was a medium in which both French and Spanish children could make joint discoveries."

In the mainstream class the children then worked on a difficult artistic text about Goya, written in French. The results achieved by this stage were shown at the annual exhibition in the local town hall (the preparation having been done in the mainstream class and in the

Spanish group). The Spanish children also visited the Goya exhibition at a nearby *Centre Culturel* and reported on it in the mainstream class. The success of this project was seen by the French teacher as what she called an *ouverture d'esprit:*

> I'll give you an example. A girl in my class went to England with her parents at Easter or on May 1st. In London she saw Trafalgar Square, and she immediately made the connection between Napoleon and Trafalgar. And that's how it is - in London you can see something to do with Trafalgar, but not in Paris: there's no Place Trafalgar in Paris! It was quite funny, the connection she made; she realised that ultimately everyone perceives the more pleasant side of things and tries to ignore whatever... The children worked on a very limited segment of history, but it was effective: I think they'll continue to enjoy making comparisons - what in France we call *vérité en-deçà des Pyrénées, erreur au-delà.* I think this is a good *ouverture d'esprit* for the children - learning that what happens in our own country is not necessarily perfect, that it can be viewed unfavourably in another, and vice versa."

What makes this project convincing is the success it had in activating the pupils, together with the cross-fertilization of "foreign lessons" and "mainstream lessons", as a result of which learning objectives that could scarcely have been formulated in a monocultural context become possible (and attainable), and the determination to acquire something of the cultural heritage of both sides without reducing it from the start.

What is present only to a limited extent in the project "Napoleon" is a link with the world in which the children actually live. The theme remains at best something that is part of world history; its connection with the pupils and their parents is only indirect and does not relate to their own situation. The project "Cavanna", which was put on at the primary school in Ivry (also with fourth-year pupils), was linked to a far greater extent to the real life of the children:

Cavanna, a famous journalist, is the author of *Les Ritals*; in this book he recounts anecdotes from his childhood in an eastern suburb of Paris as the son of an Italian worker and a French mother. The language of the book is a written version of the spoken language, interlarded with slang and above all with the "pidgin French" of the Italian father. The book touches upon a variety of themes conducive to discussion and reflection about the world in which the children live - childhood experiences, the child's understanding of the world, the relation between the mother tongue, the standard language and dialects, the role and influence of the French school, the image of the children's country of origin, the manner in which foreign workers express themselves, the kind of work they do, their living conditions, etc.

The chapter of the book selected for classwork was entitled *L'Arabe* –
an anecdote about an Arab immigrant who goes and asks for work at a
building site again and again, day after day, and can only manage to
survive because an Italian bricklayer working on the site – Cavanna's
father – gives him something to live on every day.

I know that's too good to be true. And even if it *is* true, it's too
edifying and I'd have done better not to tell the story. But I told
it because I heard it myself only a short time ago. Vivi Taravella,
who is now the boss, told me it, and I could hardly believe it
myself..." (Cavanna).

It was intended, with the help of this excerpt, to attain the following
learning objectives:

- to analyse a literary text;

- to consider the differences between the written and the spoken
  language;

- to create an awareness of the socio-economic aspects of the
  migration of workers to France;

- the create an understanding among French children of the life led
  by their non-French peers and an understanding among the latter of
  their own and their parents' situation.

The teaching unit starts with the children getting to know the book by
studying what is shown on the cover – the pictorial elements, the
author's name, the biographical information and the publisher's blurb.
Next comes the analysis of the selected chapter with the help of
analysis sheets: breaking down the action into individual scenes,
describing the characters, copying out the direct speech. This last
exercise is of special interest: the utterances of each individual
character, written out one after the other, can be used to illustrate
the characterization very clearly. Those of the Arab are confined to the
continual repetition of the word "work", "work", "work". The Italian
bricklayer, Cavanna's father, speaks to both the Arab and the boss of
the building firm in the same Franco-Italian pidgin; the two bosses
speak condescendingly in logically structured standard colloquial
French.

It is at this point that mother tongue teaching is brought into play:
the Italian pupils "translate" the father's utterances into both
standard French and standard Italian. There are only a few such
utterances, and so the pupils are not overstretched. Through this
exercise they get not only a clear insight into the language mixture
underlying this mode of expression, but also an excellent aid to the
understanding of the text itself, together with the possibility of

passing on what they have learnt to their French classmates, who have
no direct access to the Italian language.

To provide a basis for understanding and to create a link between
language teaching and other subjects, a number of complementary
materials are available, comprising short excerpts from historical
accounts of labour migration, tables showing the development of
France's immigrant population, accompanied by explanatory notes, and
photographs of migrant workers on French building sites in 1914, 1930
and 1975; in addition there are further quotations from Les Ritals, a
copy of a testimonial supplied to an Italian worker from the period
covered by the book, and the text of a poem about migrant workers by a
French-speaking Swiss author.

On 31 May 1979 Cavanna met the fourth-year pupils at the primary
school in Ivry. They had prepared for his visit by thinking up
questions to ask him, questions which related both to the book and
more generally to his work as a writer. The conversation is recorded,
and so are the author's subsequent reflections. Cavanna writes that he
was unusually nervous before meeting the children, being anxious about
their expectations. But he goes on:

"From the very first question they gave me a feeling of security.
The questions were uncannily precise. It was clear what answers I
had to give. The children gave me a lot of help. I told them
exactly what I would have told a grown-up if he had put the same
questions to me; I didn't have to use any special "children's
language". Sometimes I would be aware of having let slip a word
that perhaps not all the children understood - the word "nostalgia"
for instance - but then I would explain it, paraphrase it.

"In their naïveté, their sometimes brutal naïveté, they were all
aware of what were the important questions. When the conversation
was over I realized that it had been sufficient simply to answer
directly, without beating about the bush, in order to deal with
practically all aspects of the subject we were talking about."

The materials on this teaching unit have been published (CREDIF 1981a),
together with recommendations for teachers (CREDIF 1980a, pp 57-134).

CREDIF's final report contains a theory of intercultural teaching which
represents a considerable advance towards a further structuring of
aims, content and methods (Boulot/Fradet/Blot, in CREDIF 1979/80, vol 1,
pp 90-130). We will give here a brief account of the main ideas it
contains:

The theory has an analytical and a constructive component. The
analytical part (Boulot/Fradet, ibid. pp 90-112) sets out three possible
options for the aims of intercultural teaching, these being derived
from the experience so far available: the first (the socio-cultural

option) is to make all the pupils aware of the diversity of their socio-cultural backgrounds; the second (the pedagogical option) is to draw upon the variety of the children's knowledge and experience in order to enrich and renew the content of the subject teaching; the third (the psycholgical option) is to strengthen the self-confidence of the ethnic minority pupils. These aims may be combined with two types of content. The first type comprises the cultural stereotypes which are believed to determine the cultural identity of the ethnic minority pupils; the second comprises their specific modes of behaviour, which are believed to be culture-specific and culturally conditioned. A discussion of the dangers that arise from an excessive concentration on cultural stereotypes or specific modes of behaviour leads on to a discussion of the concept of migrant culture as a whole. This is defined as a transitional culture which is variable, unstable and reactive, arising from an attempt to balance and combine two conflicting needs - the need to integrate and the need to preserve one's ethnic identity. This attempt performs certain vital functions: it assures a minimum of social recognition within one's own society, making it possible to maintain an identity that is rooted in the past, sustaining communal morale, keeping open the possibility of returning home, and providing a focus of resistance to the forces of alienation. At the same time it is determined by the attitude of French society, which is prepared to let itself be "enriched" only superficially by elements taken from foreign cultures, while basically holding fast to its cultural ethnocentricity. One would be deluding oneself if one were to believe that it was possible to use cultural means to overcome the basic facts of economic dependency, which are in any case enshrined in the law. The question of migrant culture is thus a political rather than an educational question. Nevertheless, the apparently obvious conclusion - that the only sensible way to proceed is to deal with the children and teenagers of the ethnic minorities in political terms - is rejected. To draw this conclusion, it is maintained, would be to misjudge the real political possibilities open to the migrants, to ignore their actual cultural needs, and to overrate their capacity for political action.

It is at this point that the constructive part of the theory comes in (Blot, ibid. pp 112-27); this articulates the aims of intercultural teaching, defines its various stages and offers hints on method. Three legitimate objectives are stated:

- to note the attitudes of all the children taking part in intercultural education;

- to subject cultural stereotypes to critical examination;

- to collect critical information about cultural situations which are of interest to the children.

These aims are intended at the same time to correspond to stages in the long-term planning of the teaching. The first stage consists of subject teaching centred upon the child. At this stage it is expected that the pedagogical impulses will come principally from interaction between the pupils themselves, from the way the classroom is equipped, and from the teaching materials used, with the teacher playing the role of an observer, noting the different ways in which the children deal with space and time, with the objects around them, and with one another. At the second stage the emphasis is on communication and on the awakening of the children's awareness: they should be encouraged to comment on cultural differences (e.g. by looking at photographs and pictures, by direct teaching, and by role-playing), their comments being discussed in class and on occasion pursued further. The third stage is reached when it appears that further factual information is required, so that opinions can be assessed and ideas organized into a pattern; this involves the inculcation of cultural knowledge. This implies above all involving the pupils directly in various activities, for instance in carrying out mini-surveys, collecting press photographs, conducting interviews, and securing the active co-operation of their parents.

This theory does more than simply reflect what went on during the pilot project, and if it were to be developed further there would have to be a more explicit link between the constructive and the analytical parts. All the same, had it not been for the actual experience of the pilot project and the practice of intercultural teaching, it would not have been possible to formulate the theory. It systematizes and summarizes what was learnt during the project, but also follows up certain ideas; it may thus be said to be a product of the project, yet at the same time to transcend it.


## Home-school liaison

In the original conception of the pilot project a relatively high value was placed on home-school liaison. The memorandum issued by the Ministry states that one of the aims of the project should be to bring about a change in the attitudes of the French parents; in the bilingual teachers' timetables special provision was made for parent-teacher consultation, which was to count as part of their work-load. One of the prerequisites for setting up the pilot project was that the migrant parents should be expressly asked for their approval of the mother tongue teaching. In this way home-school liaison was defined as a third area of activity alongside mother tongue teaching and intercultural teaching.

However, as is shown by the results of the parent survey which was carried out four months after the start of the project (CREDIF 1977, p 141), the French parents were quite inadequately informed about it: at one school only 1% of those questioned stated that they had been informed about the project; at another the figure was 13%. The French teachers too confirmed that the project did not generate any notable impulse for home-school liaison work. Yet at the same time the survey reveals that among the French parents there was a genuine and even lively interest in the project, especially in the intercultural activities. The schools clearly did not take up and exploit this interest as fully as they might have done.

On the other hand, it appears that the parents of the ethnic minority children at all the schools did receive this initial information and in the main approved the aims of the project. Nevertheless, there are reports of individual cases in which migrant parents refused to allow their children to take part; the reason they gave was usually that they feared that their children's progress in the French classes would be hampered. According to reports from the schools, the attendance of migrant parents at the regular parents' meetings was generally lower than that of French parents. The principal reasons advanced for this are lack of time, the language barrier, diffidence *vis-à-vis* authority and official institutions, and a feeling that they were powerless to achieve anything; at the same time there is said to have been some dissension among the ethnic minority parents which prevented their taking any concerted action. This situation does not seem to have been improved by the pilot project. In this respect the home-school liaison undertaken specifically by the bilingual teachers represents to some extent a substitute measure; it was not aimed at encouraging the foreign parents to make use of the normal channels of parent participation. There is no doubt, however, that the efforts of the bilingual staff led more foreign parents than before to cross the threshold of the French school and discuss their children's educational problems more fully and intensively than would have been possible with the French teachers alone. However, to judge by the statements of the bilingual teachers themselves, these conversations seem to have been concerned largely with general problems arising from immigration and with the specific difficulties of individual children; only rarely was there any discussion of institutional demands which might have been met by the pilot project or the school, and which would have required the bilingual teacher to mediate between the parents and the school.


## Evaluation

The evaluation process fell into three distinct phases; their sequence was determined, however, not by a clearly conceived plan worked out in advance, but by the failure of the broadly based empirical-analytical evaluation scheme that had originally been envisaged. In keeping with the wide-ranging innovative aims of the pilot project, the aims of the evaluation had initially been defined in comprehensive terms: it was supposed to establish the effect the project had had on the achievements of the migrant pupils in their mother tongues, on the school conduct of French and non-French pupils alike and, finally, on the French teachers and on parents of all nationalities. The instruments used to elicit this information were required to be standardized - or at least to be susceptible of being standardized - and to allow a quantitative interpretation of the findings.

It was characteristic of the original plan that it aimed on the one hand at documenting the effects of the pilot project on the pupils and, on the other, at establishing the marginal conditions of the pilot project in the area of social structures and institutions. This plan did not give central importance to pedagogical questions: it was intended to provide knowledge regarding the legitimation and operation of certain practices, knowledge which could then be applied in educational policy-making. In accordance with the urge to seek optimally objective data, the evaluation in this first phase of the project was carried out strictly "from outside". Its conception, execution and supervision were in the hands of the CREDIF team and external experts; the teachers were there simply to be questioned or, where the children's conduct was being investigated, to play an ancillary role by filling in assessment sheets and carrying out language tests.

The problems which arose during and after the first year of the project were of many kinds: the amount of work involved had been under-estimated; the investigations could not be carried out on the scale that had been intended, let alone regularly repeated in order to measure any changes that had taken place. Moreover, there were obvious difficulties and errors in the methods employed. An unsuitable instrument had been used to investigate the conduct of the ethnic minority children - a scale of assessment evolved and calibrated for indigenous children. In the language tests the teachers could not be dissuaded from helping the pupils to fill in their papers, even though this was contrary to the instructions they had been given, and so it was impossible to obtain reliable measurements of their linguistic performance. It was impossible, by means of the instruments that were employed, to show whether the pupils were making progress in their mother tongues; as a result CREDIF was forced to the somewhat dispiriting conclusion that instruments of this kind, when "applied to different ethnic groups, of differing ages and with differing levels of competence in the language being taught, did not allow of any very precise analysis" (CREDIF 1979/80, vol 1, p 13).

The questionnaires sent out to French parents operated with questionable categories and superficial techniques of formulation, thus vitiating the (at times wide-ranging) conclusions that were based on the returns. It was concluded, for instance, from the fact that at the beginning of the pilot project 74% of the respondents favoured the introduction of intercultural teaching, that "the intercultural activities, if carried out consistently, would lead to considerable changes in the attitudes, opinions and behaviour of both sides towards each other" (CREDIF 1977, p 162f). The difficulty here lies not only in the causal linking of school activities and parental attitudes, but also in the fact that at the time of the survey there was no clear definition - even within the project itself, and certainly not in the minds of the parents - of the concept of "intercultural activities".

The most useful results of the survey were the responses of the French teachers. These could have been of significance for the later course of the project: the majority of the French teachers saw that ethnic minority pupils had special problems and agreed with the basic principle of integrating them as quickly and effectively as possible into the French classes, while paying due attention to the languages and cultures of their countries of origin. This theoretical approval of the principle of integration, however, contrasts with clear reservations when it comes to measures which would necessitate concrete changes in the day-to-day work of the school or the personal involvement of the teachers.

On the whole the results of the evaluation did not match up either to the claims that were made for them or to the needs of those who were involved at a practical level. In view of this it was decided at the end of the first year not to continue with longitudinal studies. These were replaced by individual investigations which employed qualitative methods involving comprehension and description, though these were no longer systematically linked. Among these projects were a case study on the conduct of two Yugoslav girls, a description of Portuguese children in three regular classes at two different schools, and interviews with migrant parents about their attitudes to the pilot project, about questions of bilingualism, about living and bringing up their children in France, about their plans for returning home, and other matters. These studies differed from those undertaken in the first year not only with regard to method, but also with regard to the fact that they involved an attempt to approach the project from the socio-psychological situation of the individual pupils. These too were conducted "from outside", i.e. by experts, the teachers themselves having no part in the planning. One problem to emerge was that such investigations did not take into account the working situation of the teachers and pupils; their aim, in other words, was to establish basic knowledge rather than the kind of practical know-how which could have been applied in the pilot project. Admittedly this would not have been feasible in any case because the time-consuming assessment, interpretation and description of the qualitative data could not be completed until near the end of the project (CREDIF 1979/80, vols 2 and 4).

Finally, in the third year, some members of the CREDIF team drew a fundamentally different conclusion, stemming from the lack of results produced by previous evaluation efforts. They gave up their role as outside experts, whose job it was to observe and report impartially, and started collaborating closely with the teachers, on a long-term basis, to evolve and test didactic models for mother tongue and intercultural teaching. "Evaluation" thus became an instrument for guiding teaching practice in the pilot project; its main aim was no longer to describe and analyse, but to discover practical teaching strategies. The borderline between evaluation and "advising" became increasingly blurred and finally disappeared. The results of this phase are described above in the section on intercultural teaching.

Characteristically the reflections which guided the CREDIF team in this phase of the project drew largely upon the general state of knowledge (as available in publications) regarding the social and institutional conditions for the teaching of ethnic minority children; the results of the evaluation carried out in the first two years - insofar as they were available - played only a minor role. In this respect too the evaluation practice adopted in the third year represents a distinct departure from the earlier evaluation attempts. The concentration on the practical needs of the teacher in the classroom is discernible even in those passages of the account given by CREDIF which are couched in theoretical terms. What is formulated here is a theory-based model for intercultural teaching: any comprehensive conception of intercultural education as a task for the education system as a whole (and not just for individual teachers or individual teaching areas), is present in the report at best by implication.

# Ethnic minority children in the education system of the Netherlands

### The legal and social framework

During much of the present century there has been a good deal of emigration from the Netherlands. An extremely high population density and a large excess of births over deaths forced the government to adopt an active emigration policy, with the result that roughly 25,000 Dutch nationals left the country every year, mainly for Australia and Canada. Immigration on a large scale did not begin until after the Second World War. Here we must distinguish between two different streams of immigration: on the one hand there were the immigrants from the former Dutch colonies, and on the other - at ε somewhat later date - the migrant workers who were recruited abroad by Dutch industry as a consequence of the country's economic development after the Second World War. These groups are not only culturally distinct, but differ also with regard to their legal and political status.

As a result of decolonization, about 330,000 Indonesians entered the country; a further 153,000 immigrants came from Surinam and the Dutch West Indies. All these had Netherlands citizenship, except for about 40,000 people calling themselves citizens of the Republic of the South Moluccas, which is not recognized under international law. Some of these immigrants regarded themselves as only temporary residents in the Netherlands, intending to return home when the political situation had changed. Hence there are widely differing attitudes to the host country.

The other group is made up of migrant workers who came to the Netherlands in the first place for the sole purpose of taking up employment for a limited period on the basis of job contracts made between Dutch industry and their countries of origin, and who do not generally have Netherlands citizenship. As their stay in the Netherlands proved more prolonged than they had originally envisaged, they sent for their families to join them. In 1976 there were 196,000 foreign nationals from those countries where migrant labour had been recruited, and by 1 January 1979 their numbers had risen to 243,000. Among these the nationalities most strongly represented are the Turks (103,541 = 43% of the total), the Moroccans (62,136 = 26%), the Spaniards (24,945 = 10%), the Italians (21,851 = 9%), the Yugoslavs (14,082 = 6%), the Portuguese (10,025 = 4%) and the Greeks (4,326 = 2%).

The migrant population is concentrated in the industrial areas of the provinces of North and South Holland (Amsterdam, Rotterdam, Utrecht) and Twente. These provinces account for two thirds of all ethnic minority residents. Within the framework of family reunification the Turks and Moroccans have led the way in sending for other members of their families to join them in Holland. Up to the present day the proportion of migrants under the age of 19 is comparatively low in relation to the total number of inhabitants in that age group (3% only, compared with 7% in the Federal Republic of Germany and 13% in Belgium). Indeed, the proportion of foreign residents in the population as a whole cannot be considered high (in 1977 it was 2.7%). It must be borne in mind, however, that the ethnic minorities from Indonesia, Surinam and the West Indies are not counted as foreign nationals. In the Netherlands, as elsewhere in Europe, there has been a drop in the birth-rate of the indigenous population, accompanied by a rise in the birth-rate among foreign nationals. In 1978 the proportion of foreign births was 6.3% (Lebon 1981, p 23).

Despite the fact that in principle migrant workers enjoy equality under the law, there remain some forms of legal discrimination, e.g. loss of one's work permit after more than a year's unemployment if one has worked in the Netherlands for less than five years. Until 1970 it was possible for migrant workers to take up employment according to the needs of the economy. Initially the government's immigration policy apparently envisaged that workers recruited abroad would stay in the country only for a limited period. Subsequently, however, as a result of economic difficulties, fear of overpopulation and the shortage of housing, measures were taken to restrict further immigration; these measures, first introduced in 1970, were tightened up in 1975 and 1979. One of the most important, introduced in 1979, was a prohibition on illegal employment, though this was accompanied by the granting of legal status to migrant workers who had been employed illegally since before November 1974. There was some discussion at the time about introducing repatriation grants, but politically this was not feasible. At the same time the rights and political status of foreign nationals living in the Netherlands were improved: after five years of legal residence and secure employment one can now apply for unrestricted right of abode, and after three years one can apply for an unrestricted work permit. In addition to this, further rights were accorded to children born to foreign parents in the Netherlands.

The social position of migrant and ethnic minority workers in the Netherlands is characterized by two special factors. One of these is the particular role played by the *stichtings* in the Dutch social system. Basically these are voluntary non-profit-making organizations which are to be found in all sectors of the welfare system, including housing, health, education and many others. Thus, although most *stichtings* are state-subsidized, the Dutch welfare system is essentially private, which makes it possible, in the context of *verzuiling* (see below, p 140) for most *stichtings* to cater solely for the needs of specific sectors of the population, e.g. Protestants, Catholics or others. For the migrant workers the *stichtings* have come to be an essential element in the personal and social welfare of their families. The other is the degree of acceptance - what is sometimes called "pragmatic tolerance" (Bagley 1973) - that they encounter among the

Dutch. This explains why, despite a certain measure of dissatisfaction, the minority communities in the Netherlands are largely satisfied with their circumstances and feel that they enjoy more public and private support there than in any other country (Bagley 1973, p 105). The large number of marriages between members of different nationalities is also regarded as a sign of successful integration (Rose 1969, p 126); so too is the exceedingly low crime rate (Rose 1969, p 128). Moreover, the Netherlands are the only European country, apart from Sweden, which officially calls itself a multicultural society.

## The education system and educational opportunities

The number of migrant and ethnic minority pupils in Dutch schools can only be estimated, since nationality cannot always be clearly established. Thus in the school year 1979/80 about 42,540 pupils of non-Dutch nationality attended Dutch schools, this being roughly 3%; to these must be added 2,519 Moluccan children and 14,500 from Surinam and the West Indies (figures from internal statistics of the Ministry of Education, 16 October 1979). Among children from migrant families the biggest groups are Turkish and Moroccan (numbering 16,412 and 8,027 respectively). The highest concentrations are to be found in the inner cities of the large industrial towns. In these areas some schools have a proportion of ethnic minority pupils exceeding 50%; in a few the figure is over 95%. For about the last five years school rolls have been falling, with the result that the relative proportion of ethnic minority pupils has been rising and will continue to rise.

The *verzuiling* of Dutch society also has its repercussions on the organization of educational provision. This term, which literally means "columniation", relates to the way Dutch society sees itself as being vertically divided into religious and ideological "columns", the most important of which are the Protestants, the Catholics and the wide spectrum of agnostics. Although, of course, these columns are themselves divided - and, today, increasingly superseded - by social class, individual loyalties are still very largely determined by denominational affiliations. Very often, on the local level, the *stichtings* are the organizational backbone of the vertically divided networks of social life.

Within this system all the large groups have their own schools; hence, in addition to the state schools, there is a large number of private schools. State financial support, however, is absolutely the same for all kinds of school. Most primary schools are independent, i.e. denominational, only a few being state-run. These denominational schools have the right to refuse admission to children of other denominations. In individual cases, in a few areas where the denominational schools exercise this right, the Turkish and Moroccan children, being Muslim, are concentrated in state schools, which are obliged to admit any child as a matter of course.

Another significant fact about the Dutch school system is that the government has no statutory right to exercise a direct influence on the way in which schools are organized or on the content of the curriculum. Its main responsibility is funding and the provision of equipment. It also supports teacher training and the school advisory services. Under the Dutch system foreign children have the same rights and obligations as Dutch children (including the obligation to attend school), and theoretically all branches of education are open to them. In order to ensure equal treatment for minorities, special support measures are required in the schools to enable migrant pupils to start attending normal Dutch classes as soon as possible, without at the same time being alienated from their own language and culture. To this end the government provides special facilities. The way in which these facilities are utilized in the individual schools is left to the discretion of the governing bodies and the schools themselves. Thanks to the considerable freedom of action allowed to the individual school, a wide spectrum of models for the teaching of foreign pupils has evolved.


## Pre-school education

The difficulty some children experienced in finding an identity and the problems they faced in their relations with their parents led the authorities to move away from their original concept of a direct and exclusive integration of the children into the Dutch schools and to place particular emphasis on the provision of instruction in their own language and culture. Moreover, it is now recognized that it is essential for schools to have good contacts with the parents of ethnic minority children.

While it is almost a matter of course for Dutch children to attend pre-school classes – 86% of all four-year-olds and 96% of all five-year-olds do so – a not inconsiderable proportion of ethnic minority children (between 30% and 50%) do not attend kindergarten. In October 1979 the number of foreign children attending pre-school institutions was 16,301 (of whom 6,137 were Turkish and 4,008 Moroccan; in addition there were about 4,200 from the West Indies). At such institutions additional teachers can be appointed to look after migrant and ethnic minority children. In general, however, no teachers from the children's countries of origin are employed, nor is there as a rule any mother tongue teaching or any instruction in the children's own culture.


## Admission of ethnic minority pupils to primary schools

Primary schooling lasts six years, the normal age of entry being five. Every school draws up its own curriculum and timetable, and private schools are entitled to formulate their own admissions policy as they think fit. The government provides funds for the implementation of particular measures for the teaching of ethnic minority children, but the actual mode of implementation is left to the schools themselves, with the result that the situation varies from one locality to another. More importantly, the schools receive extra funding for the engagement of teachers for special duties (*taakleerkrachten*). The allocation of funds is dependent on pupil numbers and varies according to the duration of the children's stay in the Netherlands, the size of the teaching groups and the children's nationality, a distinction being made between the children of migrant workers and those of Surinamese or Moluccan descent.

Some schools attach particular importance to ensuring that the children learn Dutch as quickly as possible. Children are allocated to classes corresponding to their age and given a number of additional lessons in Dutch every week. Other schools, while leaving the children in the classes they belong to according to age, provide the Dutch class teacher with the services of a teacher charged with special duties for a number of hours a week; this teacher's time is devoted to ethnic minority pupils in need of extra help. Schools that have to cater for exceptionally large numbers of ethnic minority children run special reception classes which are attended for a limited period of time. In such schools all pupils who are new to Dutch education are placed in these special classes, which are made up of between ten and twenty pupils and taught by a Dutch teacher. The ages of the children range from six to twelve. After about a year the children are considered to have made sufficient progress for them to switch to classes corresponding to their age-groups. Wherever feasible, an effort is made to organize the classes according to either age or nationality. The classes take place either locally, in the area where the children live, or, in some cases, in a centrally situated school, which they then leave for their neighbourhood schools as soon as they have acquired the requisite linguistic competence. Although the schools aim to prepare the pupils as quickly as possible for transfer to mainstream Dutch classes, specific problems constantly arise in connection with this kind of schooling. Children may also be transferred to schools of the type just described, though only with the agreement of the authorities. This makes for the development of separate schools in which particular groups are concentrated. Even in the Netherlands it may sometimes be observed that indigenous parents tend to move away from areas where the schools have a high proportion of ethnic minority children. Thus even in the Netherlands there is a danger that the various models put into practice in primary education may serve largely only to relieve the burden on mainstream classes by shunting off the ethnic minority pupils - who are thought of as problem children - into special groups or classes. In some cases, however, they are redistributed among a number of other schools; this helps to ensure that the proportion of ethnic minority children does not exceed 25% in any one school.

The high degree of autonomy enjoyed by individual schools enables them to develop their own approaches to solving their difficulties and to find the best way of responding to their particular circumstances. In April 1974, however, in order to reduce the risk of discontinuity and to facilitate nation-wide co-ordination of the means employed to cater for migrant children, the Ministry of Education appointed two co-ordinators. These were placed at the disposal of schools, inspectors and teachers in an advisory capacity, with the task of liaising with the individual groups and decision-making bodies.

Today the bilingual and the indigenous teachers working with ethnic minority children receive concrete on-the-spot help from the local and regional school advisory services (*Schooladvies Centrum*), of which there are about eighty in the country as a whole. When the number of ethnic minority pupils in a primary school rises above certain figure, additional funding is made available. The advisers' remit covers not only kindergartens and primary schools, but also seconday schools and the so-called *internationale schakelklassen* (bridging classes between different levels of schooling - for more detail see p 145 below). The advisers' task is to support the work of the teachers in the schools and encourage them to become personally involved with the ethnic minority children in their care.

## Mainstream and specific education provision at primary level

The above-mentioned "teachers for special duties" (*taakleerkrachten*) are allotted to schools on the basis of a highly complex set of fixed criteria; this makes for a degree of fluidity on the borderline between initial reception teaching and specific support measures within mainstream classes. The criteria for their allocation were improved in May 1979, with the result that, starting from the school year 1979/80, more favourable conditions were created for the implementation of additional support measures aimed at ethnic minority pupils in mainstream classes at pre-school and primary level. Where, for instance, there is only a small number of ethnic minority pupils, the support teaching is undertaken by peripatetic "teachers for special duties". This system of "flying brigades" was first tried out in Rotterdam in 1973. It has the advantage of making teaching more effective by co-ordinating the development of teaching materials as well as by centralizing the advisory facilities and in-service training available to teachers.

Since 1974 the shift of aim in the teaching of ethnic minority children from an exclusive emphasis on smooth and speedy integration into the Dutch school system to "integration without loss of identity" has led to the introduction of mother tongue teaching, though admittedly only at primary level. Originally such teaching was intended largely to prepare the migrant pupils for a possible return to their countries of origin. However, when it became obvious that the migrants were going to stay in the Netherlands much longer than had been envisaged, there was a shift of emphasis in the interpretation of the aims of mother tongue teaching. Now the main concern is to help children of ethnic minorities to develop their own identity, to promote contacts between schools and ethnic minority families, to facilitate the children's acquisition of Dutch as a second language, and to provide them with support in the process of acculturation. Mother tongue teaching is supposed to be incorporated into the regular timetable. In practice two types of mother tongue teaching have emerged: one is the "parallel" type which operates outside normal school hours on Wednesday afternoons and Saturday mornings; the other is the "integrated" type for which children are withdrawn from regular classes for some six lessons a week. To make up for this they are often given extra support teaching in the medium of Dutch, but of course this means that they are withdrawn from normal lessons yet again. Apart from these forms of mother tongue teaching there are a few cases where the consulates of the pupils' countries of origin – and occasionally the communities themselves – provide their own national teaching, which then falls outside the purview of the Dutch school authorities.

Schools with large numbers of ethnic minority pupils can sometimes appoint one or more bilingual teachers, provided that there are at least fifty pupils with the same language background. Mother tongue teaching then takes place in groups of ten to twenty pupils, who are graded according to age and ability. Occasionally children from one and the same language group are bussed to a central school for their mother tongue classes.

At first the training of bilingual teachers differed markedly from that of their monolingual Dutch colleagues. Many of them had been recruited from among those migrant workers in the Netherlands who had teaching qualifications from their home countries. If they could demonstrate some knowledge of the Dutch language and the Dutch education system, they were eligible for renewable one-year teaching contracts. It must be added, however, that they were generally less well paid than their indigenous colleagues. (None of this applies to Moroccan teachers, whose qualifications are not recognized by the Dutch authorities.) Since 1975 there have been special in-service training programmes for them, similar to those which are offered to Dutch teachers. The facilities available to the bilingual teachers consist in the main of Dutch language courses and courses designed to extend their knowledge of the Dutch education system.

In the past there was often no integrated scheme of teaching in which the mother tongue and the Dutch provision interlocked. There was also a dearth of teaching materials which might have enabled the Dutch and the bilingual teachers to work out programmes of multicultural or intercultural teaching.

Today the situation has improved considerably in certain areas. Bilingual teachers are now paid on the same scale as Dutch teachers; possibilities for the recognition of teaching qualifications from abroad have been widened; and finally there are facilities for further training which enable bilingual teachers to acquire Dutch qualifications fairly rapidly (*Beleidsplan "Cultureele Minderheiden"*, 1980, p 89).

## Admission of ethnic minority pupils to secondary schools

A special feature of the Dutch education system is the existence of the so-called *internationale schakelklassen* (ISKs) at the beginning of secondary schooling. These classes, which were instituted in 1973 and could be set up whenever more than ten migrant pupils were in the first year of secondary school, were meant to prepare migrant children who had spent one or more years in the Dutch system for the education they would receive at secondary level. They thus amounted to a form of support teaching designed to ease the transition from primary school to the various forms of schooling offered at secondary level and could therefore be regarded as a kind of orientation stage in the children's school careers. However, with an increasing number of young people aged between twelve and seventeen arriving in the Netherlands, the ISKs inevitably took on more and more the function of reception classes preparatory to secondary education. While their main function is to provide the pupils with a knowledge of the Dutch language, they also involve up to five lessons of mother tongue teaching a week. For an ISK to be set up there must be at least ten pupils at the school who do not have Dutch as their mother tongue. Since 1974 schools have employed "interpreters" who work alongside the Dutch teachers and have the task of establishing contacts between the school and the children's homes and helping to sort out any difficulties that arise at school. By 1979 about a hundred schools in 56 towns ran ISKs. In all there were 190 such classes, with a total of about 3,200 pupils. Of these 3,200 pupils, 53% were due to enter secondary education immediately upon arrival in the country, while 47% had already attended Dutch primary schools. 40% of the pupils were Turkish and 20% Moroccan.

In fact it is far from easy for ISKs to perform their intended function of integrating migrant pupils quickly and smoothly into the Dutch education system. At the discretion of the school, pupils can go on attending these classes for two years, and half of them actually do so; some are taken into secondary schooling so late that they never reach the stage of attending mainstream classes. Those who arrive in the Netherlands at the age of sixteen or seventeen, i.e. over the compulsory school age, may attend one-year or two-year courses in Dutch which are provided for their benefit.

## Mainstream and specific educational provision at secondary level

In the Dutch school system the six years of primary education are followed by secondary education. This is divided into three branches, one offering an academic education, one a general education, and one a vocational education. The first year of secondary school is regarded as the orientation stage, during which the pupils' learning achievements and attitudes are observed in order to ascertain which type of school is best suited to them. In practice, however, each type of secondary school has introduced an orientation phase of its own. The academic type of secondary education (*Voorbereidend Wetenschapelijk Onderwijs* or *VWO* - "preparatory academic education") lasts altogether six years and provides a preparation for university study. Within the type that offers a general education two sub-types are to be distinguished: one is of five years' duration and provides a higher level of general education (*Hoger Algemeen Voortgezet Onderwijs* or *HAVO* - "higher general continued education"), while the other extends over three or four years and provides a general education at an intermediate level (*Middelbaar Algemeen Voortgezet Onderwijs* or *MAVO* - "intermediate general continued education").

Most ethnic minority pupils, together with about 40% of Dutch pupils, go on after six years of primary schooling to the least demanding kind of vocational education (*Lager Beroepsonderwijs* or *LBO* - "lower vocational education"). This lasts four years and comprises technical, commercial, domestic and other branches. Approximately 80% of Dutch boys choose the technical branch, and approximately 85% of Dutch girls the domestic branch. Special emphasis is placed on general educational subjects, in particular the Dutch language. Since a knowledge of Dutch is indispensable even for those subjects which are geared to vocational training in the more restricted sense, it is often hardly possible for ethnic minority pupils to gain a leaving certificate even in this branch of secondary education. Yet some *LBO* schools run reception classes or reception groups to provide support teaching for their ethnic minority pupils in order to prepare them for the specialized training they may receive at other schools. Since August 1981 there have been special transition courses for a practically orientated kind of vocational training designed for teenagers from the ethnic minorities. There is no provision at secondary level for ethnic minority pupils to be taught their mother tongue.

**Academic achievement and vocational integration**

Only the most tentative statements can be made about the academic achievement of pupils from the ethnic minorities, as no official statistics are available and the existing studies are inadequate. There is no information about the leaving qualifications and subsequent careers of youngsters from the ethnic minorities, nor is it possible to know whether all ethnic minority children of school age actually attend school.

Nevertheless, the available statistics show that the overall situation of ethnic minority children is anything but satisfactory, and that the first steps on the road to failure are made during the early years.

146

There is thus little reason to believe that in any but exceptional
cases more promising avenues will be opened up for the 7.3% of all
migrant children in primary schools who stay there even though they
have reached the age when their Dutch peers would be found in some
branch of secondary education. The following table shows the numbers of
ethnic minority pupils, according to age and nationality, who were
attending Dutch primary schools in 1977:

| Age | 6-12 | 13 | 14 | 15 | Totals |
|---|---|---|---|---|---|
| Greek | 496 | 12 | 1 | 1 | 510 |
| Italian | 1,847 | 35 | 8 | 0 | 1,890 |
| Moroccan | 3,220 | 285 | 129 | 85 | 3,719 |
| Portuguese | 871 | 74 | 29 | 9 | 983 |
| Spanish | 2,644 | 108 | 24 | 9 | 2,785 |
| Tunisian | 63 | 3 | 0 | 1 | 67 |
| Turkish | 9,391 | 453 | 165 | 42 | 10,051 |
| Yugoslav | 488 | 12 | 2 | 3 | 505 |
| Totals | 19,020 | 982 | 358 | 150 | 20,510 |

The proportion of ethnic minority pupils aged thirteen to fifteen who
were still in primary education was thus, by nationality:

| | |
|---|---|
| Greek | 2.8% |
| Italian | 2.3% |
| Moroccan | 13.4% |
| Portuguese | 11.4% |
| Spanish | 5.1% |
| Tunisian | 6.0% |
| Turkish | 6.5% |
| Yugoslav | 3.4% |
| Overall | 7.3% |

Source: Centraal bureau voor de statistiek 1978, 35.

As the table does not indicate the quota of migrant pupils aged six to
twelve who are to be found in classes with younger children, i.e. who
are "too old for the class they are in", it may safely be assumed that
the overall proportion of migrant pupils in primary schools who are in
this type of situation is not below 30% and probably a good deal
higher. Among these, many will, upon their entry into secondary
education, be "of necessity" orientated towards those of its branches
which lead to early employment in low paid manual jobs, or to

147

straightforward unemployment. On 5 September 1980 there were 248,000 unemployed persons in the Netherlands. 9% of all unemployed Dutch males were under nineteen years of age, while the corresponding figures for Moroccan and Turkish males were 13% and 15% respectively. Of all unemployed female migrants, the under-nineteens accounted for 31%, whereas the corresponding figures were 27% for Moroccan females and 22% for Turkish females. If one breaks down the unemployment figures for males under nineteen by nationality, one finds that 79% of those out of work are Dutch by nationality and ethnic background, while 8.5% are Dutch nationals from ethnic minorities, and 12.5% are young migrant workers.

# The pilot project in Leiden (The Netherlands)

## The general framework

Leiden is not one of the Dutch towns with a high proportion of foreign inhabitants, and it was only at a late stage, in 1971/72, that it began to be faced with the problem of providing schooling for immigrant children. In 1979 the number of these in local primary schools was about 400.

The persons charged with the running of the pilot project in Leiden had been familiar with the difficulties of ethnic minority children since 1971. However, attempts to try out bicultural models in schools had come to nothing because the authorities lacked any real awareness of the problem. It was only after the future project director had stepped up the pressure on the local authorities by calling a meeting, which was attended by numerous experts as well as by representatives from the Ministry of Education, that steps were taken to set up bilingual reception classes in Leiden's primary schools. After another school had declined to take part in this scheme, the Du Rieu School was selected for the experiment with reception classes of a kind that was new to Leiden. Ethnic minority pupils attending the project classes were not recruited from within the school's normal catchment area, which is predominantly white Dutch. At the time when this school was chosen for the project the representatives of the local authority, but not the members of the project team, knew that it was due to be closed down when the project had run its course.

Towards the end of 1975 an information evening with Dutch parents had resulted in the setting up of a parents' committee, but no further steps towards the planning of the project were taken before the EC Commission had declared its willingness to support it and had engaged in talks with the Ministry of Education to examine the possibilities and pre-requisites for the conduct of the project. No agreement was reached until August 1976, and so it was only on 19 April 1977, after the parents had agreed to the scheme and the local authority had put in a formal application, that the Ministry officially agreed to the project's being implemented for a three-year period (two years for the running of the reception classes and one year for further observation and evaluation), though the possibility of terminating the experiment if it turned out to be unsuccessful was kept open.

The teaching staff for the project came from an existing institution in Leiden, the so-called "Flying Brigade", a team of full-time peripatetic teachers of Dutch as a Second Language. For the pilot project three additional posts for Dutch teachers were created; these were taken up by seven part-time teachers. The selection of teachers was in the hands of the project leader, who was responsible for both the organization *and* teaching content of the project. At his request a nine-person consultative committee was set up for the experiment and the work of evaluation, and at a later stage a commission of six persons was formed to look after the administrative co-ordination; this body was concerned not only with the pilot project, but with matters relating to the teaching of ethnic minority children in Leiden as a whole. Apart from these bodies there was an external evaluation team whose task was to report on the situation obtaining at the start of the project and on its subsequent course, and to collect data about the pupils' social background.

A special feature of the pilot project was the setting up of bilingual reception classes for Turkish and Moroccan children aged six to twelve. These classes were entirely made up of pupils who had just arrived from Turkey and Morocco and who registered for school attendance between September 1977 and February 1978. The reception classes were set up so that these children could be taught their mother tongue and Dutch to a level which would enable them to join the mainstream classes corresponding to their age in one of their neighbourhood schools. To ensure that from the start there would be contact with the areas in which the children lived, the children were meant to join in club and neighbourhood activities there while attending the reception classes. Provision was also made for a flexible transition to mainstream classes.

The general objectives of the pilot project were geared to overcoming the problems of organization and teaching content of the reception classes. The evaluation was intended to embrace not only the monitoring of school achievement in the reception classes and after the switch to mainstream classes, but above all factors of identity formation or possible identity loss in the children, as well as any possible behavioural disorders and their learning motivation.


## The pilot project

### Aims

The aims of the teaching given to ethnic minority children in the Leiden pilot project were evolved from a critical analysis of forms of reception teaching already existing in the Netherlands. One objection that was made to the customary practice of the Dutch school system was that it compelled the migrant children to adapt themselves to the school. Children who until a few days ago had lived in an entirely different cultural environment suddenly found themselves in a school and a society they did not understand. Because of the emphasis placed on learning Dutch, it was said, they lost contact with other school subjects. Such a model was therefore not appropriate to the situation of ethnic minority children arriving in the Netherlands at primary school age. "Existing teaching allows too little scope for the individual character of the foreign child. Mother tongue and cultural teaching cannot provide a solution here, since it takes place in isolation. There is insufficient awareness of the fact that the attendance of masses of ethnic minority children at Dutch lessons requires the teaching to be adapted to this new multicultural situation, and that one cannot start by trying to adapt this new and hitherto unknown category of pupil to the existing form of teaching by means of a number of support and remedial measures" (Appel et al. 1979, p 25).

Bringing in ethnic minority teachers to teach in Dutch schools, it was maintained, did not produce a bicultural situation, but had led to two autonomous and scarcely integrated teaching systems - to "doubly monocultural teaching". Responsible teaching for migrant children, by contrast, required new forms of organization at all relevant levels.

The objective was a form of teaching "for Dutch and foreign children which takes into account their present joint attendance at Dutch schools and prepares them for their joint future in a multicultural society here in the Netherlands or elsewhere in the world" (Appel et al. 1979, p 30). According to this basic concept, the school must come closer to the migrant pupil; it must pick the children up from the point they have reached educationally, socially and psychologically on arriving in the Netherlands. The first steps in the direction of this objective were to be demonstrated by the teaching concept that was tried out in the pilot project.

These aims and interests correspond to two principal areas of activity: developing a new organizational concept for reception classes and devising a curriculum that would take account of the needs of migrant children.

The aim of the reception classes in the pilot project was to guide the Turkish and Moroccan children gradually towards the neighbourhood school and equip them to join the mainstream education system of the Netherlands. The Turkish and Moroccan children were to be introduced to the Dutch language and culture without forfeiting their own culture and without being exposed to a culture shock.

The pragmatic aims were pitched differently for the two years of the reception classes. In the first year the central aim was to ensure normal progress in non-linguistic subjects by the use of the mother tongue as the teaching medium and by the teaching of Dutch as a second language. In the second year they were prepared for the transition to a local primary school or a secondary school with the help of teaching the content tailored to each child individually. These aims were to be achieved using the same number of teachers as is laid down in the statutory Dutch regulations for migrant children, in order to ensure the transferability of the model.

## Organization

This particular form of reception class was to be tried out with a Moroccan and a Turkish group. It was possible, with the help of the local residents' register, to approach the parents of Moroccan and Turkish children and explain to them that they had a choice between the Du Rieu School, which in some cases was rather far from their homes, and a normal Dutch school in their own neighbourhood.

The experiment began with 13 Moroccan and 11 Turkish children; these were divided into two classes, each with three different ability groups corresponding to the children's educational level:

Level A:  children aged six to seven, beginners in reading and writing in the mother tongue;

Level B:  children aged eight to nine with a knowledge of reading and writing in the mother tongue;

Level C:  children aged ten to eleven, some of whom would go on to a secondary school after the reception classes.

The planning required that class numbers should not exceed fifteen. After the start of the pilot project only two more children were admitted. The migrant children were bussed from their homes to the school and back. During the dinner break they stayed in the school with about twenty Dutch children.

In the first year the children remained most of the time in the class group with the teacher of their own nationality. However there were always supposed to be two ability groups simultaneously in the class, while the third was either being given special teaching in Dutch or attending integration lessons in regular Dutch classes.

Timetabling became more complex in the second year, as more of the teaching was now done by Dutch teachers and some subjects were taught in the medium of both languages: on Mondays and Tuesdays the children were taught by Dutch teachers, and on Thursdays and Fridays by bilingual teachers; on Wednesdays the teachers alternated. The system of ability groups was retained. Although the division of classes into fairly homogeneous groups of ability was generally maintained, mixed ability groups were formed for certain lessons where Turkish and Moroccan children were taught together through the medium of Dutch.

In the third year the children were integrated into their neighbourhood schools, wherever possible into a class correponding to their age. They were prepared for this transition by the teachers in the reception class and in the local school. After moving to the local school they still had the chance, if they wished, to have one half day of lessons on their own language and culture.

## Teaching

The educational principles underlying the pilot project were derived from an analysis of the situation of the immigrant child in the Netherlands and, more particularly, in Dutch schools: normally the children's educational development was interrupted when they entered Dutch education, since they had to get used to an entirely new language and an entirely new system of schooling. Hence it was seen as the prime task of the pilot project to provide support teaching for the immigrant children not only in Dutch, but at the same time in factual subjects. Moreover, this teaching was supposed to facilitate acculturation and ensure psychological stability.

This basic orientation affected the choice of languages, the choice of subjects, the appointment of staff and the use of teaching material. In the first place the model for the linguistic transition was determined by this basic orientation. In the first year of the reception classes all subjects were taught in the mother tongue, and in addition there were lessons in Dutch. For the children this represented an increased learning load, though roughly 80% of the teaching was given in the mother tongue. For the Turkish and Moroccan teachers this meant that they were employed full-time and responsible for the content not only of their mother tongue teaching, but also for the teaching of arithmetic and other subjects. Two additional Dutch teachers were available to teach Dutch as a second language and to give instruction in Dutch culture; they were supposed to maintain contact with their foreign colleagues, to collaborate with them in the preparation of joint projects, and to ensure proper liaison between the teachers and the educational experts attached to the project.

In the second year half the teaching was given in the mother tongue and half in Dutch. The choice of the linguistic medium for different subjects was not arbitrary, however: Turkish or Arabic, religion and social studies continued to be taught only in the mother tongue, while arithmetic and factual subjects were taught partly in the mother tongue and partly in Dutch, while instruction in traffic security was given solely in Dutch; there were also lessons attended by both Dutch and immigrant children and given by Dutch and bilingual teachers, as well as Dutch language lessons conducted entirely in Dutch. For the bilingual teachers this meant that they were now required to work only half days. For the Dutch part of the teaching, especially for the solution of problems involved in the transition from reception classes to main-stream schooling, another Dutch teacher was brought in.

The **mother tongue teaching** given by the bilingual teachers was based on Turkish and Moroccan materials acquired and paid for out of funds available to the pilot project. The teachers made selections from these at their own discretion, the Dutch project teachers being unfamiliar with the materials.

The **Dutch language teaching** in the first year was confined to the spoken language and conducted entirely in Dutch. (It was decided that, insofar as the children were not yet literate, they should learn to read and write first in their own languages.) For Dutch lessons the teachers in the first year used not only the normal textbooks, but also materials they had devised themselves to take account of the situation of the child learning Dutch as a second language. In the second year the reading and writing of Dutch was introduced. With the transition to mainstream classes in mind, the teachers now confined themselves to the textbooks used in the regular Dutch classes.

**Arithmetic** was taught in the first year by the bilingual teachers in the medium of the mother tongue. The original intention had been to use materials from the children's countries of origin for the teaching of arithmetic and to go over to using Dutch materials only in the second year. The foreign materials could not be obtained in time, however, and so it was necessary to resort to Dutch materials after all. A textbook was chosen which had comparatively little in the way of continuous Dutch text but came with detailed recommendations for the teacher. It proved necessary, however, to render these recommendations into a simpler form of Dutch for the benefit of the bilingual teachers, and so this textbook could not come into use until October 1978, nearly a year after the start of the project. Later on, Turkish or Moroccan material was used in parallel with Dutch material. In the second year arithmetic was taught partly in the mother tongue and partly in Dutch. A Dutch teaching method was followed which involved relatively little explanation, together with Dutch materials that had been specially adapted for use in the pilot project.

Great weight was given in the pilot project to the teaching of **factual subjects**. These involved elements of history, geography and nature study and were taught in the first year by the bilingual teachers; the teachers based their teaching on materials from their own countries and used the mother tongue as the medium of instruction. For the second year a special course was devised which would link up with the teaching of these subjects in regular classes. To this end the lessons were divided up and prepared in such a way that every week an integrated course of teaching could be given in which Dutch and bilingual teachers alternated. This was meant to help the migrant children to make use of the advantage they had over their Dutch peers, viz. the opportunity to draw comparisons between two different cultures.

Another important special feature of the pilot project was the provision of **integration teaching**. From the first year on, after a preparatory phase of three to four weeks, provision was made in the Dutch timetable for lessons in sport, art, craft and music; these were taken jointly by Dutch and bilingual teachers, each class including five or so migrant children from one of the ability groups. This teaching not only served to bring together children of different ethnic origins

and to familiarize the migrant children with what went on in mainstream lessons: it was also a valuable means of introducing elements of
intercultural education into the teaching of both foreign and indigenous
pupils. At first materials were taken from the *Thuisland* ("Homeland")
project of the NCB (*Nederlands Centrum voor Buitenlanders* - a
curriculum development and training institution based in Utrecht which
caters specifically for teachers and children in multi-ethnic areas).
These bilingual materials consist of little stories, some of them
written by children, which are very well suited to draw attention to
cultural differences and provoke discussion about them. An attempt was
made, in collaboration with a university, to evolve corresponding
materials for the older pupils in the pilot project, but nothing came of
this. In addition, joint projects were carried out with foreign and
indigenous pupils on topics like "Morocco", "Turkey", "Migration of
Workers", "Problems of Living Together", "Development Aid", "Religions of
the World", "Tourism", "Foreign Countries and Customs", "Other
Languages". The projects were prepared by the bilingual and Dutch
teachers working together. In the second year there were, in addition,
"creative afternoons" for all pupils, indigenous and migrant, in which
dancing, music-making and drama activities took place under the
supervision of Dutch and bilingual teachers.

## Collaboration between Dutch and foreign teachers

Apart from their teaching duties, the bilingual teachers were charged
with liaising with the Dutch staff on the pilot project, the regular
class teachers, the headteachers and the outside experts about
questions relating to the planning and conduct of the teaching and
about the children's problems. In addition to this they were responsible
for establishing and maintaining contacts between the ethnic minority
parents and the school.

All the Dutch staff taking part in the project had attended a
preparatory in-service course on the teaching of migrant children at
the Pedagogical Academy in Amsterdam. The bilingual teachers engaged on
the project had already had some years' experience as full-time or
part-time teachers. They had also attended a training course for
foreign teachers at the NCB. The staff received counselling at weekly
team meetings attended by the outside experts, the headteacher and the
teachers from the reception classes, and also during additional
discussions which took place weekly with the bilingual teachers and
less frequently with the Dutch staff. There were moreover a large
number of informal contacts between the project leader and the
teachers, especially the bilingual teachers.

Co-operation and counselling were not always unproblematic. "One does
not gain and maintain the confidence of bilingual teachers in a
counselling relationship that focusses on professional matters alone...
Successful counselling was therefore possible only because it was

preceded by several years of informal personal relations between advisers and bilingual teachers" (Appel et al. 1979, p 50). The bilingual teachers were given guidance and general help by individual Dutch teachers, often on a private basis. Being obliged to co-operate with their Dutch colleagues, they were able to improve their command of the Dutch language.

## Home-school liaison

The Dutch parents were informed about the plan for the pilot project and their opinions sought regarding it before the application was sent to the Ministry of Education. They were given a questionnaire with the help of which it was hoped to find out whether, as a result of the project, they would take their children out of the school or not let them start their schooling there, whether they or their children had any experience of social relations with Turkish or Moroccan citizens and what expectations or suggestions they might have regarding the project. At a parents' evening a delegation from the parents took a positive attitude to the project. At a later parents' evening a parents' committee was elected; this included two Moroccan and two Turkish parents. The remaining ethnic minority parents were informed in advance by the project leader during home visits. Shortly before teaching began a parents' evening was held specially for them.

## Evaluation

The starting point for the evaluation was to examine the special features of the Leiden project as compared with other forms of teaching involving ethnic minority pupils. Apart from describing the conduct of the project and recording the personal assessments of those involved in it, the evaluation centred upon the following:

- comparing the children in the pilot project with ethnic minority children in the Dutch mainstream system;

- comparing the Leiden model for reception classes with other specific models for the teaching of ethnic minority children.

This form of evaluation required a control group. For this purpose Turkish and Moroccan pupils in other forms of reception class and in mainstream classes in Dutch primary schools in other towns were selected. The teaching of the control group, which consisted of fifteen Turkish and twenty Moroccan children, differed considerably from that of the Leiden pupils, both in terms of organization and teaching method and in terms of curricular content. In both the project group and the control group, progress in Dutch, arithmetical skills, social relations and cultural orientation was measured. In order to eliminate the possibility that differences of social background or intelligence might be significant factors in any disparities that were resistered, data were collected about the families and their social background and about the children's intelligence. Curricularcontent, school organization and the development of the schools used in the comparison were also brought in as control variables.

By measuring the children's intelligence with the help of the Raven test (which the evaluation team itself viewed with some scepticism) it was ensured that no significant differences existed between the project group and the control group. The same was true as regards family background, e.g. the socio-economic situation and educational level of the families, circumstances of migration and future prospects. From the findings it was possible to conclude that on all these counts the situation of the pupils at the two schools was homogeneous. Big differences existed in both groups between the Moroccan and Turkish families. Differences in the abilities that were to be measured could be ascribed to the school model or the organization of teaching, since they could not be accounted for by individual factors. The children involved in the pilot project also continued to be observed for another year after moving to the neighbourhood school.

The project started out from two hypotheses which were to be tested in the evaluation:

1) The bilingual reception model has advantages for the school progress of ethnic minority pupils. It produces greater continuity through the inclusion of mother tongue teaching.

2) The bilingual reception classes of the pilot project have a favourable effect on the social behaviour and cultural orientation of the ethnic minority pupils.

The testing of both hypotheses and the discovery of a better perform-ance among the children in the project classes would demonstrate the superiority of this form of school organization. Since it was envisaged that critics would maintain that the mother tongue teaching impeded the children's progress in Dutch, their command of Dutch was also tested. The evaluators worked on the hypothesis that the children in the pilot project would perform worse than those in the control group.

To test the pupils' competence in Dutch a language test was carried out to ascertain their passive comprehension and oral competence. The material recorded on tape and in written reports was assessed according to vocabulary, word order, syntax and linguistic complexity. In addition, procedures for measuring conceptualization and command of syntax were employed. Telling stories and a conversation about out-of-school topics in the form of an open interview were incorporated into the assessment. The test results were assessed in relation to social variables such as the pupil's nationality, sex, age and length of residence.

The results after one year showed no significant differences between the pupils in the project group and those in the control group in their command of Dutch. The original hypothesis that the children in the project classes would lag behind those in the control group in linguistic skill was not borne out. This example demonstrated that a teaching model in which reception teaching is given solely in the mother tongue need not, after the lapse of a year, entail any disadvantages as regards second language learning. (For a more detailed account of this component of the evaluation research cf. Altena/Appel 1982.)

The hypothesis that teaching conducted in the mother tongue during the first reception year would lead to an improvement *vis-à-vis* the control group was tested in relation to the teaching of arithmetic. It was expected that there would be a greater continuity and a better command of mathematical concepts in the reception class. At the same time it was supposed that a command of mathematical concepts and the technical ability to solve arithmetical problems were identical. Therefore a test was used to measure technical arithmetical skills and given to the children in a Turkish or Arabic version. The Dutch version could of course also be used. The aim was to compare the arithmetical skills of the ethnic minority children with the standards demanded in Dutch schools and with the skills of Dutch pupils. The results were assessed in relation to nationality, age, sex and school model. This test did not produce the results that had been hoped for: it was clear that there were striking gaps in the arithmetical ability of all the migrant children and that the speed at which they calculated was well below that of the Dutch children.

Since it was suspected that the customary procedure by which migrant children in the Netherlands were integrated into mainstream classes led to problems, resulting especially from neglect of the mother tongue, it was intended to examine the social and psychological results of the transition. Against the background of an analysis of the socialization of ethnic minority children and a description of the concrete bicultural situation of Turkish and Moroccan pupils in the Netherlands, hypotheses were formulated relating to social development and forms of acculturation. It was supposed that at schools which favoured a gradual transition and provided a large measure of teaching in the medium of the mother tongue the following would apply:

- The children would display fewer behavioural disorders and have fewer identity problems, indicators of which were assumed to be isolation, aggression, rebelliousness and clowning;

- they would be able to develop a much stronger bicultural identity, since both languages and both cultures would be perceived as having more or less equal value in the day-to-day life of the school;

- they would be more highly motivated and more familiar with the everyday life of the school.

The methods employed consisted of semi-standardized observations, the drawing up of case-studies of individual children, and the use of semi-standardized interviews in which the children were shown photographs and drawings which reflected various cultural elements. Sociogrammes were also used. The investigations had not been fully assessed by 1980. Apart from the sociogrammes, which were also administered to both the control and project groups, none of the data which were obtained through these instruments had been fully exploited by the time of writing. The sociogrammes showed that the isolation of ethnic minority children in the multi-ethnic control groups was significantly higher in the latter than in the bicultural project groups.

## Assessment of the pilot project

Setting up a pilot project at a school which was due to be closed upon completion of the project and which, because of its geographical position, had not previously been attended by ethnic minority children created an artificial and almost insular situation. Moreover, the school had more funds than usual, since these are calculated on the basis of the number of pupils attending the school in the previous year, and for the year in question rolls had fallen. Because of this it was possible to provide a form of teaching that was highly differentiated and often highly individualized. The additional funding provided by the European Communities for the pilot project served only to cover the cost of employing outside experts, the additional material and the evaluation.

The initiative of the EC Commission came to the aid of a group of persons who had already made a number of attempts to experiment with new ways of teaching migrant children without eliciting a favourable response from the authorities. One of these was the project leader, who consequently had quite firm views as to how the pilot project should be organized; this ensured that the planning of the project would be carried out on a solid basis. The objectives of the project could be couched in practical terms, and its practical orientation could be clearly justified against a background of years of theoretical work and firm political and ethical principles. Furthermore, the validity of its findings was reinforced by the comparison with other schools.

The pilot project started from the position that teaching must be geared to the interests of the children and to the real situation in which they led their lives, not to short-term considerations of economic and social policy. The teaching must be adapted to the children, not the children to the teaching. Hence modes of teaching and forms of teaching content must be evolved which could prepare Dutch and non-Dutch children for life in a multicultural society. This led on to the demand that the migrant children should enjoy a bilingual education. The aim was to guide the children slowly towards the Dutch educational and social system and at the same time to prevent any hiatus in their factual learning. Such a concept, it was maintained, would produce psychological stability in the children, since they would see their own culture recognized as having the same value as the indigenous culture. In line with this objective was a scheme of teaching which united both cultures. This was tried out in practical teaching for the pilot project.

Less attention was paid to the fact that such a definition of aims also presupposed certain elements of teaching content and teaching method. The setting up of a new form of teaching for migrant children living in the Netherlands also requires the development of new teaching content for the school. However one gets the impression that teaching content played a subordinate role in the whole of the pilot project, since the reports concentrate on two areas: school organization and evaluation.

There are also very few statements about the individual learning areas and the didactic concepts that were applied in them. Thus in the area of Dutch as a second language - apart from the very detailed analysis of the results produced by the tests of linguistic competence - there are no reports of the teachers' experience in working with the materials which were already available or which they devised themselves, and no reports of the children's learning progress or difficulties. It would above all be interesting to have concrete information as to how the transition was made in the second year of the reception class from teaching of Dutch as a second language to the Dutch teaching given in mainstream classes at the Dutch school.

There is some obscurity too about the content of teaching given in the mother tongue. Those running the project made no stipulations with regard to the choice of materials or the methods of teaching, and the results of the teaching were not discussed. The teaching material was obtained by the bilingual teachers direct from their countries of origin. The suitability of such material for teaching Turkish and Moroccan children in the Netherlands was not discussed. Nor was it stated how one might succeed in preparing the Turkish and Moroccan children for the material used in normal Dutch classes by teaching them with the aid of textbooks from their countries of origin. No transitional curricula were devised which started from the children's prior knowledge and took into account their specific situation as immigrants in the Netherlands. Experiments were carried out in the subject known as *wereldorientatie* ("world orientation"). (This represents a child-centred approach to the exploration of the immediate and - at a later stage - the wider natural environment of the children. Both the subject and the concomitant teaching strategies are fairly well established in Dutch schools.) A course was constructed by student teachers in which material was taken from Dutch textbooks and specially revised for the Turkish, Moroccan and Dutch staff. This might have been a starting point for evolving material that was suitable for the children. No further elucidation was given of the extent to which the selection was made according to the specific learning conditions and the special social situation of the migrant children. The difficulty of harmonizing the teaching content of the Dutch schools with what could be expected of the migrant children and the bilingual teachers was especially clear in the case of arithmetic, to which those in charge of the project paid particular attention. The original hope, that if the pupils were taught initially in the mother tongue, their achievement would be higher than in other reception classes, proved unjustified. In this case it was impossible to decide whether the failure in the teaching of arithmetic was due to the initial difficulty over materials, the new method, or the difficulties the bilingual teachers had in teaching according to this method. Probably in this case a Dutch method should have been introduced and the bilingual teachers made thoroughly familiar with it; and probably also additional material should have been used which would have led on to this method from the knowledge of arithmetic which the children already had on arrival and which was built upon in the first year. Finally, it is not clear how the joint teaching of Dutch and non-Dutch pupils was conducted. The pedagogical and didactic problems it entailed are hardly discussed at all.

In all areas there is a question mark against the concrete agreements and co-operation between the foreign and Dutch teachers. From the reports and interviews one gathers that the project leader spent a good deal of his time on contacts and discussions with the teachers, but that there was not enough precise joint planning of the teaching. Joint planning and agreement was made more difficult because of the Moroccan teacher's inadequate command of Dutch. It seems too that this teacher was not properly integrated into the project.

On the other hand, co-operation between the project leader and the Dutch staff was also not without its problems. There were complaints that conference sessions often dealt solely with matters of organization and produced no agreement on teaching content. Originally the role played by those teachers who had previously worked in the "flying brigades" was judged favourably, but this changed in the course of the pilot project. The demands made on their time by attending meetings and by having to remain at school during the dinner break, as well as by having to spend extra time on preparing lessons, represented a not inconsiderable load. There were also complaints that it was extremely difficult to take up the threads if one entered the project at a later stage because documentation of the teaching was lacking and there were no written materials. Moreover the continuing work of the school was put under strain because there was a change of head and some teachers left for personal reasons.

There was a further question as to whether the in-service training of the Dutch and non-Dutch staff, which was in line with the normal in-service training given in the Netherlands, was adequate for the work involved in the pilot project. Probably in the course of this training more systematic consideration should have been given to questions relating to the co-ordination of the content of the Turkish and Moroccan curricula with that of the Dutch school system.

All those involved stated that the reaction of the Dutch children during joint lessons was extremely positive. They greatly enjoyed learning new games and getting first-hand accounts of life in Morocco or Turkey. It was stressed that the children had achieved a high degree of tolerance and a great desire for mutual understanding. The ethnic minority children too felt at home in the situation created by the pilot project and became more sure of themselves and their own worth.

According to the Dutch teachers who paid home visits, the ethnic minority parents showed great interest in what was going on. In their own countries, they said, the parents were not used to visiting their children's schools and talking about their problems. This was superficially interpreted as lack of interest. However, if one visited their homes and talked to them about these problems one saw that they really were very interested. The Dutch parents too, though at first reserved, are said to have evinced a growing interest in the situation of the migrants and their children.

# Comparative analysis and assessment

## Introducing migrant pupils to the language and culture of the host country

### The importance attached to the task in the pilot projects

Several pilot projects explored the conditions under which ethnic minority pupils could be introduced to the language and culture of the host country. This was true especially of the Genk and Leiden projects, but also in some measure of those mounted in Paris and Bedford. In the latter two it was hoped that mother tongue teaching would have a positive effect on reception teaching. In the Paris project the intercultural teaching of indigenous and migrant pupils was also accorded a reception function. All these experiments will be discussed below in connection with the general conditions obtaining in the education systems of the countries concerned.

A cursory comparison of the pilot projects in Leiden and Genk shows how they were structured in accordance with the tasks they were meant to perform. The Leiden project was aimed solely at migrant pupils of primary school age (i.e. the first six years of schooling) who had only recently arrived in the Netherlands. The Genk project was concerned with all ethnic minority children, irrespective of how long they had lived in Belgium, and above all with second-generation migrants. In its last year it took in the last pre-school year and the first three years of primary schooling.

In Leiden, ethnically homogeneous preparatory classes of two years' duration were set up for Turkish and Moroccan children. There was collaboration with mainstream classes in the joint teaching of art and craft and technical subjects towards the end of the preparatory period in the transitional period teaching provided in neighbourhood schools. In Genk the bulk of the teaching took place in mainstream classes, though there was special extra provision for ethnic minority children. The initial group was multinational and contained a high proportion of ethnic minority children.

These differences were matched by differences of emphasis in the teaching programmes. In Leiden both Dutch and the mother tongue were used as media of instruction. In the teaching of factual subjects the latter had a bridging function. Only at a later stage was it replaced by Dutch as the teaching medium. In Genk the basic concept was joint teaching in mainstream classes for all indigenous and ethnic minority pupils. Here, as a matter of principle, even actual subjects were taught in the medium of Dutch, the chief function of mother tongue teaching being to support the mainstream teaching through providing a facility for revision and consolidation.

**Defining the task**

It is only theoretically possible to separate the task of introducing migrant pupils to the language and culture of the host country from the other tasks involved in the teaching of ethnic minority children. As has been shown, the Genk and Leiden projects both started by linking these tasks, though with differences of emphasis. The concepts behind the French and English projects also show an awareness of the need for a link. Moreover, in all countries discussions and experiments are to be found which are aimed at justifying or establishing such a link. There are various reasons for this: among these are a desire to ensure a uniform schooling for all children, to avoid duplication of teaching tasks, and to foster an intercultural exchange in the classroom. A comparison between the individual countries reveals that there were four ways in which the tasks were linked to varying degrees:

- by systematic instruction in the language of the host country without recourse to that of the pupils' countries of origin;

- by conducting the teaching in the language of the host country and using reception teaching as an aid;

- by including the mother tongue to provide psychological support for the reception teaching;

- by giving equal weight to the teaching of the migrants' mother tongue and culture and to introducing them to the language and culture of the host country.

Introducing ethnic minority children to the language and culture of the host country is understood as a process which takes place in the institutionally limited sphere of the school, though it is by no means restricted to school, since it is linked with the learning and socialization processes the child undergoes outside the school context. The interplay between school and out-of-school learning necessarily means extending the functions traditionally performed by the school into the social environment, for instance in the form of home-school liaison. Introducing the pupils to the indigenous culture thus pre-supposes and includes social integration. This connection between social, cultural and linguistic integration is generally appreciated, though different aspects may be emphasized. It is dubious whether there is such a thing as a culturally neutral education in individual teaching areas. We start from the premise that the way in which the growing child perceives the world is always culture-specific. It follows from this that it is too restrictive to limit the reception process to language teaching. We also start from the premise that it is essential to interpret the task under discussion not only statically, in relation to the children's present life (i.e. their school and out-of-school environment), but dynamically, in relation to their future.

We thus arrive at the following approaches to the task of teaching the language of the host country:

- organizing it according to spheres of application - the imparting of linguistic knowledge, factual knowledge, social skills, the values and norms of the host society;

- organizing it in terms of a time scale: initial admission to the education system of the host country for immigrants of school age newly arrived from abroad, for second-generation ethnic minority children, and transition from special provision to mainstream classes or to different schools or different levels of schooling;

- organizing it according to learning areas - school life, public life, free time, vocational preparation.

The formal aim of reception classes may be characterized by the term "participation", i.e. the ability to participate in the learning areas in question. The ambiguity of the word "ability" is intentional: it denotes the process of qualification, but also the aim of the process. Reception teaching is thus not completed when the young immigrant can move into a mainstream class: it must continue after this transition. This is not to imply that it should go on indefinitely: it should be deemed to be completed when the migrant children can take part in lessons with the same success as their indigenous peers.

## Problems of organization

### Differentiation or separation?

We must consider the question of the degree of specialization that is reached in reception teaching. At first sight, this question seems to imply a contradiction, since the political and practical pedagogical solutions start from several apparently conflicting educational concepts: a concern for the social integration of migrant children would favour their admission to mainstream classes as quickly and directly as possible, whereas a concern to help them over their particular difficulties would point to the planned provision of special support measures.

In the main, the regulations arising from the educational policies of the different host countries and the schemes introduced in them take account of both aspects, though to varying degrees and for various explicit reasons. Direct integration into mainstream teaching without transitional provision may be taken as indicating either insufficient appreciation of the problem or helplessness in the face of the problems posed by reception teaching.

Provision which does not involve classroom contacts between the migrant children and their indigenous contemporaries, or in which virtually no such contacts take place, or in which contact with the language and culture of the host country is possible only during a few lessons cannot be regarded as reception teaching. Such provision is justified by various arguments: that the pupils must first learn to "think in the language", that the possibility of their returning to their countries of origin must be kept open, that the parents' wishes must be respected, that to integrate the pupils into mainstream classes too early, too directly or too rapidly leads to unnecessary social tensions, etc.

In the majority of cases an attempt is made, by differentiating between the pupils, to enable migrant children to attend mainstream classes while paying attention to their specific situation. The extent to which such differentiation contributes to their integration depends on a number of different factors, among which the following deserve special mention:

- the proportion of ethnic minority children in relation to the number of their indigenous peers. It is sometimes maintained that if one wishes to adhere to the aim of "integration" the proportion of foreign pupils in a mainstream class should not exceed a certain percentage. The growth in the migrant population in the industrial conurbations has made a shambles of this argument, leaving only an educational helplessness which settles for classes made up etirely of foreign pupils.

- quantitative and qualitative parity in the teaching of foreign and indigenous pupils. To prevent the ethnic minority pupils from lagging behind in their academic achievement, they are taught factual subjects for a limited period in their first language, which is then gradually replaced by their second language. However, this does not appear to be a satisfactory way of accelerating the process of integration and reducing the workload on the children. An alternative is to set up crash courses in the language of the host country. Here, admittedly, there is a danger that the reception process will be limited to providing for language acquisition only. The pilot project in Genk accorded the first language the function of providing practice, revision and consolidation of what was taught in the mainstream classes. It became clear, however, that the indigenous children, who remained all the time in the care of their mainstream class teacher and did not have to attend mother tongue classes, made better progress.

Mainstream class teaching with internal and external differentiation seems to be most successful when the proportion of foreign pupils in the class is not too high. A clear advantage in this respect is enjoyed by education systems which, because of their organizational structures and staff provision, and because of the curricular freedom allowed to the schools or the individual teachers, enjoy greater flexibility in attending to the difficulties, abilities and needs of pupils with special needs. An important, though still not adequate pre-condition for this appears to be the provision that is made for instance in Belgium, Sweden, the Netherlands and Denmark for the employment of additional teachers when the proportion of foreign pupils in the school increases.

**The relation of reception teaching to levels of schooling**

In most countries reception teaching is linked mainly with primary schooling. This was true also of the pilot projects sponsored by the European Communities. The Genk project was expressly charged with exploring the transition from elementary to primary level (on these terms see p 33 above). The results of this experiment confirm the special importance of supporting ethnic minority children by means of elementary education, yet at the same time it is clear that some ethnic groups have reservations about subjecting their children at an early age to an unfamiliar kind of education away from the family. This reinforces the differences that exist in any case among migrant children. In this respect France is an exception: here almost 100% of ethnic minority children attend pre-school institutions. The reason is presumably that the French pre-school system comes entirely within the state sector, and so there are no reservations on grounds of religion such as one finds in many other countries, where pre-school education is in the hands of private bodies. On the question of the transition from elementary to primary schooling even the Genk project hardly offers any answers which go beyond the organizational links between the elementary and the primary level. Of some interest are the attempts to combine the final pre-school year with the first two primary years into a "play and learning group" in order to provide a basis for a flexible transition to mainstream teaching.

In all countries we may observe that, at secondary level, ethnic minority pupils are over-represented in those branches of schooling which provide short-term preparation for low-status and badly paid menial jobs. This reinforces the trend for schools in inner-city areas to become predominantly or exclusively institutions for ethnic-minority students. Apart from forms of schooling which separate the ethnic groups and can be regarded as extensions of the solutions adopted at primary level (such as one finds in North Rhine-Westphalia, Bavaria and Sweden) most countries provide separate facilities for migrant pupils who join the system late. In organizational terms these too are usually identical with solutions adopted at primary level, and it is seldom possible to discern curricular differences. Only in those cases where migrant pupils have access to transitional support facilities which are intended also for indigenous pupils with learning problems (e.g. in Great Britain) is it possible for them to be integrated more directly into the system. For ethnic minority pupils who have already completed compulsory education according to the legislation of their country of origin, but are still of school age according to that of the host country, there is the question of whether or not their foreign leaving qualifications should be recognized or taken into account. On this point there is a lack of conclusive experience.

With the emergence of a second generation of migrants, the importance of measures for the transition from primary to secondary education acquires increased importance, since even if ethnic minority children belong to the second generation and have successfully completed their primary schooling, they need further support on moving into secondary school. This obviously applies not only to the transition to the more demanding branches of secondary education (e.g. grammar school), but also to those which offer a preparation for working life. (Cf. for example the Dutch institution of the *Internationale schakelklas* as a form of intensive support for foreign pupils, including latecomers to the system.)

So far, the measures for the transition from secondary education to vocational training or for entry into school or industrial training schemes have not been satisfactorily developed. Even where the legal pre-conditions for setting up special forms of teaching already exist, the necessary didactic concepts are lacking, and the real successes (the provision of training places or jobs) are negligible. Facilities which were originally designed to provide some support for these young people do as a matter of fact degenerate into mere parking institutions where they are confined until they reach school leaving age and are thus "ready for unemployment" (e.g. schemes such as the *Berufs- vorbereitungsjahr* - "work preparation year" - in the Federal Republic of Germany). Hence, ethnic minority pupils are increasingly unlikely, the older they get, to attend school beyond the minimum leaving age.

### Problem areas in teaching

### The function of individual subjects and learning areas in the reception process

It is axiomatic that the language of the host country is central to any programme of reception teeaching. The merit of the pilot projects in Leiden and Genk lies precisely in the fact that they went beyond this self-evident truth and focussed on the functions of other subjects in the reception process. For there is a real danger that the claims of these other subejcts will be curtailed, if not ignored, in favour of the acquisition of the language of the immigration country. There is also a danger in the merely administrative establishment of new subjects for reception teaching if their place in the curriculum is not clearly defined and the teachers not properly equipped to teach them. Examples are the intensive teaching of Dutch (*Intensief Nederlands*) in the Genk project, and also the joint teaching given to German and foreign pupils in the Federal Republic. The Austrian regulation which requires that a

168

syllabus should be submitted for approval before any organizational measure is approved deserves special mention here.

In addition to the language teaching itself, almost all subjects should be regarded as important in introducing the pupils to the language and culture of the host country. It seems that mother tongue teaching, quite apart from ensuring that the ethnic minority children acquire a knowledge of their own languages, has a favourable influence on the reception process in that it can exercise a stabilizing effect on their whole personality. Such an effect, which is reported in connection with a number of projects, seems altogether plausible, even if not strictly proven. In preparatory classes, subject teaching is often conducted in the mother tongue for a transitional period. The success of such teaching can also not be tested. What is clear, however, is that it does not prevent foreign pupils from lagging behind the indigenous pupils. To avoid the extra load which mother tongue teaching imposes on the children, an attempt was made in Genk to give the mother tongue lessons a practice and revision function in relation to the reception and mainstream teaching. However, this can be achieved only at the expense of the language maintenance function of mother tongue teaching.

The teaching of artistic and technical subjects is often thought to be particularly well suited to providing an initial contact between the pupils in preparatory classes and indigenous pupils of their own age. Experience with joint teaching in various parts of the Federal Republic, however, reveals special difficulties which arise when an attempt is made to get the pupils to do anything more than "sit next to one another". These difficulties result, in the first place, from underestimating the importance of language in the teaching of these subjects, and this inevitably has a detrimental effect on the children's performance. On the other hand, there is no doubt that such subjects do afford special opportunities for fostering social relations between the various groups of children, though excessive emphasis on this function can lead to a clash with the claims of the factual content of the lessons. It is important, especially in these subjects, for suitable bilingual teachers to be on hand to co-operate with the indigenous staff. Without such co-operation the cultural and social tensions between the different ethnic groups may easily be aggravated.

Didactic concepts of reception teaching

The development of didactic concepts for reception teaching is in the early stages in all countries. Syllabuses are mainly confined to attempts to relieve the teaching of some of the ballast or to establish starting points for co-ordinating the curricula of the host country and the pupils' countries of origin. The reception teaching in the Genk project started from a concept of comprehensive teaching to which the individual subjects and learning areas were related. This experiment, however, needs further detailed discussion before any conclusions can be drawn.

Of the many individual teaching problems, the following seem at present to be most in need of further discussion and experimentation:

- the transition from situation-related introductory teaching to subject-related support teaching;

- support for migrant children with varying degrees of integration by means of a curriculum which will allow them to join the learning process at different stages of achievement (spiral curriculum);

- the role of the first language in the learning process (bilingual learning, contrastive learning, etc);

- the increasingly pressing need, with the emergence of the second generation of immigrants, to decide on the transition from foreign-language to first-language methods in the teaching of the second language;

- the co-ordination of the processes of learning to read and write in the migrants' first and second languages.

## Teaching and learning materials

The didactic problems are directly reflected in the development of materials. In most countries there is a wealth of materials for the acquisition of the second language, yet there is a dearth of materials which do more than provide an introduction to the new situation in which the children find themselves living. For other subjects and learning areas too there is a general lack of suitable materials, especially such as are sufficiently differentiated to be used with the target groups.

There is so far no reflection of the advantages and disadvantages of the various ways of developing new materials. In all countries, materials for reception teaching seem to have been developed on a commercial basis, since publishers have recognized the strength of the market. Only exceptionally do the state education authorities appear to have given any guidance. The development of materials is often closely linked with educational practice. Thus, in Great Britain it is largely in the hands of the teachers themselves. In the main, however, the task seems to place an excessive burden on the teaching staff. Most of them lack the necessary training and experience, and they often have no chance to make up for this lack by collaborating with experts or undergoing in-service training geared to this end. However, it is also a question of how many demands one can make on the teachers, for after all the preparation of lessons for ethnic minority pupils makes far greater demands on their time than the preparation of lessons for indigenous children.

## Mother tongue teaching

### The importance attached to the task in the pilot projects

It was primarily the pilot projects in France and England that were
charged with finding answers to the question of how to teach the
language and culture of the pupils' countries of origin. In Paris, all
the institutional regulations in the pilot project can be related to
this task, and the same is true of the Bedford project. In Belgium and
the Netherlands the teaching conducted in the mother tongue was at
first conceived as having an integrative and transitional function. In
the Dutch pilot project this was to be performed by the use of the
mother tongue - in decreasing measure - as the medium for the teaching
of mathematics and other subjects, and also by the joint teaching
conducted by Dutch and bilingual staff; running side by side with these
was the mother tongue and culture teaching given by the bilingual
teachers. In the Belgian project the lessons conducted in the mother
tongue were conceived primarily as support and remedial teaching
related to that which was given in mainstream classes. Even so, this
did not prevent mother tongue teaching from acquiring a measure of
independeence and hence taking on the function of language and culture
teaching.

In a cross-national perspective, mother tongue teaching may be
classified into the following five types:

- mother tongue teaching sponsored by provate bodies, mainly parents'
  associations or other immigrant organizations;

- mother tongue and culture courses run by the consulates, usually on
  the basis of bilateral cultural agreements, organized in collaboration with the authorities of the host country, and conducted
  by teachers appointed and paid by the consulates;

- mother tongue teaching incorporated into the regular timetable of
  the school in the host country and given by teachers paid partly by
  the consulates and partly by the local authorities;

- mother tongue teaching conducted outside normal school hours, for
  which the host country bears financial and curricular responsibility;

- mother tongue teaching within the framework of ethnically homogeneous preparatory classes and special forms of schooling designed
  for ethnic minority pupils;

Finally, in addition to these five types, we should mention the general
regulation obtaining in Sweden whereby all pupils from migrant families
have a right to two weekly lessons in their "home languages".

We start from the premise that, from an educational point of view, the provision of mother tongue teaching for ethnic minority pupils is fundamentally meaningful and desirable. The arguments in favour of this premise bear upon the ethnic minority child as an individual. The Swedish example demonstrates that it is possible, within the framework of a highly developed education system, to give reality to the individual's right to mother tongue teaching, and this to a very large extent. It should therefore be the first requirement of any plans for further development that all ethnic minority pupils should be assured access to instruction in their mother tongues. Were such a right to be generally recognized, the question of who should provide the facilities would be a matter of minor consequence. An obvious corollary of such a development would be that the authorities of the countries concerned would have to assume responsibility for mother tongue teaching. It is, however, quite conceivable that such a right could also be secured through teaching provided by independent bodies and funded wholly or partly by the state.

In our opinion the chief function of mother tongue teaching should not be to preserve a way of life governed by inherited norms and values, nor should its chief aim be to maintain the possibility of the migrants' returning to their countries of origin: it should be seen rather as an educational provision relating to the pupils' life in the host country. Thos forms of mother tongue teaching for which the host country takes responsibility are more in line with this last objective than those which are determined by the official representatives of the countries of origin.

**Defining the task**

The value attached to mother tongue teaching in the education systems of the various countries, as it appears in reality, should be understood as reflecting not so much the present stage in the development of educational thinking, but rather the present stage in the conflicts between linguistic and cultural groups. The host countries have an interest in linguistic and cultural adaptation, as they are bound to be concerned, for economic reasons, with preserving the uniformity of their education systems and, for reasons of social policy, with minimizing the potential for conflict. However, counter-forces tend to develop, on the one hand in the schools, which have an interest in the smooth running of the system, and on the other among the indigenous parents, who fear a lowering of standards when the classes their children attend contain a substantial proportion of foreign children. Both of these work in favour of a tendency to relegate the schooling of ethnic minority children and young people to separate groups, and these groups can very easily acquire a degree of independence, engendering "mother tongue features" within the host country's schools. The schools and the indigenous parents come to ally themselves with the ethnic minority parents, who are interested in their children's acquiring the language they themselves speak - in preserving the integrity of their families and their self-esteem. Admittedly, it may be observed that as a rule most migrant parents set greater store by the academic success of their children than by their maintaining a command of the mother tongue. The exceptions are those politically articulate ethnic minority groups who to a greater or lesser extent demand the provision of pure mother tongue education in the host country. An interest in the acquisition of the national language (which is not necessarily identical with the children's mother tongue!) also exists as a rule among the official representatives of the migrants' countries of origin. This is clearly true of European and Arab states with emigrant citizens; it is not true - or not to any great extent - of the Asian and African states.

Given this complex web of interests, the pilot projects had the opportunity to give various definitions of the aims of mother tongue teaching. The Paris project, in its official statement of aims, was intended to combine those aims which were most likely to find public or institutional recognition. In addition to its intercultural objectives, it laid emphasis on the general educational goals which should be attained or promoted through mother tongue teaching ("development of the child's personality"); it also stressed its reception function ("freer access to the language and values of French society"), adding the further aim of keeping open the possibility of the child's returning to his own country. In practice we found a wide spectrum of approaches to the tasks of mother tongue teaching among the bilingual teachers involved in this project, and these came to exercise a decisive influence on its actual conduct. They ranged from an abbreviated form of primary mother tongue teaching, modelled on that which was given in the pupils' home countries, to attempts to come to terms with the language learning situation of the immigrant children, and finally to a consistent orientation of mother tongue teaching towards intercultural objectives - in one case to an attempt to use it primarily as a means to ensure academic success for migrant children in the French school system. The official statement of aims for the pilot project in Bedford likewise gave priority to general educational objectives, while at the same time adding reception objectives. The experimental syllabus for mother tongue teaching underlined in particular the idea of general support for the children's linguistic development (in the sense of "compensatory" or "emancipatory" language programmes). Here too there were clearly differing interpretations in the minds of the bilingual teachers, though these were not as wide-ranging as in Paris. They went some way beyond the official objectives in that they laid stress on the pupils' acquisition of their national language (Italian) or the teaching of certain elements of the culture of the society the children had come from. The relation of the teaching to the children's situation in the host country was not all-pervading, but on the whole it was more conspicuous than in the French project. In the Dutch pilot project, on the other hand, the teaching of the mother tongue was clearly directed towards the pupils' country of origin; this language teaching was not obviously related to the rest of the teaching

173

given in the medium of the mother tongue, which had a transitional reception function. In the Belgian project, by contrast, there was a continuing debate on the relation between mother tongue teaching and its reception functions; even here, however, language maintenance came to some extent to be seen as an end in itself, asserting itself over its transitional reception function.

The principles that were followed in the pilot projects corresponded in varying degrees to national policies relating relating to ethnic minorities. In Great Britain the task of mother tongue and culture teaching is seen almost exclusively as a matter for the minorities themselves; to this extent the Bedford project represented a significant departure. In Belgium too, for constitutional reasons, there is no provision for mother tongue teaching at state schools; the emphasis laid on its reception fucntion was part and parcel of the strategy of approaching the new tasks with care and circumspection. In France, by contrast, mother tongue teaching is seen as having its own educational justification, its function in language maintenance and reception being regarded as equally legitimate. The pilot project in Paris followed this principle, though it also extended it by including the notion of its having intercultural functions in the education of ethnic minority children. In the Netherlands, finally, the teaching of the language and culture of the pupils' countries of origin is seen as an independent educational task existing side by side with that of introducing them to the Dutch language and Dutch culture. The way in which the mother tongue was taught in the Leiden project was in line with this twofold approach.

The results of the pilot projects show that mother tongue teaching may contribute effectively to the psychic and social stabilization of ethnic minority pupils and hence to the successful development of their ethnic identity. It is very unlikely, however, that this aim can be permanently assured if mother tongue teaching is understood merely as a vehicle for short-term reception schemes or for subject learning at schools in the host country. This suggests that tuition in the pupils' mother tongue and culture should be defined as an autonomous task, having its own educational value *vis-à-vis* other subjects and learning areas. It is admittedly necessary to defend such a view against various misconceptions and misinterpretations. The final report of the French pilot project contains statements to the effect that, in the social environment of the project, the introduction of mother tongue teaching aroused fears among migrant parents that this might be the prelude to forced repatriation. Clearer statements of aims and more intensive home-school liaison should help to dispel such fears. To a lesser extent this applies also to the fears of some ethnic minority parents that mother tongue teaching may cause their children to miss out on the normal teaching and thus jeopardize their academic success. On this point the pilot projects have shown that satisfactory solutions can be reached by co-operation, even though, in the nature of things, there can be no perfect solution. It has to be accepted that there will be an extra mental burden on the pupils and extra calls on their time. It is therefore necessary to ensure that this additional educational task is sufficiently appreciated within the school system and society at large to ensure that the principle of equality of opportunity is not impaired. To achieve this, the pupils' performance in mother tongue classes should be awarded marks and noted in the normal school reports; these marks should be taken into consideration when decisions are made about their moving up into a higher class or orienting them to different branches of secondary education; command of the mother tongue should also be fully recognized within the framework of foreign language provision at secondary level. In the wider social context it would be useful to examine the extent to which job profiles can be devised in which a prospective employee's knowledge of the language of his country of origin would constitute a valuable qualification, and the extent to which a linguistic component can be built into the vocational training courses leading to such jobs.

Some of the countries of origin (e.g. Portugal, Yugoslavia, Greece and Italy) have issued their own guidelines on the teaching of their citizens abroad. Now, however, even these countries are increasingly taking the view that, because of the different language learning situation and different school organization, mother tongue teaching abroad cannot be seen simply as an abridged or watered-down version of the teaching given in the home country. This development is due not so much to the unfavourable learning situation in the host country as to the realization that mother tongue teaching ought not to be oriented to a way of life that is known to the pupils only through stories or holiday visits. Instead, it should be related primarily to the part played by their languages in the host country and to elements of what is - from the viewpoint of the host country - and alternative culture. Hence it should contribute to improved communication within the family, to the self-presentation and self-realization of the ethnic group in the host country, to the strengthening and developing of real ties between migrant families and their countries of origin, and to the continuing evolution of their national culture in the host country itself. Here the conditions are very varied, depending above all on the size of the linguistic minority groups in particular countries. It should also be clear, therefore, that the objectives outlined here cannot simply be understood as reflecting a given linguistic and cultural situation; their aim is rather to respond in a positive way to the existing linguistic and cultural diversity and so to contribute to the transformation of the host societies into multilingual and multicultural societies.

As educationists, however, we must not ignore the fact that there really are re-emigration movements, even though they do not involve large numbers, and that these create difficult educational situations which make it necessary to provide special help for pupils who intend to return home. Admittedly, these are problems which in our opinion cannot be solved by a kind of mother tongue teaching that is geared to the remote contingency of a return migration. They can be solved only where they actually arise, i.e. in the schools in the pupils' countries of origin, should they ever return there. The development of measures to deal with this eventuality might well be a joint responsibility of the host countries and the countries of origin. Something has already been achieved with regard to recognition by the latter of certificates and leaving qualifications obtained by their nationals abroad, but so far there has been little institutional provision and educational help (in the shape of support facilities, teaching materials or teacher training) for those pupils who do return home.

Linked with the demand for a basic orientation of mother tongue teaching to life in the host country is an issue which featured in both the French and English pilot projects - the problem of how to decide what language the children should be taught when the national standard language of the country of origin is not identical with the real mother tongue spoken in their families. To us it seems obvious that, if mother tongue teaching is to achieve its general educational objectives, it must start from the language the pupils actually speak and the living culture existing in their families. In the case of dialects, the difficulties that arise call for particular teaching methods, but the situation is different in the case of minority languages which are not officially recognized, since these represent a political problem - or in the case of varieties which exist only in speech and thus are linked to sociolinguistic issues that are not yet fully understood. However, it would be necessary to decide in the case of each language whether and to what extent transitions from the actual spoken language to the national standard language could be devised, especially if this could enhance the pupils' job prospects and were in accordance with their parents' educational expectations.

## Continuity of mother tongue teaching

Both the French and the British pilot projects were limited to primary education, and both recognized that there was a problem in continuing mother tongue teaching after primary level. In the French project there is only one report, from the school at Villejuif, that it had proved possible to arrange for a group of pupils to continue with Italian lessons at secondary school. In principle the French system provides many pupils with the opportunity to offer their mother tongue as a foreign language, since theoretically the number of foreign language options is comparatively large. In practice, however, this facility is severely restricted. In the first place, the number of secondary schools offering the relevant foreign languages is extremely limited, since the courses are intended only for French pupils, and therefore no non-French teachers can be appointed. Consequently, even where migrant pupils have the chance to attend such a course, there is no guarantee of didactic continuity, since their French classmates have to start the language from scratch. Only a very small number of foreign pupils, for whom the language of their country of origin is no longer their mother tongue, can really profit from such teaching in the sense of acquiring a knowledge of the language.

Within the British system the pilot project at Bedford endeavoured to ensure the continuation of mother tongue teaching at secondary level, though this proved possible only for a small group of Italian children who were enrolled at a private school.

## Composition and differentiation of learning groups

In all the pilot projects - and in most of the countries compared in the present study this appears to be the rule - the mother tongue groups were fairly heterogeneous. Where a minimum class size was officially laid down, this heterogeneity resulted from the need to bring together as many pupils as possible to make up the required numbers. Such a need may arise even where there is no such stipulation, since pupils belonging to one ethnic group may be scattered throughout a number of schools, so that the migrant pupils forming a class at any one school are bound to come from diverse backgrounds. Quite apart from this, however, we are faced with the problem of what criteria to use for differentiation. If children are grouped according to age, one may have to accept widely differing degrees of competence in the mother tongue. If, on the other hand, they are grouped according to linguistic competence, one may have to accept disparities of age. Both procedures were tried out in the pilot projects, and both led to difficulties. In certain notable cases it was shown that, if the groups were not excessively large, the difficulties could be overcome by varying the teaching methods (and in some cases employing a helper), but most bilingual teachers find it fairly difficult to plan and conduct differentiated teaching of this kind. There is a need here for specific in-service training.

It is impossible to decide, on empirical grounds, whether it is preferable to differentiate pupils according to age or according to linguistic competence. As a rule it will be found that there are practical reasons for adopting the former course, whereas theoretical considerations would favour the latter. Ideally we may distinguish between those pupils for whom mother tongue teaching represents a continuation of schooling already begun in their home countries (first generation), those for whom it represents a further development of the language used only in their families (second generation), and those who have to be introduced to the language (third generation). These three categories present very different teaching problems, and it would seem easier to teach groups with a wide age-range but with basically similar learning needs than to pursue very different aims in a group with no disparities of age.

**The number of weekly lessons**

The pilot project in Paris may be regarded as having demonstrated that three lessons a week are not enough to achieve measurable progress over a limited period. On the other hand it was reported from Bedford, where five weekly periods of mother tongue teaching were given, that appreciable progress was achieved. Of course such an assertion has to be interpreted with some caution. All the same, we would advocate that as much time should be given to mother tongue teaching as is allocated to a main subject in the host country (e.g. the first foreign language at secondary level). Only in this way will the right conditions be created for full recognition of the pupils' academic achievement in their own languages. It seems to us possible that, if other conditions are also improved, the aim of achieving biligualism need not remain as utopian as it largely seems at present.

**Timetabling problems**

In all countries the provision of mother tongue teaching raises certain timetabling problems. We may distinguish four models for solving them:

The introduction of mother tongue teaching into the timetable is easiest in those educational systems which already possess well developed schemes of differentiated and individualized support teaching. Such conditions are to be found above all in the Scandinavian countries, where mother tongue teaching can be run in parallel with numerous other options.

The second model - viz. incorporating mother tongue teaching into the normal timetable - entails greater difficulties. It means taking the children of one ethnic minority out of their classes during schooltime and bringing them together for a mother tongue course. This was the model adopted in the British and French pilot projects. The difficulties in this case stem mainly from the fact that the pupils miss out on some of the regular teaching: the timetables of all the classes involved have to take mother tongue teaching into account in order to ensure that the pupils do not miss lessons in subjects that are central to the curriculum. It is not an acceptable alternative to sacrifice those lessons which, though considered "less important", are most popular with the pupils. The pilot projects have shown that, given good will all round, solutions can be found which minimize the loss of vital teaching. In this connection one should mention the Belgian experiment in running mother tongue and mainstream classes in parallel, so that all the pupils could learn the same things, but in different languages. However, this solution cannot be put into practice without difficulties. It requires very precise agreements between the teachers involved - which means additional calls on their time - and even then it cannot be guaranteed that the ethnic minority children will make the same progress as their indigenous peers: it is just not possible for the former to acquire a certain quantity of factual knowledge and a certain quantity of linguistic knowledge in the same time that the latter spend solely on factual learning. A similar experiment at one of the schools in the French project was seen as a failure by those taking part for precisely this reason. The solutions found in the French and British pilot projects are directed rather at changing the timetables of the classes involved in such a way that the lessons affected belong neither to the most important nor to the most popular subjects. Yet even these solutions failed to prevent irregular attendance and fluctuating numbers at mother tongue classes.

The problems are somewhat different when mother tongue teaching takes place within the framework of separate reception classes. The loss of basic teaching may not be directly obvious, but it exists all the same. Indeed, such preparatory classes do not as a rule enable pupils to make fast enough progress in the rest of the curriculum for a perfectly smooth transition to the mainstream class.

The fourth model consists in placing the mother tongue teaching outside the normal timetable. An argument that is usually advanced against this solution is that it overburdens the pupils. In those systems where most of the teaching takes place in the mornings there are additional problems regarding school transport, meals and pastoral care. Undoubtedly any method of integrating mother tongue teaching into the normal timetable with no loss of essential teaching is to be preferred to a model which involves additional lessons. On the other hand, none of the attempted solutions, in our opinion, gets round the need to devote extra time to the strictly linguistic function of mother tongue teaching. We would suggest that it is preferable to provide extra lessons outside the normal timetable rather than simply to accept the loss of other teaching. For the spread of different solutions encountered at individual schools participating in the pilot projects is likely to come up against substantial difficulties. In our opinion it is possible to keep the additional burden on ethnic minority pupils within reasonable bounds, as is demonstrated by the "parallel" forms of mother tongue teaching which enjoy some measure of success.

## Problem areas in teaching

### Language learning goals

It is striking that the methods employed in mother tongue teaching in the host country are less well developed than those employed in second language teaching. Teachers and their advisers often try to transfer existing language teaching models to the teaching of the mother tongue. Here we may distinguish between those models which are primarily oriented to the methods used in the pupils' countries of origin, those which adopt notions of mother tongue teaching current in the the host country, and those which employ "normal" methods of foreign language teaching. Within the first model the primary aim is to teach the

179

structure of the standard written language. From the point of view of the language system the main emphasis is placed on enlarging the pupils' vocabulary. Within the second model we find objectives relating above all to the connection between thinking and speaking. Here the main emphasis lies more in the area of the spoken than the written language. It is generally expected that the development of the children's spoken command of their mother tongues will have a positive effect on their progress in their second language. Within the third model more prominence is given to systematic learning goals, the teaching being geared largely to the standard language; here too the spoken word takes precedence over the written.

Only in the British pilot project was an attempt made to draw up a detailed and binding statement of objectives for language learning. The experimental syllabus placed the emphasis almost exclusively on the general promotion of linguistic competence. Nevertheless, the bilingual teachers still had considerable scope in deciding what objectives to pursue, with the result that it is not yet possible to judge this teaching concept on the basis of experimental results. In the French pilot project the bilingual teachers had even greater scope. Here we find all three models co-existing, though they are not formulated in detail. Finally, the Belgian project likewise did not lead to an original teaching concept; here the orientation of the teaching towards non-linguistic subjects led in particular to an emphasis on vocabulary extension. Insofar as the special features of mother tongue teaching in the host country were discussed at all, they appear to have consisted primarily in a need to pitch the teaching aims rather lower than in the home country.

It is clear that there are here a number of areas requiring further enquiry and development. What is so far lacking is above all detailed knowledge of the language situation of the migrant families and effective instruments for establishing the pupils' competence in their mother tongues. Only when this lack has been made good will it be possible to formulate valid aims for particular learning groups. These aims ought to make it possible to plan for step-by-step progress in learning and be precise enough for such progress to be monitored. Undoubtedly these objectives will vary according to the language involved, the migrant generation to which the pupils belong, and the ages of the pupils, but it ought to be possible to define the degree of difficulty attaching to individual linguistic skills and to use this in measuring the pupils' competence and progress. This work will require co-operation between teachers, educationists, linguists and language teaching experts from the host countries and the pupils' countries of origin.

**Methods and media**

There is even more variety in the decisions made by the bilingual teachers over the choice of particular methods of teaching. Although as a rule only the mother tongue itself was used as the medium for mother tongue teaching, we did observe situations in which bilingual teachers helped the pupils by resorting to the language of the host country. It is true that some bilingual teachers tend to stand in front of the class and address the pupils formally to a greater extent than the indigenous teachers, but we also found group work, partner work, role-playing, project teaching, etc. Above all some bilingual teachers tend to set great store by verbal knowledge, but we also saw them working with visual materials, bringing in artistic and dramatic activities, reading stories, etc. What matters most here is that the bilingual teachers should be familiarized with the widest possible spectrum of teaching methods.

Mother tongue teaching in the host country constitutes a quite new and original task which no teacher should be expected to carry out without extra assistance. The development of teaching materials thus acquires considerable importance. The British pilot project has shown that in this sphere admirable results can be achieved by the teachers themselves. At the same time, however, it illustrates the limits of such self-help: in order to ensure the necessary breadth in the development of materials it would be necessary to complement the work done "at grass roots level" by initiatives taken at the centre, which could at the same time ensure an effective dissemination of such materials.


## Intercultural teaching

When we compare different countries it becomes clear, from considering the value attached to the teaching of the languages of the host countries and those of the pupils' countries of origin, that the development of school provision has been strongly influenced by the notions which underlie immigration policy. Those countries which were familiar, through historical experience, with the phenomenon of international migration movements or which started from the assumption that the immigrants would remain for a considerable time, perhaps even permanently, were also the countries which made the first moves towards a policy of integration in their education systems. This found expression especially in the development of organizational models for accelerating the acquisition of the language of the host country and for the quickest possible integration of the migrant children into mainstream schooling.

The languages of the migrants were virtually ignored or relegated to a marginal position and their cultures banned from normal school activities. The contention that such covert stigmatization of these cultures in schools is at least one cause of the integration problems encountered by the children is central to the "intercultural option" (Porcher): in order to improve the school achievement of ethnic minority children it is vital that their cultural heritage should no longer be ignored, but finally recognized, that it should no longer be

181

treated as a blemish, but accorded an equal place in the everyday life of the school.

The intercultural perspective is not confined to extending the catalogue of measures that are designed to facilitate the reception of migrant children and improve their educational opportunities. It is directed in equal measure at the indigenous children, whom it is intended to encourage to come to terms with the situation created by the presence of ethnic minority children in their midst and turn it to their own benefit. It does not matter whether this situation is to be found in the classroom, outside school, or in "the wider society" after schooling is over. It is not just a question of educating the children in a vague way to be "open, tolerant and understanding" towards those who are different from themselves: on the contrary, the second idea underlying the "intercultural option" is that, given the fact that a multicultural situation already exists, educational activity cannot be confined simply to enabling the ethnic minority children to come to terms with it, but that it is equally important to enable the indigenous children to do the same. To put the matter in somewhat extreme terms: the indigenous children too need a form of "reception teaching", and intercultural teaching is intended to cater for this need.

As a demand for the development of new kinds of educational provision for indigenous and foreign children alike, the "intercultural option" ultimately relates to the school itself as an institution. It seeks to create an awareness of the fact that the systems of norms existing in schools are themselves culturally determined, to examine them and broaden their scope in order to give all the children – majority and minority alike – opportunities for development which do not stop short at adaptation to the norms of the dominant majority and its educational institutions.

For this is the fourth and fundamental thesis of the intercultural approach to education: the conflict between cultures is already on, and it is taking place in the schools too. The "intercultural option" demands of the school no more and no less than that it should open itself up to this conflict – that it should give both sides a chance to speak.

These reflections should not be misconstrued as implying that intercultural education has reached the stage where it can operate with clear-cut, watertight notions, or that there are ready-made models to be put into practice and ready-made criteria to be applied. On the contrary, very little has been achieved so far. This is no reason to dwell on the inadequacies of the few experiences that have so far been acquired or to reproach them with being wildly empirical. As Porcher (1981, p 46) rightly remarks, these experiments, some of which will be discussed below, can lay claim to the merit of having gone beyond the mere affirmation of principles and having ventured to give them concrete form.

The danger that, even in intercultural teaching, ethnic minority children might be forced into the status of objects – being talked about without being free to speak for themselves – was avoided in the Paris project from the beginning, since the topics that were treated were not oriented to the problems of migration, but related to a longer historical perspective within which the *relations* between the cultures were taken as a theme for discussion. This was achieved mainly by making sure that the intercultural activities were planned and conducted jointly by the Spanish teacher and the French teacher, additional preparation work being done separately in Spanish lessons and French lessons. Conceived in this way, it was able to perform many of the functions of intercultural teaching:

- It taught the children of both groups (for instance in the teaching unit "Napoleon in Spain") a basic historical vocabulary which enabled them to arrive at an understanding of the relations between the two cultures, thus going beyond an unconnected confrontation along the lines of abstract comparisons between cultures and encouraging children to reflect upon their own position from that of another culture;

- it gave the migrant pupils the chance to experience their "differentness" in a positive way, by capitalizing on it at school, and thus to enhance their self-esteem;

- it gave the French pupils an impression of the dignity and vitality of the foreign culture;

- it created, as it were, a natural, i.e. specifically educational link between mother tongue teaching and the mainstream curriculum, thus preventing the mother tongue class from developing into a kind of ghetto within the school;

- it was at the same time a means of making the French teacher aware of the special situation of the migrant pupils – of providing her, in other words, with a kind of school-based in-service training;

- by requiring the headmistress and the whole staff to collaborate in solving difficulties of timetabling and classroom accommodation, it obliged the staff to adopt new forms of co-operation and co-ordination, thus highlighting the fact that it was the responsibility of the staff as a whole to deal with the migrant children's problems;

- it motivated the French teachers by introducing them to new learning experiences in the spheres of both teaching practice and content.

These achievements of intercultural teaching at one school involved in the Paris project would, of course, have been inconceivable had it not been for the initiative, advice and guidance provided by CREDIF. Moreover, the personality of the Spanish teacher, herself a second-generation immigrant, undoubtedly facilitated her collaboration with the French teachers – and this factor in the relative success of the experiment could not automatically reproduced in other schemes.

One criticism that has to be made of this particular experiment, however, is that not enough was made of the opportunity afforded by the participation of the Spanish teacher to offer an authentic and authoritative interpretation of migrant culture in a teaching project that was concerned with relations between the two cultures in the host country. More convincing results might have been achieved by a more "child-centred" approach, one that was related more directly to the real-life situation of the children involved.

A step in this direction has been made by the Henri Wallon School at Fontenay-sous-Bois, an experimental school which, under the guidance of IRFED, das developed a concept of "geography and history teaching with an intercultural perspective" (Padrun 1979, p 15).

Two groups of children, French and Portuguese (it is not recorded whether other nationalities were represented at the school), were first asked to bring to school various items relating to their family history (identity cards, documents, pictures, letters, etc), then to arrange them systematically and use them to establish their own family trees, as well as the family tree of the class as a whole, which was then discussed, from the most points of view, in a series of lessons planned and conducted jointly by French and Portuguese teachers (IRFED 1978, pp 74-76).

Here again we see a teaching concept that could not have been evolved without advice from outside. This was due not simply to the efforts involved in obtaining teaching materials and information, but even more to the difficulty of developing categories for analysing the material and presenting it in class. Intercultural education, so IRFED maintains, can no longer use teaching, especially in a subject like history, as a vehicle for the inculcation of patterns of moral and civic behaviour, but must generate reflection on such patterns. The subject matter for the intercultural teaching of history is not a corpus of self-contained knowledge; hence, the best way to teach it is through class projects, since this is a way to activate the pupils and exploir their curiosity (IRFED 1978, p 77). This concept of intercultural history teaching has yet another component which is not expressly mentioned by IRFED: it takes as its theme not so much the "history of states and statesmen", but the history of the peoples and their conditions of life in both countries, for in this way it is able to create a plausible link between historical knowledge and the pupils' experience of present-day life.

This particular school went a step further by providing lessons in Portuguese which were given by the Portuguese teachers to the French pupils (and teachers!) of classes comprising both nationalities. It is of course clear, considering the different learning conditions of the pupils, that the demand for a curriculum with identical coverage for all pupils comes up against certain basic obstacles. Hence, even this instruction in Portuguese was conceived as an introductory course, taking up only one lesson a week – though admittedly lasting throughout the whole of the primary school period (Padrun 1979, p 15). The main point of the scheme was not so much to teach the French children Portuguese as to enhance the status of Portuguese culture in the minds of all those connected with the school, including the French parents, who had to be convinced – not without some difficulty – that it was a worthwhile undertaking (Padrun 1979 p 16). A somewhat similar model, which we need not describe in detail, is run by a school in the XXth *arrondissement* in Paris; this is an introduction to modern Arabic for the French pupils (*Projet d'éducation interculturelle 1977*).

Finally, literacy programmes were set up at Fontenay for Portuguese migrant workers; these were open to all Portuguese residents in the town (Padrun 1979, p 16). Thus, by becoming a local communication centre for migrants, the school was taking seriously – in more ways than one – the notion of opening itself up to the world outside it: not only did it give the pupils the chance to explore the outside world under the guidance of the teacher – it let the outside world cross its threshold. Constructing such a comprehensive model of an intercultural school is patently a long-term undertaking which calls for extraordinary material and personal resources, and it clearly cannot be generalized in present circumstances. All the same, it does show clearly and convincingly what prospects and opportunities are open to intercultural education.

One proviso has to be made, however, on the basis of the experience gained in Fontenay and Paris: intercultural teaching – and to an even greater extent the building up of intercultural schools – involves deciding in favour of one of the cultures represented in the school. If a potentially limitless proliferation of teaching matter is to be avoided, if a true social and pedagogical integration of bilingual teachers is to be achieved, and if, finally, the development of migrant culture in the school is to go beyond mere token gestures, it will be necessary to decide where to place the emphasis. One possibility would be to establish bi-national schools or classes. The experience of the Paris project shows that the distribution of emphasis in a school or class need not be such as to exclude children of a third ethnic group from participating in classroom activities. On the contrary, one may surmise that even these pupils have more to gain from intercultural teaching, in the way of possibilities for development and activation, than is afforded merely by the teaching give in mainstream classes which are geared to the "normal" curriculum of the host country.

An account of the practical efforts that are being made to introduce intercultural teaching cannot pass over the concepts that have been developed - though more discussed than realized - in England under the designation "the multi-cultural curriculum", although from what one can gather from the literature, from conversations, and from visiting English schools, this notion does not as a rule match the requirements for intercultural education that are set out here. In the practice of the schools, which enjoy virtual autonomy in drawing up the curriculum, there is seldom any discussion of anything but changing the criteria that may be used to justify the choice between competing topics for lessons, and this does not entail developing new arguments in favour of particular educational or teaching concepts. There is a broad consensus that "first, the scope of the regular school curriculum should reflect the multicultural reality of Britain and the world, and, second, its portrayal of minority cultures or cultures overseas should not be token, stereotyped or otherwise inaccurate" (Jeffecoate 1979, p 8).

In the end, this often amounts to no more, for instance, than that the regular teaching should not, as hitherto, discuss only Christianity, but that a few weeks should be devoted to Islam too, or that in geography lessons the treatment of the Caribbean islands should replace that of Tierra del Fuego or the Aleutians. The fact that all this seldom goes beyond mere token gestures of respect may be gathered from the omni-presence, in English "multi-racial schools", of folkloristic stereotypes such as the Taj Mahal or Diwali. Jeffecoate, however, does not criticize this practice because it will fail to achieve its aim of inculcating in the pupils a respect for the most varied, unspecified cultures, but concentrates his attack on the aim itself, which appears to him indicative of a tendentious, indoctrinating, "bucket-filling instruction" which denies that pupils have the right and the ability to subject both their own and other cultures to a critical examination and assessment.

His basic premise - that the academic success and the self-confidence of ethnic minority children in English education is sufficiently high to make unnecessary to adopt and attitude towards them that is intent on "sparing" them - seems at least questionable in view of other findings, but need not detain us long here, since attitudes of respect for other cultures cannot in any case be justified by the need to "spare" their individual representatives.

And indeed, the central objection to Jeffecoate's argument concerns a different aspect of its logical structure: by narrowing down the concept of culture to the point where it comprises only religious, philosophical or political ideologies, he creates a basis on which they can be treated as completely unconnected systems with a formally identical status, so that in the process of examination and assessment they can be related to one another only by external logical operations. The terms in which these operations are then conducted, however, are by no means simply formal and lacking in content, but of necessity culture-specific. This becomes clear when he dismisses, without further qualification, the "atavistic obscurantism of the Rastafarian creed" (ibid., p 11). One is inclined to wonder, after such a statement, whether pupils who have been exposed to such views from their teacher will feel confident to strive for the type of "critical understanding of a rational, sensitive, evaluating human being" (ibid., p 10) which Jeffecoate suggests the multicultural curriculum should be aiming at, whether the object of study is "Afrikanerdom, Islam or Rastafarianism" (ibid., p 11). Yet the real issue is not there at all: it is in the practical relationships which "cultures" and individuals from different cultures maintain with each other. And these relationships are not, as Jeffecoate would have it, shaped by the logic of "the free play of the critical mind" (ibid., p 11), but by the logic of power – domination and resistance.

We have expatiated on Jeffecoate's argument in order to make clear once more, by using it as an example, that intercultural education can no more navigate by the stars in a sky of abstract ideas supposedly spanning all cultures than it can restrict itself to merely reflecting a cultural heritage that is remote in time and space. It is concerned with the relations between living cultures which are evolving, not without conflict, in the multi-ethnic and multilingual societies of today. Its aim is to make these relations comprehensible to the pupils and to enable the pupils to break out of the confines of power-conditioned perception and power-conditioned behaviour.

# Critical arguments for new approaches to the education of ethnic minority children

## The politics of pilot projects and educational innovation

The schools of the industrialized countries - contrary to the ideologies that determine the way they operate and underlie the political
systems of the countries themselves - do not serve all social groups
equally, in the sense that they do not ensure an equal distribution of
opportunities for access to the resources of society. It is well
established that the schools do not provide equality of opportunity,
but strengthen the social advantages already enjoyed by privileged
groups and play a substantial role in denying academic success - and
hence vocational and social success - to working class children and, to
a still greater extent, to children from marginalized groups. The
function of the schools in selecting and orienting their pupils poses a
problem that has become even more acute with the advent of growing
numbers of ethnic minority children.

Statistics from all the immigration countries demonstrate that ethnic
minority children and adolescents in mainstream education fall behind
in their school progress more often than indigenous pupils, that they
are over-represented in those forms of schooling that lead to the more
badly paid and less prestigious jobs, that they obtain fewer and poorer
leaving qualifications, and that they constitute an above-average
proportion of the young unemployed. This undesirable trend can be shown
to be independent of any differences of ethnic origin among workers
recruited abroad, of the arrangements made for their residence and
opportunities in the host countries, and of traditional differences in
educational provision, and so the conclusion can be drawn that the
nature and causes of the problem are fundamentally alike.

Attempts have been made to solve these problems, starting from
different positions which we may characterize by the antithetical
designations national vs. supranational, educational vs. administrative,
and conservative vs. innovative. The question that concerns us here is
whether the EC Commission's policy over the pilot projects worked in
favour of innovative solutions within the education systems of the
countries involved or helped to shore up the traditional administrative
machinery for dealing with the education of migrant workers' children.
To answer this question we have to start with an account of the initial
positions adopted by the EC Commission, the Council, and - though here
our account must necessarily be somewhat simplified - of the national
education systems themselves.

These systems, it is true, all have their own history of educational
conflicts and debates, also in relation to migrant pupils. Yet at the
same time the established administrative and policy-making bodies are,
on the one hand, compelled to react to the presence of migrant pupils

in the national system *and* at the same time to defend their previous decisions - whether these are of a general nature or specifically relate to the education of migrants - both against the demands of national policy on immigration and migrant employment and against the claims of supranational bodies to a say in matters of national policy.

Hence, the manifest problems confronting the national systems in the sphere of migrant education are not generally recognized for what they are, viz. indicators of structural weaknesses that have caused trouble in the past and in any case work to the disadvantage of a sizeable section of the indigenous population, because to recognize them would be to call the systems themselves into question - the criteria employed in assessment and examination, the organizational structures, the languages used in teaching, the professional self-image of the teachers, etc. The obvious dysfunctions are thus explained as due to inadequacies on the part of the migrant pupils themselves: it is they who are said lack a command of the language of the host country, to have the wrong attitudes to school, and not to fit "properly" into society. Recourse to such arguments makes it possible to narrow the problem down, so that the functioning of the system as a whole does not have to be called into question, and gives rise to the kind of responses we have come to expect: what is required, we are told, are measures that will help the migrant pupils to take their place in the system and fulfil its demands. National differences notwithstanding, attempts to compensate for the supposed inadequacies of the pupils all follow an essentially uniform strategy in education policy: the setting up of specific preparatory or remedial schemes which the pupils have to go through in order to be able to slot as smoothly as possible into the mainstream education provision of the host country - which remains unchanged.

One-dimensional reception programmes of this kind, designed to meet immediate needs, produce a twofold vindicating effect for the education systems: they legitimize and ensure the temporary segregation of pupils who, with their imperfect command of the language of the school, are unable to keep up with the mainstream teaching, *and* - what is no less important - by justifying this segregation on simplified and - as it were - erroneous educational grounds, programmes of this kind provide the basis for "explanations" of the under-achievement of ethnic minority pupils - "explanations" that boil down to putting the blame on the pupils and thus clearing the education systems of any criticisms directed at their shortcomings. If minority students do not succeed within the mainstream system, even after completing a full cycle of the reception programme, then - so the argument runs - this is surely to be seen as evidence of deficits inherent in the students themselves, who may therefore legitimately held responsible for their under-achievement. In this way, the vicious circle is closed: once more, ethnic minority students are identified as a problem group that places a burden on an otherwise just and equitable education system.

The first tentative steps taken by the EC Commission in this area were perforce confined partly to co-ordinating and supporting the policies of the individual countries, and partly to working out its own supra-national position on education policy. The history of its subsequent involvement has continued to vacillate within these confines. When the educational implications of the policy of freedom of movement within the Community came to be realized in the late sixties, this led to an attempt to enlarge the Community's powers; this had the support of the member states, in spite of its somewhat tenuous legal basis (cf. p 5f). The economic interest of the member states in improving the conditions for migration was consonant with the accompanying measures in the sphere of education policy, and the result of this was relative harmony between Community policy and national policies. Equal treatment for indigenous citizens and the citizens of other member states continued to be a feature of the policy of freedom of movement, even when narrow national interests came to indicate a need to restrict immigration. Not being hampered by any history of its own in the field of educational policy-making, the Commission felt free to demand the introduction of educational innovations so as to improve the academic achievement of migrant workers' children. Moreover, being under an obligation both to the host countries and to the migrants' countries of origin, it was able to set about devising a programme for the education of migrant workers' children which involved specific educational provision, both as a token of genuine equality and as a means to achieve it. Being oriented, in its own interests, to the creation of European laws, it was able to give this programme a meaning which visibly went beyond a merely economic rationale and to justify the educational measures it wished to promote on grounds of social policy. This is evident in the numerous submissions made by the Commission (cf. Wittek 1982, pp 41-44) and also in the draft text of the Directive (see above pp 7-12). The main features of this are:

- the express formulation of the dialectic relation between equality and individuality in the process of educating migrant workers' children: "a training ... which is adapted to their particular situation and assures them access to all levels of the education system" (draft preamble);

- the justification of mother tongue teaching on the ground of the children's linguistic and cultural situation and opportunities for development, not solely, or indeed primarily, with a view to their eventually returning home;

- the notion that the children had individual rights to education;

- the applicability of the proposed educational norms to the children of all migrants, not just to those of migrant workers from other EEC member states.

190

In the period of restrictive immigration policies, i.e. from 1973/74 onwards, this liberal, reformist stance adopted by the Commission gradually came to contrast with the tendency of the national education systems to resolve issues in the education of ethnic minority children by resorting to segregationist or assimilationist policies.

In the resulting controversy the Commission found itself increasingly at a disadvantage as economic conditions in the member states came more and more to suggest the need to put a brake on the mobility of labour. In the conflicts over the final formulation of the Directive (cf. above, pp 13-16) the interests of the member states represented in the Council prevailed over the position that had been adopted by the Commission. The political, legal and financial arguments that carried the day have had the effect of promoting a defensive approach to migrant education, limited to individual measures designed to remove problems, measures such as are enumerated in the final wording of the Directive: introductory teaching and training, in-service training for the staff responsible for the teaching, and instruction in the mother tongue – all subject to the internal conditions of the member states.

Although national interests clearly prevailed, it must be borne in mind that although the Commission's scope for action was thereby restricted, it was not completely removed, and that the Council, by declaring that it did not wish the Directive to be implemented in such a way as to create discriminatory structures in the education systems of the member states, kept the door open to an eventual redefinition of its political intentions.

One must remember that the education of migrant workers' children is not a matter of great political moment in which uniformity of approach is considered essential: it is an area of policy-making where decisions are made on an *ad hoc* basis and are dependent on the wider political context. Just as in this question the positions of the Commission and the Council were at variance, so too there are differences between the member states, and even within these, educational policy-makers differ in the extent to which they allow wider political considerations to override their educational convictions. There are groups who hope that they will benefit from supranational support, and there are also educationists whose see their ideas better represented in supranational initiatives than in the traditional approaches of their national education system. Hence it was possible for the debate to continue on quite different levels, one of them being related to the pilot projects on migrant education which emerged from the 1976 action programme. Both the hidden and the explicit aims and contents of the projects were determined partly by demands for innovation and partly by the limitations imposed by national traditions. Just as decisions taken at European level must not be seen one-dimensionally as expressing a uniform intention, so too at national, local and school level it was possible to perceive or create some room for manoeuvre in which innovative educational strategies could be developed for the benefit of ethnic minority pupils. In these circumstances the Commission was able to take advantage of whatever institutional autonomy it enjoyed.

The procedures by which the pilot projects were approved and the course they followed must therefore be examined in order to ascertain whether this room for manoeuvre was in fact perceived and exploited. Were the pilot projects, in their national and local context, given opportunities to evolve viable innovations? How far were these opportunities seized, and how far did they fail as a result of institutional conservatism? To what extent were the innovations that had been introduced allowed to be distorted during the course of their implementation in a way which strengthened rather than weakened existing assimilationist and/or segregationist tendencies? In each case we have to ask whether, and to what extent, the policy of the Commission gave extra power to the forces of educational innovation within the pilot projects themselves and within the context of education policy in which they were set up.

In the cases with which we are concerned here, these questions can be answered only insofar as we have access to information about the approval and implementation of the individual pilot projects - in other words, only to a limited extent. However, the sources available to us justify the contention that - with the exception of the Bedford project - the overall orientation of the projects was very largely determined by the preceding formulation, either by central government (as was the case in France) or by local groups of experts (as in Leiden and, to a lesser extent, in Genk), of a specific policy which was able to inform the planning and implementation of a particular innovation.

This may be shown most clearly in the case of the French pilot project, where the ministry's note setting it up described it in so many words as an opportunity for the further development of the provision for integrated mother tongue teaching that had existed in primary schools since 1975 with a view to introducing classroom co-operation between indigenous and bilingual teachers. To this end it was made possible, for the first time in France, for foreign teachers to be employed by a French authority - though not, as is customary in the case of French teachers, by the rectorate of the Academy, but "only" by the *Ecole Normale* in Paris (the reason being that there were no relevant legal precedents). These teachers not only gave mother tongue instruction: part of their working time was to be used in fostering contacts with parents and engaging in intercultural teaching, in order to bring the migrant parents closer to the French school and to make French schools in general more sensitive in their treatment of ethnic minority pupils (see above, p 113). In this way, a programme was laid down for the project which - especially in this last point - went a fair way beyond the objectives formulated in the Directive or in the EC's 1976 programme of action. By taking this line, the department of the Ministry of Education responsible for the project was acting contrary to the immigration policy of the government in power, which was at the time preparing to move away from a policy of consolidation to an avowed policy of repatriation (see above, p 100f): "A prerequisite for the attempt to integrate this teaching is a systematic sensitizing of French schools to the presence of children of different ethnic origins, a profound acceptance among French teachers, pupils and parents which should lead to the creation of a genuine openness to the values of the groups in question." However realistic one judges these formulations in the Ministry's note to be, they clearly start from the assumption that migration is just as much a "problem" for French society as it is for the migrants themselves - a problem, moreoever, which will not be substantially altered by policies of "encouraging" return migration. As such initiatives went well beyond the aims that had been set out officially in the action programme, the Commission was not to be expected to take such initiatives by itself. Yet it has supported them unreservedly.

The pedagogical integration of mother tongue teaching into the wider activities of the school was at least partially successful in Paris (see above, pp 121-29). We would regard the intensive counselling and formative evaluation work as having been essential preconditions for this, together with the fact that the head teachers and inspectors of the schools involved actively encouraged the work that went into the development of the project (cf. above, p 118) and that it proved possible, during the project, to sustain and even to enlarge a basic consensus with regard to the importance of this work and the goals it should seek to attain. There is no denying that the achievement of such intense, long-term co-operation was due in part to chance circumstances such as personal friendships, shared languages, etc, but this does not disprove the thesis that, in the education systems we are concerned with, innovations in the sphere of migrant education cannot be introduced and sustained solely at the level of the individual teachers and their teaching, but require the active support of the institutional hierarchy. This may be illustrated by one positive and one negative example: the (admittedly only temporary) integration of the Portuguese teaching at one school, which was made possible by the energetic intervention of the inspector (cf. above, p 126f), and the permanent isolation of the Yugoslav teacher, whom none of the participant schools was prepared to rescue from the ghetto of a totally marginalized mother tongue course. The isolation of this foreign teacher need not have been intentional, but it is a not altogether surprising consequence of the ethnocentricity of the curriculum, the conditions under which the teachers have to work, and the social discrimination to which minorities are subject; therefore it is bound to happen nearly "automatically" as long as there are no positive policies to counter it. In those cases where continuing support for the teachers' work was forthcoming from expert advisers, head teachers and inspectors in the Paris project - in the Italian and Spanish teaching especially - a degree of co-operation was made possible that resulted not only in investing the agreed objectives with a concrete educational content, but also in the formulation of additional concepts which have provided a stimulus for changes in educational practice and subsequent pilot projects in France (cf. Boos-Nünning et al. 1984). We would therefore wish to hold up this pilot project as a model of how a certain "scope for manoeuvre" may be created by an interplay of forces at the most varied levels of the political and administrative system and then exploited to carry out the successful occupation of an area of disputed educational territory through the deployment of a convincing innovation.

As a counter-example we may take the Bedford project, where the forces of educational innovation blocked one another at the intermediate level and thus substantially impeded potential educational developments at the teaching level. There was undoubtedly scope for developments in educational policy: the Bedfordshire LEA was in direct partnership with the EC Commission and, by virtue of the lack of centralization in the English education system, it could act autonomously in accepting and implementing the pilot project. In the event, however, this scope for action could not be purposefully exploited. The reasons for this – apart from fortuitous factors arising from personal relations – lie in the fact that, in this particular case, there was no way of synchronizing local, national and supranational developments in migrant education.

This was due not least to the fact that the advocates of mother tongue teaching in the administration were unable to refer to a political decision by the County Council or even the Education Committee in favour of introducing mother tongue teaching in Bedford schools or experimenting with its introduction. The pilot project in Bedford thus lacked not only any institutional and political legitimation on which the other projects – all of which were carried out with political approval – could rely; nor had there been (by contrast with the situation in Leiden and Genk) any local debate among experts on reforms in education policy which might – even without the initiative taken by Brussels – have prepared the ground for the implementation of the project.

In these circumstances it is altogether understandable that an attempt should have been made to fill this local gap by seeking guidance from the EC Commission in the form of a more precise statement of objectives (cf. above, p 80f and 97), but this was to misjudge the extent of the Commission's influence and to underrate the importance of informal factors. By approving a pilot project on mother tongue teaching in maintained schools, the Commission had pursued the intention of promoting a contribution to the practical educational development of this subject, which had so far been more neglected in Great Britain than in any other member state. However, the Bedford authorities had not only ventured into an area in which they could hardly expect support, but rather delaying tactics, from the DES, but committed themselves to the experiment at a time when the so-called "mother tongue debate", stimulated by the increasingly insistent demands of the minorities and by the parliamentary discussion surrounding Article 3 of the draft directive, was just beginning to make itself felt in British educational and academic circles. (The very first academic publication on the subject (Saifullah Khan 1976) appeared in the year the pilot project was started; the cautious formulations of the Bullock Report on the needs of bilingual pupils (DES 1975, p 286), which British educationists now like to cite as an early official reaction on the part of the system, had certainly not made a significant impact by that stage.) This explains why local minority groups did not ally themselves with the official advocates of mother tongue teaching, though such an alliance would have been quite conceivable, or rather why such an alliance came to nothing – as witness the fate of the Punjabi petition (cf. above, p 93).

In educational circles at national and local level the pilot project was thus somewhat isolated, lacking as it did any political or symbolic legitimation. Despite the courage shown by the LEA in taking up the Commission's invitation, it seems to have been more or less inevitable that it should produce so few results. It is impossible to judge whether and to what extent this relative isolation can be held responsible for bringing a degree of conflict into the internal structure of the project, but it is reasonably certain that it is one of the reasons why the Bedford project did not play any significant part in the "mother tongue debate" which was subsequently to become so wide-ranging and intense (Tomlinson 1983, pp 111-14; Linguistic Minorities Project 1983, pp 19-25. – It remains to be seen what the response will be to Tosi's publication of 1984, which is based to a large extent on his work in the pilot project.)

The Leiden project occupies a special position in that its political and institutional legitimation was in all essentials achieved by a group associated with the later project leader (cf. above, p 149f). This group, which had to negotiate with the local authority, the Ministry and the EC Commission, obviously knew how to win over first the Commission and then, with the latter's help, the Ministry, in order to overcome the delaying tactics of the local authority. It is true that, by selecting a school which was due to close because of a shortage of pupils, the local authority produced a situation in which the innovation was unlikely to be effective in the long term. Admittedly this must have been to some extent a tempting choice for the authority, since another school had declined to take part, and the Du Rieu School, which had not previously had any ethnic minority pupils, was interested in increasing its rolls. It is not our contention that the choice of school in itself was detrimental to the experiment and the pupils involved in it, but that it was in effect a pre-emptive move against the continuation of the pilot project and the more general application of its results, since it was clear from the start that it would not be possible for the experiences and insights gained by the teachers at the school during the course of the project to be systematically exploited. Instead of using its resources to make the implementation of the project an

attractive proposition to a school that was not threatened with closure
and was situated in an area inhabited by ethnic minorities, the local
authority took the line of least resistance. The political significance
of this very common mode of procedure is revealed in a remark made by
Overberg, who recalls in another context that the Leiden project took
place at a time which "can be seen as the borderline of an era in Dutch
education of moving from the stage of perceiving multicultural
education as an additional service for a specific target group to
perceiving it as a structural rebuilding of education for all children
in the schools" (Overberg 1980, p 34). However, such transitions do not,
as Overberg's formulation suggests, take place inevitably as though
they were part of the programming of social development: on the
contrary, they are characterized by an intensification of social
conflict. In this conflict an interim compromise was reached in Leiden
for the duration of the pilot project: the Ministry, by agreeing to its
implementation, was able to appease a restive group of critics who were
opposed to its policy on migrant education and pressing for
innovations to be introduced, and at the same time present the
Commission with a model which was conceptually so advanced that it
could be put into practice at short notice without any sacrifice of
standards in terms of content; the local authority could pride itself on
this potentially prestigious project, without having to face the
necessity of drawing any long term consequences from it.

Meanwhile the Netherlands have extended voting rights in local
elections to foreign residents and so taken a step in the sphere of
social affairs which will favour developments in the direction
indicated by Overberg. The group of experts in Leiden was obviously not
content with the limited success they achieved in the pilot project: the
project leader gave a lecture in Enschede which prompted the town to
try out a project very similar to the one in Leiden; this has since
been introduced in Enschede as a regular model for the reception of
migrant children (cf. Boos-Nünning et al. 1984).

In Genk, finally, the original position was that for some time before
the start of the pilot project, a local group of experts had been
concerned about the unsatisfactory situation in which mother tongue
teaching was organized by the consulates outside normal school hours,
yet all their attempts to integrate it into the mainstream curriculum
had come up against an apparently insuperable obstacle: the language
regulations which became law in 1983 (cf. above, p 33f) are the outcome
of a laboriously negotiated compromise, which has brought some order
into the language controversy that has been smouldering in Belgium
since the state was founded, though it has not put an end to it; any
deviation from these regulations is liable to revive the latent
conflict, which has at times threatened national unity. And this is the
background against which we should view the Limburg project: the
exemption of the pilot project from the normal language regulations
must undoubtedly be seen as an act of political daring in which the
Ministry was probably prepared to indulge only because the EC Directive

on the education of migrant workers' children was already under discussion and likely to have consequences in education policy which in the long run the Ministry could not evade. At the same time it could justify itself to its critics at home by pointing to the growing supranational consensus. In this sense the Belgian pilot project is the clearest evidence for the thesis that some areas offering scope for manoeuvre have only been opened up by the political intervention of the Community.

On the other hand, the use of mother tongue teaching as a means of facilitating the admission of ethnic minority pupils into Belgian mainstream classes also shows how existing patterns of legitimacy in the national education system ensure that innovations are interpreted within the framework of traditional educational objectives and can be bent, as it were, to fit in with tradition. Whereas the original intention was to relieve the extra burden which the additional lessons in the mother tongue placed on the migrant children, its integration into the mainstream curriculum also deprived mother tongue teaching of its autonomy. This becomes especially clear from the original ministerial order for the setting up of the pilot project, which expressly excluded the teaching of reading and writing from mother tongue lessons given at school. Characteristically, the objections of the bilingual teachers, made on educational grounds, only succeeded when they were given the backing of their embassies (cf. above, p 47).

We have shown how some schools pursued the logic of the pilot project and developed further schemes for restoring a certain measure of independence to mother tongue teaching. Today, now that the project has been run a second time (again with the support of the EC Commission) at a larger number of schools (cf. Boos-Nünning et al. 1984), it has become a model for schemes throughout the province of Limburg, and it is now being tried out in secondary schools too. For the French-speaking area, Marques Balsa reports that in 1982 all pre-school institutions and primary schools wanting to incorporate mother tongue teaching into the mainstream curriculum were given a general dispensation from the 1963 language regulations, and that stages of development could already be discerned: first, the integration of teaching in the medium of the mother tongue into the normal timetable, then the incorporation of these courses into the curricula, and finally the integration of the bilingual teachers into the staff body (Marques Balsa 1984, p 138): "The changes in the Belgian school system outlined here were at first only just within the law, yet they now have the status of educational experiments; they were not instigated by educational considerations, however, but resulted primarily from outside pressure which was brought to bear upon the education system - particularly by the immigrant groups and supranational bodies" (ibid., p 139). We concur in this analysis.

Thus in definable political circumstances the pilot projects, by following their own pedagogical logic, have set in motion innovations which go beyond the terms of the Directive. These innovations are the outcome of continued reflection on the tasks of reception teaching and mother tongue teaching in the host country and of increasing experience in the field. The impetus thus given to innovation demonstrates that even the most ambitiously conceived tasks, if they are continually thought through and developed, can point the way forward beyond themselves, thus influencing other areas of educational provision and ultimately the education systems of the host countries as a whole.

## Reception teaching

The purpose of reception teaching is to introduce migrant pupils to the language and culture of the host country: this is a proposition that will command universal assent, with at most minor reservations. The earliest forms of teaching designed specially for migrant children were in fact characterized by the naïvely optimistic assumption that the children's problems could all be solved by providing instruction in the language of the host country for a single limited period. It is a patent fact that ethnic minority children - not only new arrivals, but some second-generation immigrants too - lack competence in the language of the host country, and it is probably because their inability to communicate in it is so striking that "language" comes to be seen as the most pressing problem, beside which everything else pales into insignificance; hence,in practice reception teaching usually amounts to no more than language teaching. The aim of introducing the migrant children to the society and culture of the host country, which figures as an additional requirement in the government orders, is treated as relatively unimportant and soon turns into the practice of unreflecting and ill-informed adaptation, becoming effective under the obscure guise of the "hidden curriculum". This basic interpretation of the problem, which makes language difficulties the chief justification for specific schemes  designed for migrant children, provides a legitimation for administrative measures such as the setting up of special classes, the validation of special curricula and finally the training of specialist teachers. These again constitute an obstacle to reception - taking the term in a comprehensive sense - in that reception comes to be seen as a function performed by special structures rather than as something that takes place when the pupils are received into the schools through their normal structures and into society through its schools.

Such arguments are usually countered, on the one hand, by reference to the real need (which nobody would wish to deny) for specific measures and, on the other, to the short-term nature of the measures in question. It is plausibly argued that preparing migrant children for mainstream teaching is an indispensable stage in the process of integration, at any rate for new immigrants of school age. In practice, however, there is a tendency to confuse the means with the ends: the mere completion of a preparatory course, symbolized administratively by the transfer of the pupils to mainstream classes, is equated with successful integration, there being no general provision for continued support after the pupils have been transferred.

To put the matter in positive terms: we are not criticizing specific reception schemes in themselves, but arguing the case for a reception curriculum that would allow a flexible and differentiated approach to the various needs of the migrant pupils and lead to concrete measures, especially at the stage when the migrant pupils move into new areas of schooling.

The pilot projects in Genk and Leiden attempted, by initiating collaboration between teachers in the different forms of reception teaching, to create a sensitivity among the Belgian and Dutch staff to the needs of the migrants in the sphere of language learning. The most interesting result was the emergence of a new understanding of what was meant by "reception" – a clearer appreciation of the fact that it proceeds by stages and overlaps with other processes. An admirable example was set by the head of the VLS Genk-Winterslag, who managed to get his staff to co-operate and come up with their joint reflections on the educational questions involved; these reflections led to independent curricular developments in the form of the *afspraakboekjes*. Under such conditions the reception of migrant children was no longer a short-term task for specialists, but tended to become just one dimension in the teaching in all subjects.

Also belonging here, from another point of view, are the experiments that were carried out in Genk and Leiden in combining reception teaching with pedagogical concepts that belong to the tradition of educational reform in both countries and are subsumed by the term *wereldorientatie* ("world orientation"): all language teaching must have a content of some sort and therefore inevitably involves introducing the pupils to a particular culture. These initiatives deserve further consideration; this would mean consciously taking account of the factual and cultural content involved in the language teaching and incorporating it into lessons as elements of an "introduction to the culture of the host country". Schools and school systems which traditionally include the exploration or the social environment in the content of their teaching will have little difficulty in adopting this approach if "reception teaching" is to be understood in this comprehensive sense. One consequence will be a narrowing of the gap between the content of mainstream teaching and that of specialist reception teaching.

The pilot project in Leiden also evolved a scheme for bringing the migrant and the indigenous children together by stages; this scheme provided for joint projects, joint attendance at integration lessons in mainstream classes, and finally a visit to the neighbourhood school which the children would attend after completing their preparatory course. This showed in exemplary fashion that specific prepatatory teaching need not be bought at the price of social isolation, but should be complemented, during the reception process, by steps in the direction of joint learning.

These examples illustrate the essential aspects of a development which removes reception teaching from the confines of mere language acquisition and pedagogical isolation - reception as a joint task for both indigenous and bilingual teachers, as a process of classroom integration, and as a comprehensive introduction to the school and its environment, and to the language and culture of the host country. Once more it must be clearly stated that none of this was consciously envisaged by the pilot projects; what we have tried to demonstrate is simply that the developments which took place in the projects lead one to conclude that reception teaching has a natural virulence, which can infect not only other subjects, but the learning processes of a whole class, and indeed of the whole of the teaching staff. If this infection is allowed to spread, it may result in a fresh and more coherent approach to education and bring about important changes in school life.

## Mother tongue teaching

Mother tongue teaching too can help in combating discrimination, in that it can provide the clearest possible indication that the language and culture of the migrants are recognized as having the same value as those of the host country. Admittedly, the fact that mother tongue teaching is widely (if somewhat loosely) incorporated into the curriculum of migrant pupils was due less to developments in educational thinking than to bilateral developments in the sphere of foreign policy, whereby the countries of origin took advantage of their responsibility for their citizens abroad and the host countries responded to a greater or lesser extent to their representations. Thus, mother tongue teaching was not viewed primarily as an educational task, but as a political arrangement - an arrangement, however, which furnished both parties with an educational alibi. The sometimes blind adherence to the curriculum of the host country, the obsession with re-migration (which runs counter to the aims of both reception and mainstream teaching), the barriers between the bilingual teachers and their indigenous colleagues, the relatively poor resources (by the standards of the host country) allocated to mother tongue teaching - all these are symptoms of an approach which derives essentially from merely political and administrative considerations. The marginal position accorded to mother tongue teaching within the education systems of the host countries is obvious upon even the most superficial analysis. Yet surprisingly few analyses have so far been made; even rarer are attempts by educationists to think beyond the present situation; and there has been an appalling dearth of pedagogical experiments which might have contributed to genuine improvements in teaching.

Several of the host countries have tackled the problem of integrating mother tongue teaching into the mainstream curricula of their schools; such integration has gone farthest in France, and rather less far in the Netherlands and the Federal Republic of Germany. It is certainly not without significance that the curriculum should have been modified and classrooms redistributed in order to accommodate mother tongue classes for migrant pupils, but it remains a matter of organization – amounting to no more than the creation of the material conditions for a development that has still to get under way, viz. the development of a kind of educationally integrated mother tongue teaching which effectively serves the needs of bilingual children and recognizes their academic potential. What we have in mind is, in the first place, a kind of mother tongue teaching which will no longer be tied to the curriculum of the pupils' countries of origin, the development of autonomous methods of teaching the mother tongue to emigrant children: this was the objective pursued in all the pilot projects described here. In the second place, what is envisaged is the formal recognition of mother tongue teaching as a continuing element in the curriculum of schools in the host countries, together with all that this would entail for the credentialling system.

What we also have in mind, however, is the infectiveness of mother tongue teaching and the changes it may induce in the education systems of multilingual societies. The pilot projects, especially those in Genk and Paris, may be taken as evidence for the contention that whenever serious consideration is given to the aims of mother tongue teaching, with a view to making changes in teaching practice, this results in its being accorded a function *within* the education system of the host country, since this is the only way to end its marginal status. The ways in which it is combined with other components of the curriculum may vary. One option explored in the pilot projects was that of assigning to it the function of supporting the reception process, whether as remedial teaching related directly to mainstream classes or as a contribution to more general educational aims – or, to use our own terminology, as a means of strengthening the pupils' psycho-emotional stability. This option may be considered as the obvious antithesis to the unsatisfactory provision of teaching which relates chiefly to the pupils' countries of origin – to a remote culture and an unreal future – and as the more sensible and realistic variant of an educational approach directed towards adaptation and compensation.

If we take the mother tongue teaching in Genk-Waterslag as an example, it is interesting to note how even here, where it was assigned a somewhat restricted function, it had repercussions on both reception and mainstream teaching: consultation between bilingual and indigenous staff about the content and aims of their teaching led quite logically to the need to recognize that the knowledge and experience that the children already had "on board" could not and should not be kept out of the reception process, and that aspects of a particular topic which were at first dealt with only in mother tongue lessons should be brought into the mainstream teaching too, in order to establish or maintain a meaningful link between the two kinds of teaching. When this is done, the migrant pupils see their special knowledge and experience taken up and pursued in the mainstream classes, while the indigenous children learn about additional aspects of a given topic which not only broaden their horizons by adding a dimension of distance, but sharpen their perception of their immediate social environment; for the relevance of what they learn in this way consists in the fact that it derives from the knowledge and experience of their present classmates.

The use of the mother tongue as an additional instrument in the reception process leads to a change in the quality of the process itself. This idea may be given a more general formulation: through the incorporation of mother tongue teaching, the curriculum of the host country is changed in a more fundamental sense than it would be by, say, the provision of an extra foreign language or a scientific subject. It implies that the school is beginning to take a broad view of the educational experience of the migrant pupils and declaring itself responsible for their future development in these terms. It thus ceases to adhere to the naive equation of the acceptable culture with the target culture, which even in a monocultural context leads to the implied superiority of middle-class values over lower-class values, and in a multicultural context goes so far as to deny the value of any form of socialization which is not linked to the dominant culture - which means that culturally the pupils are, as it were, cut in half. By giving up this equation, the school puts the educational opportunities of its pupils above the educational demands of society. (This is one more reason why mother tongue teaching should start from the language that is actually spoken by the pupils and the living culture that exists in their homes: it is the pupils themselves who matter - *their* personalities and *their* repertoire of abilities.) Such a change of attitude necessarily has consequences for the other linguistic and humanities teaching. As an example we may take the Franco-Spanish teaching at the school in the rue Hamelin during the Paris project: through the combination of mother tongue teaching with mainstream teaching it proved possible, at a stroke, to get away from the ethnocentric teaching of history and culture and evolve something more humane - something with a palpable content, which involved the use of selected texts that were readily comprehensible and was presented in a varied and vivid manner. Here too we have a "functionalizing" of mother tongue instruction, but this time with the aim of evolving a kind of teaching for which national and cultural variety is recognized as a vital prerequisite and a new objective is envisaged; here it has an essential and not just an ancillary function.

The principle of justifying educational activity by reference to the pupil, rather than to society, can easily lead to the growth of pedagogical parochialism. This is not what we have in mind here: school must be school, not a kind of nature reserve for the language and culture of the mother country; it must provide linguistic and cultural knowledge that is useful and vocationally exploitable, and it must provide pupils with the ability to assert themselves, as bilingual speakers, in a society which largely refuses to recognize its own linguistic diversity and thus makes this very diversity the basis for perpetuating or creating social inequalities. A more progressive form of training for bilingual teachers will make possible a type of mother tongue teaching which will be successful, in the first place, because it will start from the language spoken in the children's homes and promote their communication skills within a group of pupils who speak the same language, thus developing an awareness of the existence and uniqueness of this group. This will provide a foundation for language teaching with a literary and cultural content, which will enable those who have been exposed to it to use the knowledge and skills they have acquired in international communication. When once the schools have been opened up to the linguistic and cultural diversity in our society, and when once bilingual and indigenous teachers are given joint in-service training, part of the pupils' time will be spent acquiring specific knowledge and insights linked to a particular language medium; they will then bring this knowledge and these insights into joint learning processes, which will draw their vitality to the very variety of the knowledge and insights that inform them. In the conflicts that ensue, and by virtue of the potential for successful communication that is thereby created, school life will become the model for a plural society open to evolutionary change.

This educational model should not simply be dismissed as utopian. Quite independently of the interests of the migrant pupils, both the host countries and the countries of origin may well have an interest in such a development. It would afford the host countries an opportunity to enhance the quality of their foreign language potential - a potential which is needed not only for communication between the different ethnic groups within the population, but also for technical, commercial and scientific communication between nations. And here we need not think only in terms of continuing to teach young people their mother tongues: these mother tongues may become the second languages of indigenous pupils when the education system can guarantee the necessary provision. The countries of origin, insofar as they remain interested in exercising their sovereignty over their expatriate citizens, will for their part discern, in the enlightened self-interest of the host countries, an opportunity to prevent their languages from gradually dying out there. The demand for language maintenance will then no longer spring from national nostalgia, but be seen as an obvious outcome of the lively exploitation of linguistic resources.


## Towards intercultural education

The "culture of the home country", often described as the "culture of origin" and conceived as a mere replica of a quasi immutable and totally unified culture of "there" and "then", has no viable future in the host country. Wrenched out of their historical and social context, the individual elements which give the culture its dynamism tend to atrophy and become mere artefacts, which can at best serve as emblems of a culture that was once a living entity. Any form of intercultural education which equated the emblem with the reality would miss the central motive of the concept - which is not only to widen the horizons of knowledge and to promote tolerance in the abstract, but to create real empathy, a genuine sensitivity to what at first seems disturbingly alien. This means that intercultural teaching must direct its attention to the cultures of the ethnic minorities in the form in which they actually express themselves in the host country.

A theory of migrant culture has yet to be evolved by scholars concerned with migration research; it is possible, nevertheless, to outline two central factors. Cultures maintain relations of relative autonomy with the social order to which they belong; therefore cultural and social change hardly ever occur synchronically, cultural developments sometimes racing ahead of and sometimes lagging doggedly behind social change. Yet it is the social structure of the society underlying any given culture that gives it vitality and meaning. Therefore cultural change inevitably takes place whenever individuals - and, *a fortiori*, large groups of individuals - move away, for whatever reason, from the social and geographical context in which their culture is rooted. Changed living conditions have to be made sense of and structured with the help of inherited patterns of interpretation (*Deutungsmuster*), but at the same time - sometimes imperceptibly, sometimes so conspicuously as to generate dramatic conflicts - the changed living conditions exercise their own influence on the traditional patterns of interpretation, affecting not only the ways in which the world is perceived and made sense of, but also the ways in which interpretations of the world are arrived at. Whether the new cultural patterns that emerge are to be seen as composite or autonomous forms, whether they are to be located "between" different cultures or whether they are to be seen as being "of" two (or more) cultures, is an entirely dogmatic question that need not concern us here at all, for these new patterns will find their meaning and significance in future exchanges and conflicts between the cultural groups involved. It is important for us to highlight the second dimension of our concept of ethnic minority culture. The "changes in living conditions" to which migrants are subjected are not politically innocent; they are not to be seen as being changes from one climatic zone to another, nor merely as changes from agrarian to highly industrialized societies: for Europe's new ethnic minorities migration has meant, first and foremost, being exposed to an experience that was fundamentally new to them - the combination of structural disadvantage and racial discrimination which characterizes much of their experience. True, they are often familiar with misery and oppression, as it was these which impelled them to emigrate in the first place; yet to be faced with discrimination as "foreigners" - *Kanaken*, Pakis, *Bougnouls*, to use the racist newspeak of Western Europe - is an entirely new experience to them. Migrant and/or

204

ethnic minority culture, we would argue, must in the first place be construed as resulting from this situation, and as being the minorities' means of coping in it. Reactions are unlikely to be uniform: not only will different orientations prevail according to the migrants' ethnic, religious and social backgrounds, as well as to their age and sex, but the orientation patterns themselves will be coloured both by conservatism and modernity, both by a readiness to adapt and a conscious determination to resist.

To categorize the migrants by reference to stereotyped notions of "their" "original cultures" - and thus symbolically confine them within the scope of "their" cultures - seems to be rapidly becoming an established pattern of the "host" societies' official discourse on migration and ethnic minorities. Yet the naively romantic idea of this or that group's cultural homogeneity seems to reflect a public nostalgia for the days when it had not yet become obvious that to conceive of one's own culture as something self-contained and free from internal contradictions was nothing but an illusion. This is the hidden function of stereotyping which prevails in "our" discourse about the "original" cultures of the ethnic minorities: it enables "us" to maintain the concept of each of "our" cultures - French, British or German - as undivided and "one" in an almost metaphysical sense. These too are issues which are at stake in intercultural education, and they must not be ignored. Stereotypes of this kind have real potency in the minds of those concerned, for they are - albeit in an unenlightened and illusory way - ways of coping "somehow". It would be arrogant to understand the questionable nature of this "somehow" as anything but a reflex of the questionable nature of the situation itself. Whatever symbolizes belonging to a national culture retains its identity-conserving or identity-creating function even though the meaning of the symbols may be obscure and their representation trivial.

Although it is necessary, in intercultural education, to be aware of these conditions and of the questionable "coping strategies" which come in their wake, it would be wrong to look down one's nose at those stages in its practical development which are still attached to inter-pretations deriving from the folklore of "ethnic" culture. Yet, in the long run, to make the step from that paradigm in intercultural education which is still related to the "cultures of origin" to the alternative paradigm of "migrant and/or ethnic minority culture" is a prerequisite for posing the question of the social origins and the political meanings of the interpretations we have tried to outline above, and it is a prerequisite for the attempt to develop non-reductionist ways of perceiving and participating in contemporary cultural developments.

Undoubtedly these developments are shaped by hierarchic relations and by contradictions and conflicts between the cultural groups. Hence, the political dimension of intercultural education consists in trying not to ignore or - worse - to deny these conflicts, but in tracing and understanding their development with care, sensitivity and accuracy, and in trying to create opportunities for all the contending parties to view alternative positions in an informed way and - where possible - to understand and appreciate the position of "the other" as a possible way of feeling, thinking and acting. Only in this way can intercultural teaching come anywhere near its goal, which is to contribute to the humanizing of relations between majorities and minorities.

The limits of such objectives must be clearly drawn. Politicians in all the host countries display a tendency to expect the education system - in other words the teachers - to prevent conflicts between the ethnic groups which would allegedly break out were it not for prophylactic measures taken in the schools. Whether such conflicts do flare up - or, to put it in more general terms, how the relations between majorities and minorities will develop - depends on policies which are not of the schools' making. Education must defend itself vigorously against attempts to make it the scapegoat for failures in policy-making.

Intercultural teaching should not seek to spare individuals and groups from predictable conflicts. There are, for instance, contradictions in the sphere of sexual morality between systems of cultural relations which cannot be removed by compromises which seek to embrace both positions and in which (at least as long as one takes seriously the assumption that the opposing cultural groups, though not equally powerful, are to be seen as possessing equal dignity) there is no criterion for deciding within which cultural horizon the "right" answers are to be discerned. In such conflicts, intercultural education cannot and must not arrogate to itself any adjudicatory authority. All it can do is create conditions under which pupils - and teachers - can be helped to think and feel their way into one another's cultures and to know what practical help it is possible to give (or to accept), to know that in any such case any kind of help or advice may lead to further conflict, and to know that ultimately any decision will be in the sphere of individual responsibility of the persons involved. In intercultural conflicts, moral safety nets exist less than anywhere else.

Intercultural education is culturally open: this means that it must offer all parties a chance to express themselves and define their identity. Its psychological aim, which is to arouse interest and empathy for other ways of life, is thus complemented by two further aims: to enable the pupils to come to terms with their own personal history and to have the courage to make conscious decisions. This notion of cultural openness must be distinguished from both cosmopolitan sophistication and "cultural neutrality". An advanced kind of intercultural education such as we envisage here can by definition take place only in multicultural - or at least bicultural - classes: for its success it has to rely on the possibility of the cultures to speak for themselves. It is a learner-centred form of education in which the teacher abandons his role as the possessor and guardian of legitimate knowledge in order to give scope to an interplay between pupils from different cultural backgrounds. Thus, as was demonstrated in the pilot project in Paris, the pupils can function as the producers – or at least the purveyors – of authentic information about their own culture. Thus, indigenous and migrant parents can be brought in, not just as targets of home-school liaison, but as credible partners in the education process itself. And so, finally, partnerships can be built up between the schools and institutions belonging to the communities.

This is why the authentic representation of the cultures is so vital, because only the concrete exchange of information and (perhaps controversial) views between the groups involved can produce at one and the same time both distance from and proximity to one's own and other cultures. This is a situation in which features of the different cultures can be discussed and be shown to be equally legitimate, and in which controversy about these elements – in other words criticism of them – need no longer be taboo. In all this the abiding problem is that the majority culture enjoys a superior status, which makes the free self-presentation of the minority cultures so much more difficult. It is therefore of great advantage if, as happened in the Paris project, a well trained bilingual teacher, co-operating on equal terms in the planning and implementation of the teaching programme, can support the migrant pupils in their effort to assert themselves.

Co-operation between teachers in different subjects, as practised in Paris by the Portuguese teacher and French art teacher in the rue Keller, opens up the additional possibility of widening substantially the aspects under which a topic is handled and hence of presenting components of the migrant culture and the indigenous culture in all their rich variety and not just in watertight compartments. Teaching projects spanning different subjects not only call for co-operation between teachers: they also make it easier to leave the formalized social framework of the school and explore the environment, thus linking the teaching more closely to the world in which both the migrant and the indigenous pupils live, and presenting them with authentic material drawn from their own experience. Such projects, with their combination of different features, thus represent the most characteristic and demanding, and hence the most privileged form of intercultural teaching.

It would of course be dogmatic and formalistic to regard the aspects of content and method that we have listed and sought to justify here as a set of criteria for "correct" intercultural teaching. It is true that we are interpreting the "intercultural option" here entirely as an educational concept which has definite curricular consequences, but this option amounts to more than an enumeration of concrete practicalities, however well thought-out and mutually consistent they may be. It comes alive only when the interaction of individual factors produces that special something which is the essential feature of intercultural practice in the school: we will try to describe this special something as an intercultural ethos existing in the school. (We are aware that a more effective way to describe it would be to write a documentary novel which could illustrate, by reference to one case, what we, in default of other talents, are obliged to describe in the abstract jargon of the educationist, with all the over-simplifications and distortions that this entails.)

Anyone who has been to school knows how soul-destroying this institution can be, how anxiety and fear can stifle any burgeoning of curiosity and individuality. Ethnic diversity, in a school which was not explicitly founded or conceived as a multicultural school, can easily increase the occasions for incomprehension and miscomprehension; the natural reactions to these are insecurity and defensiveness, which are soon transformed into anxiety and submission. The intercultural school thus has to be sensitive towards ethnocentrically constricted forms of perception and the concomitant risk of causing harm to the pupils. And it needs the courage not to let itself be intimidated by what is alien and at first not understood in whatever other culture is present. Anyone who has been to school himself will, however, be able - though perhaps not without difficulty - to remember moments when the delight of discovery and the opportunity to listen and talk freely combined to provide an inkling of what concentrated learning could be, learning which had dispensed with compulsion, though not with effort. In the intercultural school this conception of learning takes on a characteristic form of its own. Pleasure in variety and openness to deviations from the norms of monoculturalism and monolingualism are the typical features of the intercultural ethos, which opens up the intercultural school to freer forms of learning. This does not mean that freedom from inner and outer compulsion is taken for granted. On the contrary, multicultural schools are as a rule situated in residential areas in which an accumulation of social disadvantage and racial discrimination produces cycles of deprivation in which the lives of the migrant children end up willy-nilly. Without presuming to attempt the impossible and to put an end to this cycle of deprivation, the intercultural school provides strategies of self-assertion and resistance - self-assertion against unreasonable demands for adaptation made by the dominant majority, and resistance to stigmatization and discrimination. The intercultural school is well aware that the indigenous children, even though they may constitute a minority group in a given school, can rely on the social dominance of the majority culture; it therefore tries to prevent situations arising in relations between different ethnic groups, when the frustrations of the indigenous children turn into aggression towards the minorities.

Since all this takes place primarily at school, those on the receiving end of the pupils' self-assertion and resistance are sometimes the teachers themselves. This aspect of "pupil culture" - this measuring up to the teachers, half in fun and half in earnest, which is a form of learning through action, a kind of trial run for settling conflicts - can be understood and allowed to happen only if the pupils are actually given a chance to quarrel, in fun or in earnest, with recognizable rules. It is not a question of trying to abolish the school rules - which would in any case be impossible in the long run - nor is it merely a question of operating the existing rules in a more flexible and less authoritarian manner: it is a question of making them transparent and examining them as components of a dominant culture.

Thus we have for the last time outlined the concepts which have determined our argumentation throughout this chapter: intercultural education attempts to draw serious conclusions from the analysis of the problematic situations in which the schools of the host countries have been landed by the appearance of migrant pupils on the scene. In doing so, it comes more and more to adopt arguments derived from other traditions of educational thinking. Thus, insofar as it evolves concepts of educational reform and argues for their introduction, it has to discover these educational traditions as allies, in order to understand its position as one current of educational reform among many.

# Bibliography

## I. General (migration, comparative education and evaluation)

Bastenier, A., and Dasetto, F., *L'étranger nécessaire. Capitalisme et inégalités*, Louvain la Neuve 1977.

Berger, W., *Die vergleichende Erziehungswissenschaft. Einführung - Forschungsskizzen - Methoden*, Vienna/Munich 1976.

Bernard, P. J. (ed), *Les travailleurs étrangers en Europe occidentale*, Paris/The Hague 1976.

Berstecher, D., *Zur Theorie und Technik des internationalen Vergleichs. Das Beispiel der Bildungsforschung*, Stuttgart 1970.

Boos-Nünning, U., Gogolin, I., Hohmann, M., Reich, H. H., and Wittek, F., *Vergleichende Evaluation von Modellversuchen zum Aufnahmeunterricht, zum Muttersprachlichen Unterricht und zur Curriculumentwicklung für den Unterricht von Migrantenkindern in Mitgliedsstaaten der Europäischen Gemeinschaften* (8 vols), Essen/Landau 1984.

Busch, A., Busch, F. W., Krüger, B., and Krüger-Potratz, M. (eds), *Vergleichende Erziehungswissenschaft. Texte zur Methodologie-Diskussion.* Pullach nr. Munich 1974.

Castles, S. and Kossack, G, *Immigrant workers and class structure in Western Europe*, Oxford 1974.

Council of Europe, Resolution on the Teaching of Languages to Migrant Workers, (68)18, Strasbourg 1968.

Council of Europe, Resolution on the Return of Migrant Workers to their Home Country, (69)7, Strasbourg 1969.

Council of Europe, Resolution on School Education for the Children of Migrant Workers, (70)35, Strasbourg 1970.

Council of Europe (ed), Standing Conference of European Ministers of Education. Records of the Proceedings of the Ad Hoc Conference on Migrants' Education, Strasbourg, 5 - 8 November 1974 (CME/IX (75)7), no place, no date (Strasbourg 1975).

Council of Europe (ed), Resolutions and Texts adopted by the Standing Conference 1959-1977 (CME/XI (79) 2), Strasbourg 1979; including Resolution No. 2 on Migrants' Education, Ninth Session of the Standing Conference (Stockholm, 9-12 June 1975).

Court of the European Communities, Judgment in cause 9/74 (Donato Casagrande vs. Land Capital Munich) of 3 July 1974, in *Collection of Judgments of the Court 1974-75*, pp 773-80.

European Communities, Regulation (EEC) no. 1612/68 of the Council on the education of migrant workers' children, *Official Journal of the European Communities*, no. C 213, 17 September 1975.

European Communities, *The Education of Migrant Children*, Doc. XII/226/76 - E, hectographed Brussels 1976.

European Communities, Resolution of the Council and the Ministers of Education present in the Council with an action programme in the area of education of 9 February 1976, *Official Journal of the European Communities*, no. C 38, 19 February 1976.

European Communities, Directive of the Council of 25 July 1977 on the education of migrant workers' children (77/486/EEC),*Official Journal of the European Communities* no. L 199, 6 August 1977.

Hamilton, D., Jenkins, D., King, C., MacDonald, B., and Parlett, M., *Beyond the numbers game. A reader in educational evaluation*, London 1977.

Hans, N., *Comparative education. A study of educational factors and traditions*, London 1958, repr 1971.

IRFED (Institut internationale de Recherche et de Formation: Education et Développement), *La dynamique d'éducation interculturelle*, Paris 1978 (hectographed).

Jeffcoate, R., "A multicultural curriculum: beyond the orthodoxy", in *Trends in education*, Winter 1979, pp 8-12.

Kandel, I. L., *Comparative education*, Boston 1933.

Klaassen, L. H., and Drewe, P., *Migration policy in Europe. A comparative study*, Westmead 1974.

Kubat, D., Mehrländer, U., and Gehmacher, E. (eds), *The politics of migration policies. The First World in the 1970s*, New York 1979.

Mitter, W., and Weishaupt, H. (eds), *Strategien und Organisationsformen der Begleitforschung. Fallstudien über Begleituntersuchungen im Bildungswesen*, Weinheim/Basle 1979.

Mollenhauer, K. and Rittelmeyer, C., "'Empirisch-analytische Wissenschaft' versus 'Pädagogische Handlungsforschung': eine irreführende Alternative", *Zeitschrift für Pädagogik* (1975) 685-93.

Nieke, W., *Bericht über das Kolloquium zu Methodenproblemen bei der international vergleichenden Evaluation von Modellversuchen zu Erziehung und Unterricht für Kinder von Wanderarbeitnehmern in den Mitgliedsstaaten der Europäischen Gemeinschaften vom 20.-21.11.1980 in Brüssel*, Essen no date (1981).

Padrun, R., "L'expérience d'éducation interculturelle de Fontenay-sous-Bois", in *alpha-info* 9 (April 1979) 13-20.

Porcher, L., *L'éducation des enfants des travailleurs migrants en Europe: L'interculturalisme et la formation des enseignants*, Strasbourg 1981.

Projet d'éducation interculturelle, *migrants formation*, 22 (1977) 8E - 12E.

Reich, H. H., "Überlegungen zur Konzeption für eine koordinierte Evaluation" in: Nieke, W., op. cit. pp 78-86.

Rex, J., *Race, colonialism and the city*, London 1973.

Röhrs, H., *Forschungsstrategien in der Vergleichenden Erziehungs-wissenschaft. Eine Einführung in die Probleme der Vergleichenden Erziehungswissenschaft*, Weinheim 1975.

Scheuch, E. K., "Society as context in cross-cultural comparisons", *Social Science Information* 6 (1967/5) 7-23.

Schütz, P., *Fragen der Begriffsbildung in der Vergleichenden Erziehungs-wissenschaft. Analyse und Kritik ausgewählter vergleichender Unter-suchungen*, Weinheim 1976.

Société Française pour le Droit International (ed), *Les travailleurs étrangers et le droit international*, Paris 1979.

Thomas, E.-J. (ed), *Les travailleurs immigrés en Europe: quel statut? Etude comparative de la condition des travailleurs immigrés en Europe*, Paris 1978.

UNESCO (Deutsche UNESCO-Kommission), *Ausländer in unserer Stadt. Arbeitsberichte aus dem Modellschulprogramm der UNESCO* (ed H.-W. Rissom), Cologne 1977.

Wittek, F., "Eine europäische Dimension von Ausländerbildungspolitik - Zur Richtlinie der EG vom 25.7.1977", *Recht der Jugend und des Bildungswesens* 1982, 1, pp 40-50.

Wulf, C., "Ausgewählte Beispiele zur Evaluation" in: Wulf, C. (ed), *Evaluation. Beschreibung und Bewertung von Unterricht, Curricula und Schulversuchen*, Munich 1972, pp 262-66.

Wulf, C., "Funktionen und Paradigmen der Evaluation", in Frey, K. (ed), *Curriculum Handbuch*, vol II, Munich/Zurich 1975, pp 580-600.


## II. The situation in the individual countries.
(Since the pilot projects and our investigations were completed in 1980, subsequent studies are not generally cited.)


### 1. Belgium

Beckers-Schwarz, W., *Das Enseignement Technique/Technisch Onderwijs in Belgien. Beschreibung und Analyse einer kooperativen Ordnung der Berufsbildung*, Dissertation Frankfurt am Main 1977.

Bemelmans, F., *Orientation scolaire et professionelle des enfants de travailleurs étrangers et immigrés. Bericht für die Kommission der Europäischen Gemeinschaften*, Brussels 1978.

Bika, P., *Expériénce d'enseignement du français aux enfants des immigrés*, Liège 1979.

Braeckman, C., *Les étrangers en Belgique*, Brussels 1973.

Claes, B., *De sociale integratie van de Italiaanse en Poolse immigranten in Belgisch-Limburg*, Hasselt 1962.

Conféderation Générale des Enseignants (ed), *L'immigration. Sensibilisation aux mécanismes et aux pays d'origine*, Brussels 1979.

Deloff, E., *Das Bildungswesen in Belgien*, Brussels 1977.

Depoortere, J., "Het projekt Vernieuwed Lager Onderwijs in Belgie. En poging tot systematische en globale onderwijsvernieuwung", *Pedagogische Studien* 53 (1976), 33-48.

Devos, M., *Belgium. Socio-cultural information*, Strasbourg (Council of Europe DECS/EGT (79) 103 - E), 1980.

Ducoli, B., et al., *Lire l'immigration*, 5 fascicles, Brussels (no date).

Herrel, J., "Werken mit migrantenkinderen in het stedelijk onderwijs te Gent", *Persoon en Gemeenschap* 31 (1978/79) 446-57.

Janssens de Bisthoven, K., *L'immigration en Belgique*, Brussels 1976.

de Keyser, C. C., et al., "Belgien", *Standaard Encyklopedie voor Opvoeding en Onderwijs* (edited by von de Blok et al.), Part 1, Antwerp 1973.

Marques Balsa, C., *Les besoins et aspirations des familles de migrants* (5 vols), Louvain 1979.

Marques Balsa, C., "Zum Verhältnis von muttersprachlichem und interkulturellem Unterricht in Belgien", in Reich, H. H. and Wittek, F. (eds), *Migration - Bildungspolitik - Pädagogik*, Essen/Landau 1984, pp 133-50.

Pedagogisch Centrum Gent (ed), *Gastarbeiderskinderen in ons Onderwijs*, Ghent 1978.

Pollain, J., *La population étrangère en Belgique. Répartition régionale*, Liège 1979.

Provinciale Dienst voor Onthaal van Gastarbeiders (POG) (ed), *Het Onderwijs en Belgie*, Hasselt (no date).

Roosens, E., et al., *Omtrent de achterstelling van de immigranten in Belgie*, Louvain 1979.

Rosiers-Leonard, M., and Pollain, J., *Gesamenlijke nota betreffende de situatie in Belgie* (Report for the EC Commission), Hasselt/Liège 1979.

Warzee, L., *The socio-cultural situation of migrant workers and their families in Belgium* (Council of Europe DECS/EGT (79) 104 - E), Strasbourg 1980.

Willems, J., *Les conditions des familles immigrés en Belgique*, Louvain la Neuve 1977.

## 2. Great Britain

Bell, R., and Grant, N., *Patterns of education in the British Isles*, London 1977.

BIS (British Information Services) (ed), *Immigration into Britain*, London 1977.

Blackie, J., *Inside the primary school*, London 1967.

Bolton, E., "Education in multiracial society", *Trends in Education* 1979, Winter, pp 3-7.

Brügelmann, H., "Die englischen Teachers' Centres. Dezentralisierung der Curriculum-Entwicklung auf lokaler Ebene" in: Kröll, U. (ed), *Institutionalisierte Lehrerfortbildung. Konzepte, Modelle und ihre Praxis*, Weinheim/Basle 1980, pp 189-203.

Burgess, T., *Inside comprehensive schools*, London 1970.

Campbell-Platt, K., *Linguistic minorities in Britain* (Runnymede Trust Briefing Paper 6/78), London 1978 (hectographed).

COI (Central Office of Information) (ed), *Race relations in Britain* (COI Reference Pamphlet 108), London 1977.

CRC (Community Relations Commission) (ed), *Housing in multi-racial areas. Report of a Working Party of Housing Directors*, London 1976.

CRC (ed), *The education of ethnic minority children*, London 1977.

CRE (Commission for Racial Equality) (ed), *Ethnic minorities in Britain. Statistical background*, London 1978 a.

CRE (ed), *Caring for under-fives in a multiracial society*, London 1978 b.

Cross, C., *Ethnic minorities in the inner city. The ethnic dimension in urban deprivation in England*, London 1978.

CSO (Central Statistical Office) (ed), *Social trends 9*, London 1978.

Dent, H. C., *Education in England and Wales*, London 1977.

Derrick, J., *Language needs of ethnic minority Children. Learners of English as a Second Language*, Slough 1977.

DES (Department of Education and Science) (ed), *Children and their primary schools. Report of the Central Advisory Council for Education (England)*, London 1967.

DES (ed), *The education of immigrants* (Education Survey 13), London 1971.

DES (ed), *Education: a framework for expansion* (Cmnd. 5174), London 1972 a.

DES (ed), *The continuing needs of immigrants* (Education Survey 14), London 1972 b.

DES (ed), *Educational disadvantage and the educational needs of immigrants. Observations on the Report of the Select Committee on Race Relations and Immigration* (Cmnd. 5720), London 1974.

DES (ed), *A language for life. Report of the Committee of Inquiry appointed by the Secretary of State for Education and Science under the Chairmanship of Sir Alan Bullock* ("The Bullock Report"), London 1975.

DES (ed), *Education in schools. A consultative document* (Cmnd. 6869), London 1977.

DES (ed), *Statistics of education 1977*, Vol 2: School leavers, CSE and GCE, London 1979.

Dummett, A., *A new immigration policy*, London 1978.

Edwards, V., *The West Indian language issue in British schools*, London 1979.

Evans, K., *The development and structure of the English education system*, 2nd ed, London 1978.

Halsey, A. H. (ed), *Educational priority*. Vol 1: E.P.A. Problems and Policies, London 1972.

Hodges, L., "Off to a prejudiced start?", *The Times Educational Supplement*, 24 February 1978.

Home Office (ed), *White Paper on "Racial discrimination"* (Cmnd. 6234), London 1975.

Home Office (ed), *Racial discrimination. A guide to the Race Relations Act 1976*, London 1977.

Home Office (ed), *Proposals for replacing Section 11 of the Local Government Act 1966. A consultative document*, London 1978 (hectographed).

Hopkins, A., *The school debate*, Harmondsworth 1978.

Jeffcoate, R., "Schools and prejudice", *Trends in Education*, 1975/3, pp 3-9.

Jeffcoate, R., *Positive image. Towards a multiracial curriculum*, London/Richmond 1979.

Jones, C., *Immigration and social policy in Britain*, London 1977.

Kirp, D. L., *Doing good by doing little. Race and schooling in Britain*, Berkeley/Los Angeles/London 1979.

Kogan, M. *The politics of educational change*, London 1978.

Lester, A., *Citizens without status*, London no date (1972).

Little, A. N., "Performance of children from ethnic minority backgrounds in primary schools", *Oxford Review of Education* 1/2 (1975) 117-35.

LMP (Linguistic Minorities Project), *First progress report*, University of London Institute of Education 1980 (hectographed).

LMP, *Linguistic minorities in England*, London 1983.

OECD (Organisation for Economic Co-operation and Development) (ed), *Educational development strategy in England and Wales*, Paris 1975.

Prashar, U., "The need for reform" in: Dummett, A., *British Nationality Law* (Runnymede Trust's Guide to the Green Paper), London 1977.

Rees, T., "The United Kingdom" in: Kubat, D., Mehrländer, U., and Gehmacher, E. (eds), *The politics of migration policies. The First World in the 1970s*, New York 1979.

Rees, O. A. and Fitzpatrick, F., *The origin and development of the Mother Tongue and English Teaching Project* (Mother Tongue and English Teaching Project Working Paper No. 1), University of Bradford 1980 (hectographed).

Rex, J., and Moore, R., *Race, community and conflict. A study of Sparkbrook*, London/New York 1967.

Rosen, H., and Burgess, T., *Language and dialect of London school children*, London 1980.

Rutter, M., et al., "Children of West Indian immigrants. Rates of behavioural deviance and of psychiatric disorder", *Journal of Child Psychology and Psychiatry* 15 (1974), 241-46.

Saifullah Khan, V., "Provision by minorities for language maintenance" in: *Bilingualism and British Education* (CILT Reports and Papers 14), London 1976, pp 31-37.

Saifullah Khan, V. (ed), *Minority families in Britain. Support and stress*, London/Basingstoke 1979.

Schools Council (ed), *SCOPE. English for immigrant children*, London 1969ff.

Schools Council (ed), *Concept 7-9. Teaching English to West Indian children*, London 1972.

Schools Council (ed), *GCE and CSE. A guide to secondary school examinations for teachers, pupils, parents and employers*, London 1973 (updated 1975).

Singh, P., "City centre schools and community relations", *Trends in Education* (May 1974) 27-30.

Smith, D. J., *The facts of racial disadvantage. A national survey*, London 1976.

217

Tomlinson, S., *Ethnic minorities in British schools. A Review of the literature 1960-1982*, London/Exeter 1983.

Tosi, A., *Immigration and bilingual education. A case study of movement of population language change and education within the EEC*, Oxford 1984.

Townsend, H. E. R., *Immigrant pupils 'n England. The LEA Response*, Slough 1971.

Townsend, H. E. R., and Brittan, E. M., *Organization in multiracial schools*, Slough 1972.

Verma, G. K., and Bagley, C. (eds), *Race, education and identity*, London/Basingstoke 1979.

### 3. France

Abou Sada, G., et al., *La condition de la deuxième génération d'immigrés*, Lille 1976.

Baudelot, C., and Establet, R., *L'école capitaliste en France*, Paris 1971.

Berthelier, R., "Les enfants de travailleurs migrants – problèmes psycho-pédagogiques et médicaux-sociaux". in CEFISEM Lyon (ed), *Compte rendu des journées d'études sur les problèmes posés par la scolarisation des enfants de travailleurs migrants*, Lyon 1976, pp 32-37.

Blot, B., *La situation socio-culturelle des migrants et de leurs familles en France* (Council of Europe DECS/EGT (79) 110 - F), Strasbourg 1980.

Boulot, S., Clévy, J., and Fradet, D., *Scolarisation des enfants étrangers. Enseignement public - enseignement privé. Statistique 1978/79*, CREDIF, Saint-Cloud 1980 a.

Bourdieu, P., and Passeron, J -C., *La réproduction*, Paris 1970.

Charlot, M., et al., *Mon avenir? Quel avenir? Témoignages de jeunes immigrés*, Paris 1978.

Chazalette, A., and Michaut, P., *La deuxième génération de migrants dans la région Rhône-Alpes*, Lyon 1976

Clévy, J., et al., *Questions-réponses sur la scolarisation des enfants de travailleurs migrants*, Paris 1976.

Doll, J., *Entwicklungen und Reformtendenzen im französischen Bildungswesen*, Vienna 1976.

Gokalp, A., "Le problème de l'identité culturelle", in *Scolarisation des enfants de travailleurs immigrés. Vers de nouvelles perspectives*, CEFISEM Douai-Lille 1976, pp 65-72.

Granotier, B., *Les travailleurs immigrés en France*, Paris 1970 (5th ed 1979).

Gratiot-Alphandéry, H., and Lambiotte, B., "Retard scolaire", in Girard, A., and Charbit, Y. (eds), *Les enfants de travailleurs migrants en Europe* (Centre International de l'Enfance, Colloque du 19 au 22 mars 1973), Paris 1974, pp 68-71.

Hamburger, F., "Zur Situation ausländischer Arbeiterkinder in Frankreich", in *Deutsch lernen* 78/3, pp 51-55.

Huart, M., *France. Données socio-culturelles*, (Council of Europe DECS/EGT (79) 109 - F), Strasbourg 1980.

Lebon, A., *Immigration et VII* plan* (Coll. "Migrations et Sociétés", ed. by the Ministry of Employment), Paris 1977.

Le français aujourd'hui 44/1978: "Dans toutes nos classes des enfants d'immigrés".

Le Pors, A., *Immigration et développement économique et social* (Etudes prioritaires interministérielles), Paris 1976.

Limage, L. J., *Langage et alphabétisation: Education pour des sociétés multiculturelles. Le cas de la France, OCDE-CERI (Document provisoire)*, Paris 1979.

migrants-formation, Paris: Centre National de Documentation Pédagogique 1973ff.

Minces, J., *Les travailleurs étrangers en France*, Paris 1973.

Ministère de l'Education Nationale: S.E.I.S., Série "Etudes et Documents", no. 38/1976.

Porcher, L. (ed), *La scolarisation des enfants étrangers en France*, Paris 1978.

Samman, M. L., *Les étrangers au recensement de 1975* (Coll. "Migrations et Sociétés", ed. by the Ministry of Employment), Paris 197.

Schriewer, J. (ed), *Schulreform und Bildungspolitik in Frankreich*, Bad Heilbronn/Obb 1974.

Tapinos, G., *L'Immigration étrangère en France*, Paris 1975.

## 4. The Netherlands

Amersfoort, J. M. M. van, *Immigratie en minderheidsvorming. Een analyse van den Nederlandse situatie 1945- 1973*, Alphen aan de Rijn 1974.

Bagley, C., *The Dutch plural society. A comparative study in race relations*, London/New York/Toronto 1973.

Berg-Eldering, L. van den, *Marrokaanse gezinnen in Nederland*, Alphen aan de Rijn 1978.

Brinkmann, G., *Tradition und Fortschritt im niederländischen Bildungswesen*, Weinheim 1975.

Centraal Bureau voor de Statistiek, *Leerlingen met buitenlandse nationaliteit bij het kleuteronderwijs en gewoon lager onderwijs, 16 Januari 1978*.

Contactorgaan voor de Innovatie van het Onderwijs (CIO) (ed), *I.S.K. Bulletin. Informatiebulletin voor scholen voor voortgezet onderwijs, die anderstalige leerlingen in de groepen hebben*, den Bosch 1979 ff.

Gemeente Enschede (ed), *Bi-Cultureel Onderwijs aan Turkse en Marokkaanse kinderen*, Enschede 1979.

Kloostermann, A. M. J., *Naar meer struktuur in de Internationale Schakelklassen*, Amsterdam 1979.

Kruyt, A., *Orientatie en den vreemdelingen wetgeving*, Utrecht 1979.

Lebon, A., "The impact of migrants, especially second-generation migrants, on trends in the demographic situation in selected countries of employment" in: UNDP/ILO European Regional Project for Second-Generation Migrants (ed), *Tripartite Technical Seminar on Second-Generation Migrants* (Lisbon, 4-9 May, 1981), preliminary version, hectographed.

Ministerie van Onderwijs en Wetenschappen (ed), *Konturen eines neuen Unterrichtssystems in den Niederlanden*, The Hague 1978.

Ministerie van Onderwijs en Wetenschappen (ed), *Wet op het basisonderwijs (Concept-Wetontwerp)*, The Hague 1976.

Ministerie van Onderwijs en Wetenschappen (ed), *Conceptnota beslispunten t.a.v. het beleid onderwijs aan culturele minderheden*, The Hague 1978.

Ministerie van Onderwijs en Wetenschappen (ed), *Concept-Beleidsplan. Culturele minderheden in het onderwijs*, s'Gravenhage 1981.

Ministerie van Onderwijs en Wetenschappen (ed), *Beleidsplan culturele minderheden in het onderwijs*, s'Gravenhage 1981.

Ministry of Home Affairs, *Summary draft discussion document on minorities*, April 1981 (no place).

Nederlands Centrum Buitenlanders (ed), *Fragmenten uit de rijksbegroting 1977 (1978, 1980) over buitenlanders*, Utrecht (no year). NCB-Documentatie Nr. 8 (Nr. 9, Nr. 12).

Rose, A. U., *Migrants in Europe. Problems of acceptance and adjustment*, Minneapolis 1969.

Sociaal en Cultureel Planbureau, *Bevolkingsprognose Allochthonen in Nederland* (S.C.P. cahier no. 19) Rijswijk 1980.

Schumacher, P., *De Minderheden. 600.000 vreemdelingen in Nederland*, Amsterdam 1980.

Triesscheijn, T. J. M., *Netherlands. Socio-Cultural Information* (Council of Europe DECS/EGT (79) 117-E), Strasbourg 1980.

Triesscheijn, T. J. M., *The socio-cultural situation of migrants and their families in the Netherlands* (Council of Europe DECS/EGT (79) 118-E), Strasbourg 1981.

*Vademecum Onderwijs Anderstaligen*, 's Hertogenbosch 1980.

Wetenschappelijke Raad voor het Regeringsbeleid (WRR), *Ethnische Minderheden*, 's Gravenhage 1979.

## III. The Pilot Projects

### 1. Genk (Belgium)

Coel, J., Cambergh, M. J., and Ooteghem, C., *Een experimentele Vorm van Opvoeding en Onderwijs voor de Kinderen van de multi-ethnische Gemeenschap te Genk-Winterslag* (no place or date) (Hasselt 1982).

COB (Commissie Onderwijsvernieuwing Basisonderwijs), *Pilootexperiment van de EEG, Pedagogische Opvangvormen voor Migrantenkinderen in het Basisonderwijs, Overgang van het Kleuteronderwijs naar het Basisonderwijs met bikultureel Karakter, Jaarlijks Evaluatierapport: Schooljaar 1977-1978*, VLS Genk (Winterslag) (no place or date).

COB, *Pedagogische Opvangvormen voor Migrantenkinderen en het Basisonderwijs. Eindevaluatie: Schooljaaren 1976-77, 1977-78, 1978-79*, Gesubsidieerde Vrij Onderwijs (no place) 1979.

*Experiment Bi-Cultureel Onderwijs Migrantenkinderen* (the schools' application to the Ministry), 21 June 1976.

Haesendonckx, A., *Pilootexperiment van de EEG, Pedagogische Opvang-vormen voor Migrantenkinderen in het Basisonderwijs, Overgang van het Kleuteronderwijs naar het Basisonderwijs met bikultureel Karakter, Jaarlijks Evaluatierapport: Schooljaar 1977-1978*, RLS Genk (Waterschei) (no place or date).

Haesendonckx, A., de Vriese, J., and Poncelet, E., *Pilootexperiment van de EEG, Pedagogische Opvangvormen voor Migrantenkinderen in het Basisonderwijs, Overgang van het Kleuteronderwijs naar het Basisonderwijs met bikultureel Karakter. Eindevaluatierapport*, RLS Genk (Waterschei): Schooljaren 1976-77/1977-78/1978-79 (no year) (1979).

MNO (Ministerie van Nationale Opvoeding), *Experiment in het kleuter- en lager onderwijs te Genk: pedagogische opvangvormen voor het onder-vangen van de socioculturele problematiek bij immigrantenkinderen* (Note of 25 August 1976).

MNO, *Experiment bi-cultureel onderwijs in het kleuter- en basis-onderwijs te Genk* (Note of 28 July 1977).

MNO, "Experiment bi-cultureel onderwijs in het kleuter- en basis-onderwijs te Genk" (The Minister's Note, 1978) in: COB, *Pedagogische opvangvormen voor Migrantenkinderen en het Basisonderwijs. Eind-evaluatie: Schooljaren 1976-77, 1977-78, 1978-79, (no place) 1979, Appendix 7*.

POG (Provinciale Onthaaldienst voor Gastarbeiders), *Onderzoek naar de problemen gesteld in de Lagere Scholen met starke concentratie van migrantenkinderen in het Limburgse middengebied*, Hasselt 1972.

POG, *Vergadering Bi-cultureel Onderwijs* (minutes of the meetings of 10 June, 4 November and 24 November 1976 and 20 January and 9 March 1977), Hasselt 1976f (hectographed).

POG, *EEG Pilootexperiment en het kleuter- en lager onderwijs te Genk: Pedagogische opvangvormen voor immigranten kinderen. Jaarlijks Evaluatierapport Schooljaar 1976-77*, Hasselt 1977.

POG, *Pilootexperiment van de EEG, Pedagogische Opvangvormen voor Migranten kinderen in het Basisonderwijs, Overgang van het kleuter-onderwijs naar het Basisonderwijs met bikultureel karakter. Jaarlijks Evaluatierapport: Opinie-Onderzoek bij de Ouders, Schooljaar 1977-78*, Hasselt 1978.

POG (ed), *Pedagogische Opvangvormen voor Migrantenkinderen in het Basisonderwijs. International Colloquium onder de Auspicien van de EEG.*

222

*Diepenbeek 20.-22.06.1978*, Hasselt 1978. This contains the following documents:

1) *De Doelstellingen van de Provinciale Onthaaldienst voor Gastarbeiders Limburg (POG) in het algemeen in de plaats van de POG en het EEG Pilootexperiment.*

2) *Toespraak gehouden door de Heer J. Coel, Kantonaal Inspekteur Gesubsidieerd Vrij Onderwijs - Gebied Genk.*

3) COB (Commissie Onderwijsvernieuwing Basisonderwijs), *Vrij Gesubsidieerd Jongens- en Meisjesschool. Tussentijds Evaluatierapport, Periode 1976-77.*

4) Schaerlaekens-Dekeersmaker, C., *Evaluatiegegevens van de Gesubsidieerde Vrije Lagere Scholen te Genk. Deel I: Een jaar experiment in het eerste leerjaar, Schooljaar 1976-77. Deel II: Het experiment in het kleuteronderwijs, Schooljaar 1977-78.*

5) *Praktische Gegevens en Uitbow van het Pilootexperiment van de EEG.*

6) Poncelet, E., *Evaluatierapport - Rijksscholen Genk.*

7) Haesendonckx, A., *Verslag van het eerste Experimentjaar 1976. R.L.S. Waterschei, Genk.*

8) *Experiment Bi-Cultureel Onderwijs in de Vrije Gesubsidieerde Lagere Scholen Winterslag: Taalproef, samengesteld door Juffr. Directrice Caubergh en Br. Directeur van Ooteghem, onderzoek naar de beginsituatie en evaluatie. Beschrijving van de taalproef, resultaten, conclusies.*

POG, *Pilootexperiment van de EEG, Pedagogische Opvangvormen voor Migrantenkinderen in het Basisonderwijs met bikultureel karakter. Eindevaluatierapport, Rijksbasisschool Genk-Waterschei, Schooljaren 1976-77, 1977-78, 1978-79*, Hasselt 1979.

POG, *Aantal Vreemdelingen verblijvend en de Provincie Limburg op 31.12. 1975 en 31.12.1977*, Hasselt (no date).

∙POG, *Aantal Vreemdelingen in de Provincie Limburg, telling per Nationaliteit en per Gemeente op 31.12.1971, 31.12.1975 en 31.12.1977*, Hasselt (no date).

## 2. Bedford (England)

Bedfordshire Education Service, *EEC Project: Mother tongue and culture*, June 1979 (hectographed).

Bourne, R., and Trim, J., *European Communities Bedfordshire Mother Tongue and Culture Project*, Cranfield Institute of Technology, 24-27 March 1980 (hectographed).

Burrows, G., *Mother tongue teaching and the education of minority group Children* (unpublished MSc thesis, Cranfield Institute of Technology 1979).

Cave, D., *EEC Mother Tongue and Culture Project, Bedfordshire Education Service, Preliminary Report*, Cambridge Institute of Education 1977 (hectographed).

Oertel, B., *A study of the Punjabi component of an EEC Mother Tongue and Culture Project in Bedford* (unpublished MA thesis, King's College, University of London 1978).

Simons, H., *EEC Pilot Project Mother Tongue and Culture in Bedfordshire, Evaluation Report Jan. 1978 - Sept. 1978*, Cambridge Institute of Education (revised) Oct. 1979 (hectographed).

Simons, H., *EEC-sponsored Project, Mother Tongue and Culture in Bedfordshire, Second External Evaluation Report, Sept. 1978 - July 1980*, Cambridge December 1979 (hectographed).

Tansley, P., *EEC-sponsored Mother Tongue and Culture Pilot Project, Bedfordshire Education Service, Final Evaluation Report, Sept. 1979 - July 1980*, NFER 1980 (hectographed).

## 3. Paris (France)

Boulot, S, Clévy, J., and Fradet, D., "Les cours intégrés de langues: difficultés - réussites - propositions", in *migrants-formation* 38-39/1980 (b), pp 14-21.

CREDIF, *Enseignement de la langue et de la culture d'origine des enfants étrangers fréquentant des écoles élémentaires françaises*, Paris 1977 (hectographed).

CREDIF, *Unterricht ausländischer Kinder in der Sprache und Kultur ihres Herkunftslandes*, Paris 1978 (hectographed).

CREDIF, *Langue et culture d'origine des enfants de travailleurs migrants. Colloque organisé à Paris sous les auspices de la Commission des Communautés Européennes*, Paris 1978 (hectographed).

CREDIF, *Projet pilote. Commission des Communautés Européennes. "Langue et culture d'origine des enfants de migrants"*, Paris 1979/80:

Vol 1, Les établissements scolaires. Réflexion sur les langues et cultures des pays d'origine (Dec. 1979).

Vol 2, Effets psychologiques de l'expérience (Oct. 1979).

Vol 3, Rapports des évaluateurs étrangers (June 1980).

Vol 4, Les parents étrangers et l'expérience multilingue. Eléments d'évaluation (June 1980).

Vol 5, Démarches pédagogiques (announced).

CREDIF, *Une expérience d'enseignement de la langue et de la culture italiennes. Points de repère e illustration.* By S. Boulot, J. Clévy, D. Fradet, A. Perotti, Paris 1980 (a).

CREDIF, *Une année d'enseignement de la langue et de la culture espagnoles à des enfants espagnols scolarisés dans une école élémentaire de Paris (année scolaire 1978-1979).* By S. Boulot, D. Fradet, S. Obispo (4 vols), Paris 1980 (b).

CREDIF, *Une activité pédagogique franco-italienne. LES RITALS de Cavanna.* By S. Boulot, D. Fradet and A. Perotti. Paris 1981 (a).

CREDIF, *Une activité pédagogique franco-espagnole. GUERNICA.* By S. Boulot, D. Fradet and S. Obispo:
   *Réalités linguistiques et sensibilisation culturelle*, Paris 1981 (b).
   *Cahier de l'élève*, Paris 1981 (c).

Ministère de l'Education Nationale, *Note (n° 1) sur l'expérience, en 1976-1977, d'enseignement des langues nationales dans les écoles élémentaires de Paris*, 6 September 1976 (hectographed).

Perotti, A., *Rapport pédagogique sur l'expérience d'enseignement de l'italien dans des écoles françaises de banlieue parisienne (année scolaire 1978-1979)*, Paris 1979.

Perry, P., "Was diesseits der Pyrenäen wahr ist, ist jenseits falsch. Interkultureller Unterricht in einem französischen Grundschulprojekt", *Ausländerkinder in Schule und Kindergarten* 4 (1982) pp 13-16.


### 4. Leiden (The Netherlands)

Appel, R., Everts, H., and Teunissen, J., *Onderzoek van het gewoon lager onderwijs aan Marokkaanse en Turkse kinderen:*
   *Interim-rapport 1* (no place) (Utrecht) September 1978.

*Interim-rapport 2* (no place) (Utrecht) April 1979.

Appel, R., and Altena, N., *Tweede Taalverwerving van Turkse en Marokkaanse kinderen. Werkrapport 4: Over de Nederlandse Taalvaardigheid van kinderen. Mit verschillende onderwijsmodellen na twee jaar.* Instituut voor ontwikkelingspsychologie, Utrecht Feb. 1980.

Everts, H., *Verslag van de vragenlijst die en december 1976 aan Nederlandse ouders van de Du-Rieu-School werd voorgelegd.*
*Verslag van het eksperiment met opvangklassen aan de Du-Rieu-School te Leiden over de periode van 01.01.-01.06.1978.*
*Verslag over de periode tot 01.01.1978* (no place or date) (hectographed).

Ministerie van Onderwijs en Wetenschapen, *Eksperiment anderstaligen - Leiden* (letter of 23 February 1977 to the Mayor of Leiden).

Overberg, H., *The Leiden experiment - An evaluation*, Rusden State College of Victoria 1980 (hectographed).

*Voorstel tot een eksperiment om aan een openbare school voor gewoon lager onderwijs te Leiden een Turkse en een Marokkaanse opvangklas te verbinden*, (no place or date) (application for the pilot project, Leiden 1976).